TIGERS AT WAR

BY
BOB CARRUTHERS

C◆DA
BOOKS LTD

C⊕DA
BOOKS LTD

www.codabooks.com

This edition is published in Great Britain in 2012 by

Coda Books Ltd., Office Suite 2, Shrieves Walk, 39 Sheep Street,
Stratford-upon-Avon, Warwickshire CV37 6GJ

www.codabooks.com

Copyright © 2012 by Coda Books Ltd.

A CIP catalogue record for this book is available from the British Library.

ISBN: 978-1-78158-278-7

CONTENTS

TIGER I IN COMBAT

THE TIGEFIBEL

TIGER I
IN COMBAT

BY
BOB CARRUTHERS

INTRODUCTION

The Tiger I was the most famous heavy tank used in World War II. It was developed in great haste during 1942 by the Henschel & Sohn company as the answer to the unexpectedly formidable Soviet armour encountered during 1941 in the closing stages of Operation Barbarossa - namely the ominous T-34 and KV-1 tanks to which the German tank designs of the time could provide no answer. The 50mm calibre high velocity gun of the German Mark III lacked projectile mass and penetrating power while the low velocity gun mounted on the German Mark IV was incapable of penetrating the well sloped armour of the T-34 at anything but the shortest range. The high velocity 88mm anti-aircraft gun, which had been forced into action in an anti-tank role in Russia and the western desert, was the only gun which had demonstrated its effectiveness against even the most heavily armoured ground targets such as The KV1.

Rushed into service in August 1942 the Tiger I design at least gave the Panzerwaffe its first tank capable of mounting the fearsome 88mm gun as its main armament. For the hard pressed men of the Panzewaffe however there was a very high price to pay for the Tiger in both literal and metaphorical terms. The highest price of all, or course, was paid by the slave labourers who were forced to build the Tiger.

The Roman numeral I was only officially added in 1944 when the later Tiger II entered production. The initial official German designation was Panzerkampfwagen VI Ausführung H ('Panzer VI version H'), abbreviated to PzKpfw VI Ausf. H. Somewhat confusingly the tank was redesignated as PzKpfw VI Tiger Ausf. E in March 1943. It also enjoyed the ordnance inventory Sonderkraftzug designation SdKfz 181.

The Tiger I first saw action on 22nd September 1942 near Leningrad. Under pressure from Hitler, the tank was driven into action in unfavourable terrain, months earlier than planned. Many early models proved to be mechanically unreliable; most broke down. More worryingly two others were easily knocked out by dug-in Soviet anti-tank guns, and one disabled tank was almost captured intact by the Soviets. It was finally blown up in November 1942 to prevent it falling into Soviet hands. The Soviets used the battlefield experience well and used the time to study the design of the Tiger and begin to prepare a response. The fearsome Josef Stalin heavy tank which would emerge, and prove equal to the Tiger in every respect.

One of the most famous studies of the Tiger I. This early production model appears to be in almost factory fresh condition.

A Tiger I with the turret number 133 of 1. SS-Pz.-Korps Leibstandarte Adolf Hitler in transit by road march; in the foreground is Schwimmkübel; PK 698.

PRODUCTION OF THE TIGER

Production of the Tiger I began in August 1942, and 1,347 were built by August 1944 when production ceased. Production started at a rate of 25 per month and peaked in April 1944 at 104 per month. Battlefield strength peaked at 671 on 1st July 1944. Generally speaking, it took about twice as long to build a Tiger I as any other German tank of the period. However, none of the obvious lessons concerning the need to husband scarce resources were learned and astonishingly when the "improved" model began production in January 1944, the Tiger I was soon phased out in favour of an even more resource hungry monster in the form of the massive, less efficient and even more resource intense Tiger II.

The major problem with the Tiger I was that it simply used too many scarce resources in terms of both manpower and material, especially when compared with the spartan simplicity of the T-34. As a general rule of thumb each the Tiger I cost over twice as much as a Panzer IV and four times as much as a StuG III assault gun. Each Tiger I actually cost 250,000

A rare photograph shows the interior of the Tiger I factory Henschelwerk III at Kassel-Mittelfeld.

OPERATIONAL STATUS OF TIGERS ON
1st SEPTEMBER 1942

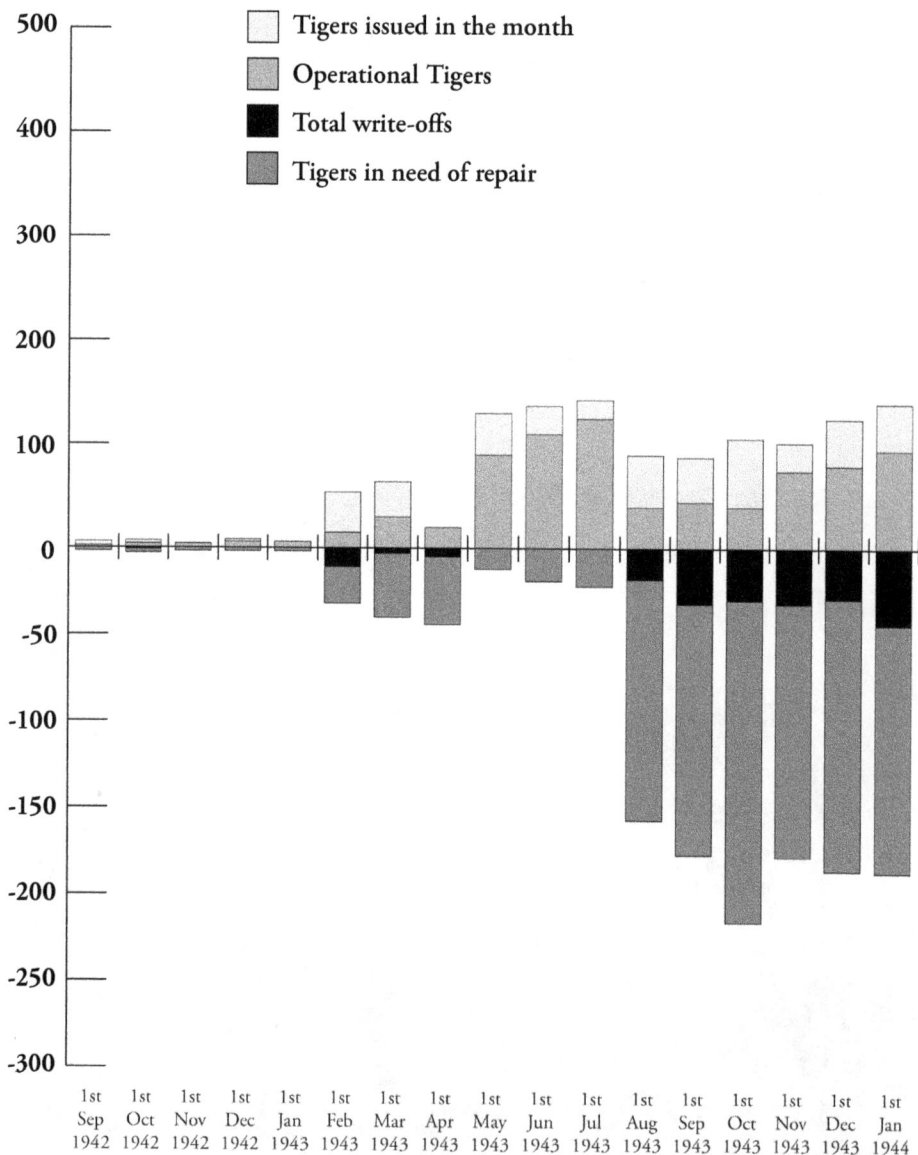

Legend:
- Tigers issued in the month
- Operational Tigers
- Total write-offs
- Tigers in need of repair

THE EASTERN AND WESTERN FRONTS

TO 5th APRIL 1945

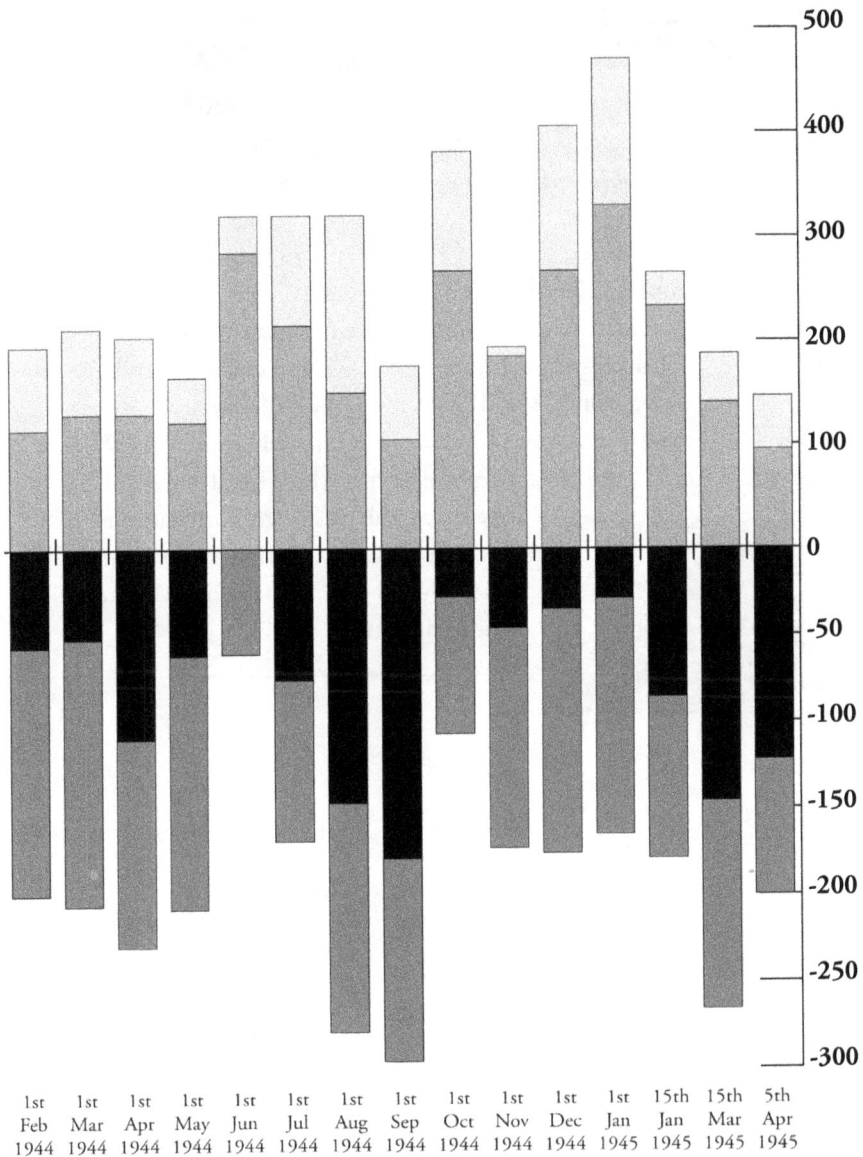

| 1st Feb 1944 | 1st Mar 1944 | 1st Apr 1944 | 1st May 1944 | 1st Jun 1944 | 1st Jul 1944 | 1st Aug 1944 | 1st Sep 1944 | 1st Oct 1944 | 1st Nov 1944 | 1st Dec 1944 | 1st Jan 1945 | 15th Jan 1945 | 15th Mar 1945 | 5th Apr 1945 |

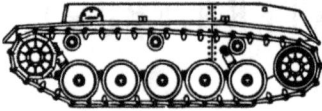
DW 1

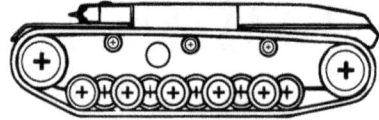
VK 6501

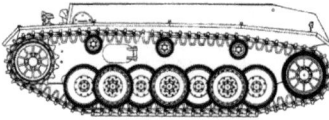
VK 3001 (H)

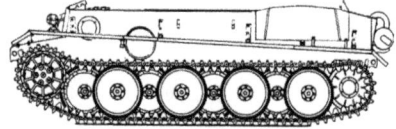
VK 3601

Early development prototype hulls for the Henschel heavy tank programme which ultimately produced the Tiger I.

Reichsmarks as compared to the 103,500 it cost to manufacture a Panzer IV. The Tiger I was also significantly over engineered which made it difficult to manufacture at a fast rate. The result was an increasing production gap which Speer's hard pressed German tank industry could never hope to close. During the Second World War, over 58,000 American Shermans and 36,000 Soviet T-34s were produced, compared to just 1,347 Tiger I and 492 Tiger II. The closest counterpart to the Tiger from the United

States was the M26 Pershing around 200 of which deployed during the war and the Soviet IS-2 of which about 3,800 were built during the war.

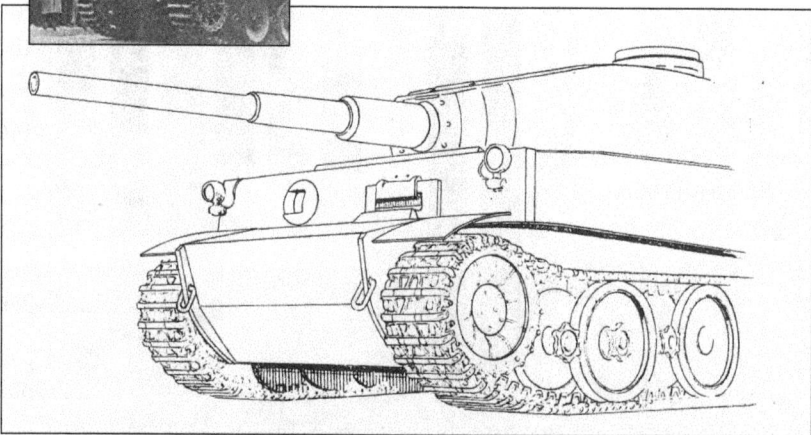

The War Office commissioned this illustration on the basis of a photograph from the German newspaper above published in December 1942. Note the lack of muzzle brake on the gun.

THE DEVELOPMENT PROCESS

Henschel & Sohn began development of the vehicle that eventually became the Tiger I in January 1937 when the Waffenamt requested Henschel to develop a *Durchbruchwagen* (breakthrough vehicle) in the 30 metric ton range (see DW 1 hulk opposite). Only one prototype hull was ever built and it never was mounted with a turret. The general configuration and suspension of the Durchbruchwagen prototype in many respects resembled the Panzer III. The proposed turret also bore similarities to existing machines and,had it been completed, it would have greatly resembled the early Panzer IV C turret which sported the short barrelled 7.5cm L/24 cannon.

Before Durchbruchwagen I was completed, however, a new request was issued for a heavier 30 tonne class vehicle with thicker armour; this was known as the Durchbruchwagen II (see VK 6501 opposite). This tank would have carried 50mm of frontal armour and have mounted a Panzer IV turret with the standard 7.5cm L/24 cannon. Overall weight would also have been approximately 36 metric tons. Again only one hull was ever built and a turret was never actually fitted. Development of this vehicle was cancelled in the autumn of 1938 in favour of the more advanced VK3001(H) and VK3601(H) designs. However, both the Durchbruchwagen I and II prototype hulls were used as test vehicles until 1941.

Prototype drawing for the Porsche version of the Tiger I. There were numerous problems with this design including the forward location of the turret that made manoevering difficult. There were also many mechanical breakdowns during testing.

On 9th September 1939, with the invasion of Poland underway, Henschel & Sohn received permission to continue development of a VK3001(H) medium tank and a VK3601(H) heavy tank, both of which apparently pioneered the overlapping and interleaved main road wheel concept as adapted for tank chassis use. Interleaved road wheels were already being used on German military half-tracked vehicles such as the SdKfz 7 although there was very little comparison with regard to the weight of a heavily armoured tank compared to a lightweight half track.

The VK3001(H) was intended be produced in three main variants the first of which was to mount a 7.5cm L/24 low velocity infantry support gun, the second was intended to carry a 7.5cm L/40 dual purpose anti-tank gun, and the third a 10.5cm L/28 artillery piece in a Krupp turret. Overall weight was to be 33 metric tons. The armour was designed to be 50mm on frontal surfaces and 30mm on the side surfaces. Four prototype hulls were completed for testing. Two of these were later used to create the 12.8cm Selbstfahrlafette L/61, also known as Sturer Emil.

The VK3601(H) was intended to weigh 40 metric tons, and carry 100mm of armour on its frontal surfaces, 80mm on turret sides and 60mm on hull sides. The VK3601(H) was also intended to appear in four variants adapted to house a 7.5cm L/24, or a 7.5cm L/43, or a 7.5cm L/70, or a 12.8cm L/28 cannon in a Krupp turret that looked very similar to an enlarged Panzer IVC turret. One prototype hull was built, followed later by five more prototype hulls. The six turrets intended for the prototype hulls were built but never actually fitted and ended their working lives as static defences mounted the Atlantic Wall. The development of the VK3601(H) project was discontinued in early 1942 in favour of the VK4501 project. German combat experience with the French Somua S35 cavalry tank and Char B1 heavy tank, and the British Matilda I and Matilda II infantry tanks in June 1940 showed that the German Army needed better armed and armoured tanks. In 1940 superior tactics had overcome superior enemy armour, but Rommel had endured a nasty shock on the form of a successful British counter attack at Arras. The German tank designers however, took notice of the lessons from the battlefield. Accordingly on 26th May 1941, at an armaments meeting, Henschel and Porsche were asked to submit designs for a 45 tonne heavy tank, to be ready by June 1942. Porsche worked hard and fast to submit an updated version of their VK3001(P) Leopard tank prototype while Henschel worked to develop an improved VK3601(H)tank. Henschel built two prototypes. A VK4501(H) H1 which used the 88mm L/56 cannon and a VK4501(H) H2 which used the 75mm L/70 cannon.

THE UNPLEASANT SURPRISE

On 22 June 1941, Germany launched Operation Barbarossa, the invasion of the Soviet Union. The Germans were shocked to encounter Soviet T-34 medium and KV-1 heavy tanks which completely outclassed anything the Germans were then able to put into the field. The T-34 was almost immune frontally to every gun in German service except the 88mm FlaK 18/36 gun. The Panzer Mark III with the 50mm KwK 38 L/42 main armament could penetrate the sides of a T-34, but had to be very close to do so. To have any chance of penetrating the frontal armour the Panzer III had to close to suicidally short range. The KV-1 was even more heavily armoured and in consequence almost immune to anything but the 88mm FlaK 18/36. The emergence of the Soviet T-34 and KV-1 was a very unpleasant surprise and the shock of the discovery was later recalled by the lead Henschel designer

Dr. Erwin Aders (front row right) was head of Henschel's Tiger I development and construction project and the Tiger's chief designer, tours shop 5 in company with high ranking army officers on September 5th, 1942.

Erwin Aders, *"There was great consternation when it was discovered that the Soviet tanks were superior to anything available to the Heer."* In the scramble to come up with an strong defensive alternative to the Russian armour an immediate weight increase to 45 tonnes and an increase in gun calibre to 88mm was ordered. The due date for new prototypes was brought forward to 20th April 1942, Adolf Hitler's birthday.

Porsche and Henschel submitted prototype designs, Tiger (P) and Tiger (H), and they were put through their paces at Rastenburg before Hitler. The Henschel design was accepted as the best overall design. The Porsche gasoline-electric hybrid power unit performed poorly on the day with frequent breakdowns. It also used large quantities of copper, a strategic war material which was in very short supply. The contract was duly awarded to Henschel & Sohn.

Unlike the later Panther tank however, the designs for the Tiger did not incorporate any of the design innovations incorporated into the T-34: the defensive benefits of sloping armour and the corresponding saving in terms of weight were absent from both the Henschel and the Porsche designs, with the thickness and weight of the Tiger's armour making up for this oversight.

A newly completed Tiger is lowered on to a railway carriage ready to commence its journey to the front.

With the contract in the bag there was no time to loose and Henschel began production of the Panzerkampfwagen VI Ausf. H in August 1942 at its tank factory Henschelwerk III in Kassel-Mittelfeld.

The official designation from March 1943 onwards was Panzerkampfwagen VI SdKfz 181 Tiger Ausf E until Hitler's order, dated February 27th, 1944, abolished the designation Panzerkampfwagen VI and ratified the use of the new designation Panzerkampfwagen Tiger Ausf. E. This was to remain the official designation until the end of the war. For common use the name was frequently shortened to Tiger - the name purportedly given to the machine by its frustrated rival designer Ferdinand Porsche.

The firm of Henschel & Sohn was established in the early 1800s as a builder of locomotives and it was only during World War I that the firm undertook the business of armament manufacturing for the first time. The company kept up the new operations during the inter-war years and by the time Hitler was ready to re-arm Germany Henschel was ready and waiting to oblige. By the time of the second World War, the company was producing locomotives, tanks, diesel engines, trucks, aeroplanes and artillery pieces. Henschel manufactured all of the main battle tank types with the exception of the Panzer IV. This meant that at various times the Panzer I, II and III as well as the Panther, Tiger I and Tiger II all rolled off the Henschel production lines.

The firm of Henschel & Sohn incorporated three huge engineering works in and around Kassel. Werk I in Kassel was devoted to locomotive assembly and gun production, Werk II in the Rothenditmold area consisted of a large foundry, boiler and other locomotive component shops and Werk III in Mittelfeld was primarily devoted to tank assembly and component manufacture.

The Mittelfeld Werkes were situated on both sides of a railway line running north to south. Looking south, those buildings on the right side of the railway line were used for manufacturing locomotive components and truck and engine repair. The main storage area for tank components was also on the right side of the track including sheds that held Tiger hulls and turrets. On the right side of the track were 4 main shops numbered 1, 2, 3 and 5. (Shop 4 was planned but never built.). Tiger manufacturing took place in shops 3 and 5.

At its peak the factory employed a total of over 8000 workers for tank production. Sadly, extensive use was made of slave labour and the victims were treated abominably being effectively worked to death. The Henschel works were in production round the clock seven days a week. The labour force, both slave labourers and willing workers performed two exhausting 12 hour shifts but the night shift for a variety of reasons produced only 50% of the output of the day shift.

A manufacturing process known as the *"takte"* system was used in the assembly shops. That system relied on a timed rhythm for each step in the manufacturing process. There were nine steps or *takte* used in manufacturing the Tiger I. In surviving factory photos the reader should note the takte signs on the shop wall denoting which step is being performed in that location.

Each *takte* took six hours. The total time to complete a Tiger, including the various machining processes, was estimated to be 14 days and incorporated 300,000 man hours. An average of 18 to 22 tanks were carried at any one time in the hull assembly line and approximately ten tanks were carried in the final assembly line.

The first 4 *takte* revolved around hull machining and preparation. Henschel itself did not have the capability to weld or bend the massive heavy armour plates used in the Tiger and actually received the raw hulls and turrets from sub contractors. The turrets were manufactured by Wegmann und Company, which was conveniently also located in Kassel. The raw hulls were manufactured by two firms, Krupp and Dortmund-Hoerder Huettenverein. The hull processing steps all took place in shop 3.

A particularly fine study of a Tiger I in profile.

THE CONTEMPORARY VIEW NO. I
NEW GERMAN TANKS
EXTRACTED FROM
TECHNICAL AND TACTICAL TRENDS NO. 18, 1943

Several new types of German tanks have been reported to be in existence:

a) Mark I (C) - No details are known but it is probable that this is a redesigned Mark I intended for airborne or landing operations. The original Mark I tank weighed about 6 tons.

b) Mark II Special - The original Mark II tank (weight about 9 tons) has for some time been considered obsolescent as a combat tank. The new tank probably has thicker armour and a more powerful engine. One of the most important features is that it is reportedly armed with the long-barrelled 50mm gun which is used in the new Mark III tanks. The result should be a comparatively light, fast tank with adequate striking power, probably suitable for use as a tank destroyer.

c) Mark VI - This is a heavy tank. No details other than the actual nomenclature are known, but it seems probable that this model is an entirely new departure in German tank design. It has been anticipated for some time that the Marks III and IV might be superseded by a new type incorporating the best features of each model and introducing features borrowed from British and possibly American designs. Having obtained a tank gun of first quality in the long-barrelled 75mm tank gun (40), the weapon mounted in the new Mark IV tanks, it is probable that this weapon or an 88mm weapon is the principal armament. The basic armour may be as thick as 80 or 100mm, and spaced armour, at least in front, is probably incorporated. There may also be skirting armour. Face-hardened armour is probably used, and the speed is not expected to be under 25mph.

Reports of a German heavy tank have been received over a considerable period of time. Apparently the most recent is the statement of a German captured in Tunisia. According to the prisoner, he belonged to an independent heavy tank battalion, which consisted of a headquarters company and two armoured companies. Each armoured company was equipped with nine 50 ton tanks. The tanks were armed with 88mm guns and were capable of a speed of 50 kilometers (about 30 miles) an hour. Whether or not this is the Mark VI tank is not known.

DEPLOYMENT

Besides Russia, the Tiger was also deployed in Tunisia as it was this theatre which gave the western allies their first glimpse of the tank in the field. Prior to the arrival of the Tiger in Tunisia allied intelligence had been forced to rely on carefully placed German newspaper stories and limited intelligence provided by the Soviets. The first widely circulated intelligence report (see page 17) appeared in the US army intelligence publication entitled *Tactical and Technical Trends No. 18* which was published on 11th February 1943 some five months after the Tiger had first appeared in combat in Russia. It is interesting to note that the name Tiger had not yet come to be associated with the tank.

As the Tunisian campaign developed, Tiger tanks began appear more frequently on the battlefield albeit in limited numbers. However, their heavy armour and powerful armament allowed them dominate the initial tank battles fought in the open terrain of North Africa, but their mechanical unreliability and lack of numbers meant that they were never to be massed in great numbers and that they served in a primarily supporting role.

The following pages feature a further U.S. intelligence report describing the German Tiger tank originally appeared in *Tactical and Technical Trends*,

A Tiger I deployed in Tunisia. Note the bemused locals to the right.

The Tiger was deployed late in August 1942 but first saw action on 22nd September 1942. The machines were operating in the Army Group North sector near Lenningrad where the terrain was marshy and entirely unsuited to a colossus such as the Tiger I. This rare photograph gives a vivid impression of the type of terrain which the first Tigers were expected to traverse.

No. 20 on 11th March 1943. By this time, accurate information on the Tiger tank was starting to be received from destroyed remnants of Tigers captured by the British forces in Tunisia. This is the second glimpse of how allied intelligence reported the arrival of the Tiger on the battlefield. At this stage the name Tiger was still not in use and the Americans did not use the Roman numerals with the new machine being simply refereed to as the PZ.KW. 6

THE CONTEMPORARY VIEW NO.2
GERMAN HEAVY TANK
IN ACTION IN TUNISIA

As reported in the press and as previously indicated in Tactical and Technical Trends (No. 18, p.6) a German heavy tank has been in action in Tunisia. So far as can be definitely determined, this is the first time the Germans have used a heavy tank in combat. Whether or not it is the Pz.Kw. 6 cannot be definitely stated. At least one heavy tank has been captured, and while complete details are not yet available, there is sufficient reasonably confirmed data to warrant at least a partial tentative description at this time.

The chief features of this tank are the 88mm gun, 4-inch frontal armour, heavy weight, and lack of spaced armour. The accompanying sketch roughly indicates the appearance of the tank, but should not be accepted as wholly accurate.

The tank has a crew of 5. It is about 20 feet long, 12 feet wide, and 9 $\frac{1}{2}$ feet high. The gun overhangs the nose by almost 7 feet. It is reported that the weight is 56 tons or, with modifications, as much as 62 tons.

The power unit is a single 12-cylinder engine. A speed of at least 20 mph can be achieved. Two types of track are thought to exist: an operational track 2 feet 4.5 inches wide, and a loading track which is just under 2 feet. The suspension system consists of a front driving sprocket, a small rear idler, and 24 Christie-type wheels on each side giving it an appearance similar to the familiar German half-track suspension system. There are 8 axles.

There is no armour skirting for protection of the suspension. The armour plating is as follows:

Lower nose plate	62mm (24 in)	60° inwards
Upper nose plate	102mm (4 in)	20° inwards
Front plate	62mm (24 in)	80° outwards
Driver plate	102mm (4 in)	10° outwards
Turret sides and rear	82mm (3.2 in)	Vertical
Lower sides (behind bogies)	62mm (24 in)	Vertical

Upper sides	82mm (3.2 in)	Vertical
Rear	82mm (3.2 in)	20° inwards
Floor	26mm	(1 in)
Top	26mm	(1 in)

The turret front and mantlet range in thickness between a minimum of 97mm (3.8 in) to a (possible) maximum of 200mm (7.9 in). It appears that the armour is not face-hardened.

The armament of the tank consists of an 88mm gun and two 7.92mm (.315-in) machine guns. The 88mm has a double-baffle muzzle brake and fires the same fixed ammunition as the usual 88mm AA/AT gun. As already indicated, the gun overhangs the nose of the tank by almost 7 feet. The turret rotates through 360 degrees and is probably power-operated. Three smoke-generator dischargers are located on each side of the turret.

COMMENT

From the above characteristics, it is apparent that the Pz.Kw. 6 is designed to be larger and more powerful than the Pz.Kw. 4. As far as known, a Pz.Kw. 5 tank has not been used in combat. The noteworthy differences between the Pz.Kw. 4 and Pz.Kw. 6 are as follows:

Armour	Pz.Kw. 4	Pz.Kw. 6
Minimum	20mm	26mm
Maximum	50 to 80mm*	102mm**
Principal Armament	75mm (long-barrelled gun)	88mm (AA/AT gun)

A 360-degree rotating turret is used in both the Pz.Kw. 6 and Pz.Kw. 4.

The appearance of the Pz.Kw. 6 indicates that the Germans continue to see the need for a fully armoured vehicle equipped with a weapon capable of dealing with hostile tanks as well as with other targets that might hold up the advance of attacking elements.

This tank is undoubtedly an effective weapon, but not necessarily formidable. In the first place, a vehicle weighing from 56 to 62 tons presents many difficult logistical problems. Also, it is reported that one heavy tank was destroyed by a British six-pounder (57mm) antitank gun at a range of about 500 yards; out of 20 rounds fired, 5 penetrated the tank, 1 piercing the side of the turret and coming out the other side, and another penetrating an upper side plate at an angle of impact of about 15 degrees.

*Attained by attaching extra armour plate to protect critical points on the tank.

**Basic armour plate. The turret front and mantlet may possibly be 200mm thick.

A Tiger I deployed to supplement the Afrika Korps operating in Tunisia, January 1943.

THE MECHANICS OF THE TIGER I

The Tiger was essentially at the prototype stage when it was first hurried into service, and therefore changes both small and large were made throughout the production run. A redesigned turret with a lower, less bulky commander's cupola was the most significant early change. To cut costs, the submersion capability was reduced and an external air-filtration system was dropped.

The rear of the tank held an engine compartment flanked by two floodable rear compartments each containing a fuel tank, radiator, and fans. German industry had not developed an adequate heavy diesel engine, so a fuel hungry petrol power plant had to be used. The initial engine was a 21 litre (1282 cu. in.) 12 cylinder Maybach HL 210 P45 with 650 PS (641hp, 478kW). Although a good and reliable engine, it was inadequate for the size and weight vehicle. From the 250th production Tiger Chassis 250251, this engine was replaced by the updated HL 230 P45 (23 litres/1410 cu. in.) with 700 PS (690hp, 515kW). The engine was in V-form, with two cylinder banks at 60 degrees. An inertial starter was mounted on its right side, driven via chain gears through a port in the rear wall. The engine could be lifted out through a hatch on the hull roof. The engine drove two front sprockets, which were mounted low to the ground.

The eleven-tonne turret had a hydraulic motor the drive for which was powered by mechanical drive from the engine. Rotation was slow and took about a minute to swing through 360°. The suspension used sixteen torsion bars, with eight suspension arms per side. To save space, the swing arms were leading on one side and trailing on the other. There were three road wheels on each arm, giving a good cross-country ride. However the smoothness of the ride was bought at a high price. The constant need to remove the front road wheels in order to gain access to the rear wheels was to become the bane of Tiger I crews from day one.

The problem from the crew's point of view was that the heavy wheels which had a diameter of 800mm (31 in) were overlapped and interleaved. Removing one inner wheel that had lost its tyre, which was a fairly common occurrence, could therefore require the removal of up to nine outer wheels. This was bad enough under calm conditions but it meant there was no way of making a fast change in the combat zone and many precious Tigers were blown up which could otherwise have been saved. The wheels could

The cumbersome road wheel assembly of the Tiger I can be clearly seen in this photograph taken at the Henschel works. It is easy to understand why these wheels could become jammed solid with mud, ice or snow requiring huge efforts to repair.

also become packed with mud or snow that could then freeze. Eventually, a new 'steel' wheel design, closely resembling those on the Tiger II, with an internal tire was substituted, and which like the Tiger II, were only overlapped, and not interleaved.

Another new feature which was to cause problems was the untested Maybach-Olvar hydraulically-controlled pre-selector gearbox and semi-automatic transmission. The extreme weight of the tank also required a new steering system. Instead of the clutch-and-brake designs of lighter vehicles, a variation on the tested and proven British Merritt-Brown single radius system was used. The Tiger I, like all German tanks, used regenerative steering which was hydraulically operated - the separate tracks could therefore be turned in opposite directions at the same time, so the Tiger I could pivot in place, and completely turn around in a distance of only 3.44 meters (11.28 ft.). Since the vehicle had an eight-speed gearbox, it thus had sixteen different radii of turn. If an even smaller radius was needed, the tank could be turned by using brakes. There was an actual steering wheel and the steering system at least was robust, reliable, easy to use and ahead of its time. The British T. I. Summary No. 104 was issued on 16th May 1943 gave the British troops in the field a pretty accurate summary of the type of tank they were facing.

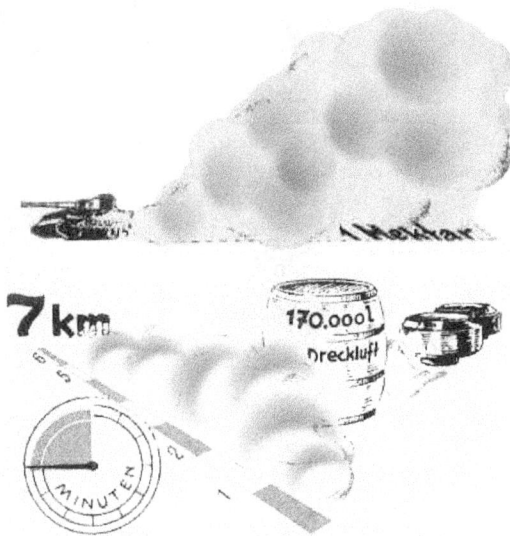

An extract from the Tigerfibel, the commander's manual: "If you travel 7km, your wide tracks will throw up the dust from 1 hectare of land. You will be recognised from far away and will lose your most efective weapon - surprise."

During action the laborious process of re-fuelling and re-arming the Tiger I was a never ending task for the hard pressed crew members.

PRODUCTION HISTORY

While the Tiger I was justifiably feared by many of its opponents, it was also over-engineered, used expensive labour intensive materials and production methods, and was time-consuming to produce. Despite its lasting reputation the tank was actually produced in relatively small numbers. Only 1,347 were built between August 1942 and August 1944 when production ceased. Throughout its brief life the Tiger I was particularly prone to certain types of track failures and immobilisations, it was unreliable mechanically reliable and ferociously expensive to maintain and complicated to transport. Due to its wide tracks powered by interlocking and over lapping road wheels the Tiger I required that a total of eight road wheels consisting of the outer four road wheels on both of the vehicle were to be removed if it was to be transported by rail.

The other huge drawback of the Tiger was the enormous fuel consumption associated with such a heavy vehicle. The 1943 log book a captured Tiger circulated by the British M.I.10 intelligence unit which

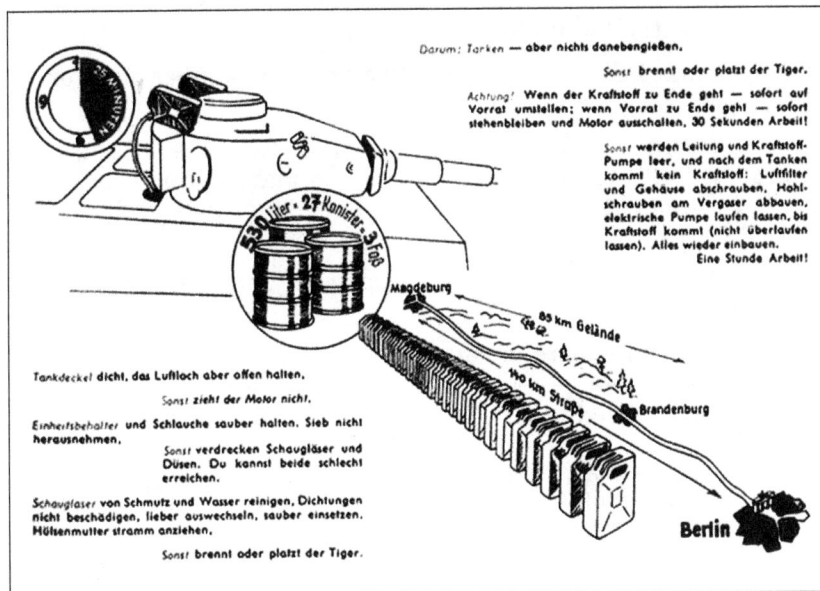

The humorous instruction manual for the tank, the Tigerfibel, was somewhat unorthodox by Third Reich standards. Full of risque sketches and irreverant statements, this is one of the more conventional pages which compares the tank's cross country capability against a road march.

THE CONTEMPORARY VIEW NO.3
Pz. Kw. VI

The following additional information on the Pz. Kw. VI has been collated from captured documents and reports from Russian and North Africa:

(a) The tank can be submerged to a depth of up to 16ft for fording rivers and other water obstacles. Further information on this development is contained at Appendix C.

(b) An automatic fire extinguisher is provided. Heat-sensitive elements are arranged in suitable positions in the engine compartment. If fire breaks out, one of these elements will cause an electric circuit to operate the extinguisher which will there upon discharge a fire-extinguishing agent for a period of seven seconds. If the fire is severe, the circuit will remain closed and the process will be repeated one or more times until either the fire is put out or the reservoir of the fire extinguisher is exhausted. The reservoir holds 9lbs of extinguishing agent.

(c) The gearbox is preselective and is cooled by a fan which also cools the manifold.

(d) Standard German petrol with an octane number of 74 or 78 is used for the engine.

(e) Reference summary 102, appendix D, North Africa now reports that the total amount of 8.8cm ammunition carried is 92 rounds stowed in racks and bins, 46 rounds each side of the tank.

(f) It is confirmed that the 8.8cm tank gun is electrically fired.

(g) Oil capacities are as follows:

Engine	28 litres (6.2 galls)
Gearbox & steering units (common sump)	32 litres (7 galls)
Final drive units	8 litres (14 pints)
Turret traversing gear	5 litres (8.75 pints)
Fan drive	6 litres (10.5 pints)

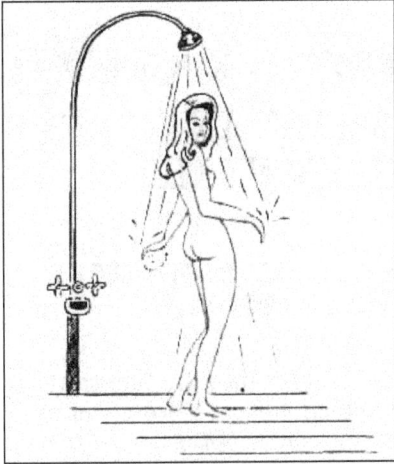

A typical risque illustration from Tigerfibel: "Like a fresh shower, the water flushes through the case and removes the heat accrued by combustion and friction, taking it to the radiators."

gives a fascinating insight into the fuel consumption characteristics of the Tiger I. The British report is shown overleaf on page 30.

With the conclusion of the Tunisian campaign there was adequate time to study the battlefield results achieved by the Tiger. Captured vehicles provided a wealth of accurate technical information A far more detailed account of the Tiger in combat was reported by the US army intelligence service in their monthly update for June 1943 which refers to the vehicle, for the first time, as the "Tiger". This US report appears on page 31.

During the course of the war, the Tiger I saw combat on the three main German battlefronts. It was usually deployed in independent tank battalions, which on occasion proved to be extremely formidable. In the right hands the Tiger I could be relied upon to turn some spectacularly one sided tactical situations in favour of the hard pressed men of the Heer. At the operational level however, there were never enough Tigers to affect the outcome of a major battle. In the tactical arena the Tiger I demanded good handling by experienced crews who knew and respected the limitations of the machine. Even with the very best crews it was soon apparent that the Tiger I was by no means a miracle weapon. It was always vulnerable to regular battlefield weapons such as the British 6 pounder which could prove deadly if the Tiger I was within range as this account from the US intelligence briefing update *Tactical and Technical Trends* reproduced on page 22 clearly demonstrates. American reports tended to favour the use of the Arabic numeral 6 as opposed to the German designated VI.

NOTE ON ENTRIES IN LOG BOOK OF PZ.KW.VI (H)

M I.IO GERMANY RCD.AT D.T.D SEPT 43

PZ.KW.VI(H) TIGER MECHANICAL BEHAVIOUR UNDER SERVICE CONDITIONS

Entries show that 4917 litres of petrol went into the fuel tanks of this vehicle during a period in which 489km were covered. In other words the apparent petrol consumption was over 10 litres per km. Even if it is assumed that the tanks (total capacity 530 litres) were empty at the start and full at the finish, the consumption would still work out at about 9 litres per km.

These figures are higher than the petrol consumption quoted in the official German specs, viz:

Roads	4.5 litres per km	1.58 galls per mile
Cross Country	7.8 litres per km	2.76 galls per mile

The following additional points have been noted in the log book:

120 km - Log started

136 km - Wireless Tested

160 km - Test run by workshops company

200 km - Wireless Tested/Engine oil and air cleaner oil

343 km - New gearbox fitted

365 km - Tooth sprocket ring (offside sprocket) changed

482 km - New engine & new nearside fan drive clutch fitted

609 km - Log closes

THE CONTEMPORARY VIEW NO.5
NEW GERMAN HEAVY TANK

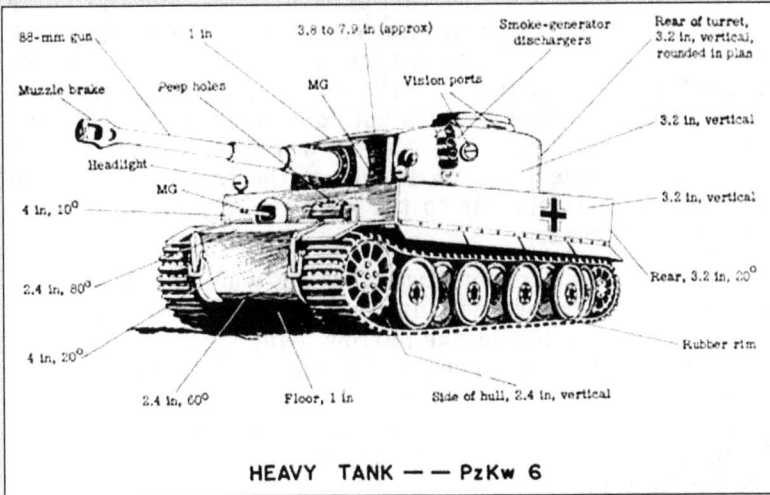

88-mm gun

Muzzle brake

Headlight

MG

4 in, 10°

2.4 in, 80°

4 in, 20°

2.4 in, 60°

1 in

Peep holes

3.8 to 7.9 in (approx)

MG

Vision ports

Smoke-generator dischargers

Rear of turret, 3.2 in, vertical, rounded in plan

3.2 in, vertical

3.2 in, vertical

Rear, 3.2 in, 20°

Rubber rim

Floor, 1 in

Side of hull, 2.4 in, vertical

HEAVY TANK — — PzKw 6

In Tunisia the German Army sent into combat, apparently for the first time, its new heavy tank, the Pz. Kw. 6, which it calls the "Tiger". The new tank's most notable features are its 88mm gun, 4-inch frontal armour, great weight, and lack of spaced armour. Although the Pz. Kw. 6 has probably been adopted as a standard German tank, future modifications may be expected.

The "Tiger" tank, which is larger and more powerful than the Pz. Kw. 4,1 is about 20 feet long, 12 feet wide, and 9 1/2 feet high. The barrel of the 88mm gun overhangs the nose by almost 7 feet. The tank weighs 56 tons in action (or, with certain alterations, as much as 62 tons), and is reported to have a maximum speed of about 20 miles per hour. It normally has a crew of five.

The armament of the Pz. Kw. 6 consists of the 88mm tank gun (Kw. K. 36), which fires fixed ammunition similar to, or identical with, ammunition for the usual 88mm antiaircraft-antitank gun; a 7.92mm machine gun (MG 34) which is mounted coaxially on the left side of the 88mm; and a second 7.92mm machine gun (MG 34) which is hull-mounted and fires forward.

In addition, a set of three smoke-generator dischargers is carried on each side of the turret.

The turret rotates through 360 degrees, and the mounting for the gun and coaxial machine gun appears to be of the customary German type.

The suspension system, which is unusually interesting, is illustrated in figure 4. The track is made of metal. To the far right in figure 4 is the front-drive sprocket and to the far left the rear idler. There are no return rollers, since the track rides on top of the Christie-type wheels, which are rubber rimmed. It will be noted that there are eight axles, each with three wheels to a side, or each with one single and one double wheel to a side. There are thus 24 wheels - 8 single wheels and 8 double wheels on each side of the tank. The system of overlapping is similar to the suspension system used on German half-tracks.

The tank is provided with two tracks, a wide one (2 feet, 4.5 inches) and a narrow one (just under 2 feet). The wide track is the one used in battle, the narrow being for administrative marches and where manoeuvrability and economy of operation take precedence over ground pressure. The dotted line in figure 4 indicates the outer edge of the narrow track. When the narrow track is used, the eight wheels outside the dotted line can be removed.

The armour plating of the Pz. Kw. 6 has the following thicknesses and angles:

Lower nose plate	62mm (24 in)	60° inwards
Upper nose plate	102mm (4 in)	20° inwards
Front plate	62mm (24 in)	80° outwards
Driver plate	102mm (4 in)	10° outwards
Turret front and mantlet	Up to 200mm (8 in)	Rounded
Turret sides and rear	82mm (3.2 in)	Vertical
Lower sides (behind bogies)	60mm (24 in)	Vertical
Upper sides	82mm (3.2 in)	Vertical
Rear	82mm (3.2 in)	20° inwards
Floor	26mm (1 in)	
Top	26mm (1 in)	

The angular (as opposed to rounded) arrangement of most of the armour is a bad design feature; reliance seems to be placed on the quality and thickness of the armour, with no effort having been made to present difficult angles of impact. In addition, none of the armour is face-hardened. The familiar German practice of increasing a tank's frontal armour at the expense of the side armour is also apparent in the case of the Pz. Kw. 6.

Undoubtedly the Germans developed the "Tiger" tank to meet the need for a fully armoured vehicle equipped with a heavy weapon capable of dealing with a variety of targets, including hostile tanks. Although the "Tiger" can perform these duties, its weight and size make it a logistical headache. It is entirely probable that the Germans, realizing this disadvantage, are continuing to develop tanks in the 30-ton class. Further, it is interesting to note that the Pz. Kw. 6 has proved vulnerable to the British 6-pounder (57mm) antitank gun when fired at a range of about 500 yards.

A Tiger captured by Allied Forces near Tunis, 1943. It was vehicles such as this which allowed the Allies to unlock the secrets of the Tiger I.

DESIGN FEATURES

The Tiger I differed from earlier German tanks principally in its design philosophy. Its predecessors all sought balance mobility, armour and firepower, and as a result were being outgunned by their opponents. The Tiger I represented a brand new approach which emphasised firepower and armour at the expense of mobility. Nonetheless the new heavy tank was surprisingly sprightly and was not that much slower than the best of its opponents. However, with over 50 metric tons dead weight, suspensions, gearboxes and other vital items had clearly reached their design limits and as a result Tiger I breakdowns were infuriatingly frequent.

Design studies for a new heavy tank had actually been started in 1937, but had stalled long before production planning stage was reached. Renewed impetus for the Tiger was provided by the discovery of outstanding battlefield qualities of the Soviet T-34 encountered in 1941. Although the general design and layout were broadly similar to the previous medium tank, the Panzer IV, the Tiger weighed more than twice as much. This was due to its substantially thicker armour, the larger main gun, greater volume of fuel and ammunition storage, larger engine, and more solidly-built transmission and suspension. Unfortunately for the Panzerwaffe not all of the lessons from the T-34 were absorbed. Sloping angular armour deflects most shots away from the vehicle and can therefore afford to be thinner and lighter. The Armour plates on the Tiger were mostly flat, with interlocking construction however the armour joints were of high quality, being stepped and welded rather than riveted which overcame one of the main disadvantages of riveted construction found in many allied tanks of the early war period.

The nominal armour of the Tiger at its thickest point on the gun mantlet was 200mm and an unprecedented 120mm thick on most of the mantlet. The Tiger I had frontal hull armour 100mm (3.9in) thick and frontal turret armour of 120mm (4.7in), as opposed to the 80mm (3.1in) frontal hull and 50mm (2 in) frontal turret armour of contemporary models of the Panzer IV. It also had 60mm (2.4in) thick hull side plates and 80mm armour on the side superstructure and rear, turret sides and rear was 80mm. The top and bottom armour was 25mm (1in) thick; from March 1944, the turret roof was thickened to 40mm (1.6in).

The gun's breech and firing mechanism were derived from the famous German "88" dual purpose flak gun, the Flugabwehr-kanone. The 88mm

Kampfwagonkanone 36 L/56 gun was the variant developed for the Tiger and was the most effective and feared tank guns of World War II. The Tiger's gun had a very flat trajectory and extremely accurate Leitz Turmzielfernrohr TZF 9b sights (later replaced by the monocular TZF 9c). In British wartime firing trials, five successive hits were scored on a 16 by 18 inch (410 by 460mm) target at a range of 1,200 yards (1,100m). Tigers were reported to have knocked out enemy tanks at ranges greater than 2.5 miles (4,000m), although most World War II engagements were fought at much shorter ranges.

Ammunition types :

    i) 8.8 cm KwK 36# Ammunition (General Issue)
    ii) PzGr.39 (Armour Piercing Capped Ballistic Cap)
    iii) PzGr.40 (Armour Piercing Composite Rigid)
    iv) Hl. Gr.39 (High Explosive Anti-Tank)
    v) Sch Sprgr. Patr. L/4.5 (Incendiary Shrapnel)

The 88mm ammunition carried by the Tiger I was exceptionally bulky and an ingenious array of stowage solutions were incorporated which allowed the tank to accommodate up to 100, and sometimes more, of these space consuming rounds.

THE CONTEMPORARY VIEW NO.6
ATTACK AGAINST GERMAN HEAVY TANK Pz. Kw. 6

The following report by an observer on the Tunisian front furnishes some comments as a guide to training in antitank action against this tank.

It appears that the first of these tanks to be destroyed in this theatre were accounted for by British 6-pounders (57mm). An account of this action, as reported by a British Army Officer, follows:

"The emplaced 6-pounders opened fire at an initial range of 680 yards. The first rounds hit the upper side of the tank at very acute angles and merely nicked the armour. As the tank moved nearer, it turned in such a manner that the third and fourth shots gouged out scallops of armour, the fifth shot went almost through and the next three rounds penetrated completely and stopped the tank. The first complete penetration was at a range of 800 yards, at an angle of impact of 30 degrees from normal, through homogeneous armour 82mm (approximately 3 1/3 inches) thick. Ammunition used was the 57mm semi-AP solid shot.

"One element of this action contains an important lesson that should be brought to the attention of all AT elements and particularly tank destroyer units."

(a) "The British gunners did not open until the enemy tank was well within effective range."

(b) "In addition to opening fire with the primary weapon - the 57mm - the AT unit also opened with intense light machine-gun fire which forced the tank to button up and in effect blinded him. His vision apparently became confused and he was actually traversing his gun away from the AT guns when he was knocked out for good.

(c) "Once they opened fire, the British gunners really poured it on and knocked out one more heavy tank and six Pz. Kw. 3s. Also, for good measure, one armoured car."

The conclusions to be drawn from this action, according to the British officer quoted, are:

(a) "The unobstructed vision of the gunner in a tank destroyer gives him a very real advantage over his opponent squinting through the periscope or narrow vision slits of a tank.

(b) "The tank destroyer unit must force the enemy tank to 'button up' by intense fire from every weapon he has, including machine-guns, tommy guns, and rifles."

The size and weight of a tank such as the Pz. Kw. 6 present many problems. It has been indicated from unofficial enemy sources that extensive reconnaissance of terrain, bridges, etc., was necessary before operations with this tank could be undertaken. Bridges have to be reinforced in many cases, and soil conditions must be good for its effective operation. It can therefore be assumed that its field of operation is limited.

Reports so far indicate that the use of this tank is chiefly to support other armoured units, including employment as mobile artillery. As a support tank it is always in rear of lighter units. In one reported skirmish in Tunisia, the lighter units formed the spear-head; as soon as enemy tanks were decoyed into range the lighter tanks fanned out, leaving the heavier tanks in the rear to engage the enemy units.

The Pz. Kw. 6 is now considered a standard German tank. Present production figures are believed to be at a maximum of 800 per month.

A tank commander confers with supporting infantry from the Waffen-SS. This shot was taken in the summer of 1943 .

GETTING TO THE BATTLEFIELD

The problems of moving the Tiger tank from place to place were significant and were especially marked in relation to rail movement by rail. The Tiger's width placed the vehicle at the very limits of the abilities of Europe's rail systems to cope with the vehicle and special transit tracks had to be developed if the tanks were to be moved at all. In order to support the considerable weight of the Tiger, the tracks were an unprecedented 725mm (28.5in) wide. Which was too wide to be carried by rail. To meet rail-freight size restrictions, the outer row of wheels had to be removed and special 520mm (20in) wide transport tracks installed. With a good crew, a track change took 20 minutes. British intelligence was bolstered by the 1944 interrogation of a POW who had experience of the enormous difficulties entailed in moving the Tiger by rail.

Another early U.S. report on the German heavy Tiger tank, Pz. Kw. 6 was featured in *Tactical and Technical Trends*, 6th May 1943 while the Tunisian campaign was coming to a close. By now the Tiger I was becoming increasingly familiar on the battlefields and as a result the intelligence reports were increasingly accurate.

As German prisoners began to be taken in Tunisia so the knowledge available to the allies increased. *Notes On Tank Tactics* was derived from interrogations of these prisoners and was published in April 1943 by the R.A.C. liaison unit. By this stage more and more detail was beginning to emerge on the exact statistical role in which the Tiger I was employed in Tunisia.

The first reports of the Tiger I in combat in Tunisia had actually begun to filter in from January 1943. From the speed at which the German battlefield tactics were altered it appears fairly clear that the German tank crews were quickly disabused of the notion that the new tank was invincible. The Tiger I was without a doubt a strongly built tank with many superior attributes, but it could be easily destroyed by regular battlefield weaponry, especially if the crew were not constantly vigilant for attacks from the rear or the side. This further extract from a British intelligence report from M.I.10 dated September 1943 underlines the fact that the British were fast learning the weaknesses of the Tiger in action.

Routine maintenance of the Tiger I was incredibly difficult and required a mobile crane as it was necessary to remove the turret in order to change the gear box. This was a frustratingly frequent occurrence.

PRISONER OF WAR
DESCRIBES RAIL EMBARKATION

A PW states that the narrow loading tracks for Tiger tanks belong permanently on the special platform truck and are put back on it when the truck returns to its home station.

Tiger tanks only just fit on the width of the truck and are secured by laying wooden beams against the inner sides of the trucks and securing them to the flooring by means of heavy bolts passing through prepared holes.

One PW described the loading of Tiger tanks at Maille-Le-Camp (France) early in Feb 44 and the unloading a few days later at Ficulie (Italy).

"Conditions at both ends were very bad. Deep mud, rain or snow, and biting winds hindered operations and made the job very trying.

The 80 ton platform truck was shunted up to an end loading ramp and secured in position.

By means of an 18 ton half tracked towing vehicle, the narrow loading tracks were towed off the platform truck and manoeuvred into position on the ground in echelon and at the correct width apart. One broad track was then undone and the tank driven forward on one track so that the bogie wheels on the opposite side ran off the broad track onto the narrow track.

The intended joining point of the narrow track was between the driving sprocket and the ground. To bring the upper run of the track round the rear idler and over the tops of the bogie wheels, the sprocket hub was used as a capstan by passing a wire rope round it. With the broad track locked and the sprocket on the opposite side rotating slowly, the crew pulled on the end of the wire rope and so brought the track up and over.

Having joined the first narrow track, the broad track on the opposite side was undone and the tank driven forward on the narrow track until the bogie wheels ran over the second narrow track.

Once the tank was fitted with the narrow tracks, the crew had to remove the four outside bogie wheels on both sides.

When this had been done, the half tracked towing vehicle had to tow the broad tracks side by side in front of the loading ramp.

The Tiger was then driven forward so that it straddled the tracks on the ground. Wire ropes were attached to the two lifting eyes at the front of the turret, passed over the front armour and secured at their other ends to the tracks.

The Tiger was finally driven up the ramp, towing its own broad tracks underneath it between the narrow tracks. Once it was in position on the platform truck the ultimate operation was to bring up the overhanging ends of the broad tracks over the rear armour of the tank, a feat accomplished by wire ropes and pulleys, with the attendant towing vehicle providing the motive power.

Before the tank was ready to travel, the turret had to be traversed to approx 5 o'clock to allow for the right-handed tunnels which are mostly encountered on the route from France to Italy.'

The cumbersome process of preparing the Tiger I for rail transport included removing the outermost road wheels, changing the wide combat tracks to fit the narrow guage tracks shown here.

GERMAN HEAVY TANK – Pz. Kw. 6

The accompanying sketch of the tank is based on photographs of a Pz. Kw. 6 knocked out on the Tunisian front.

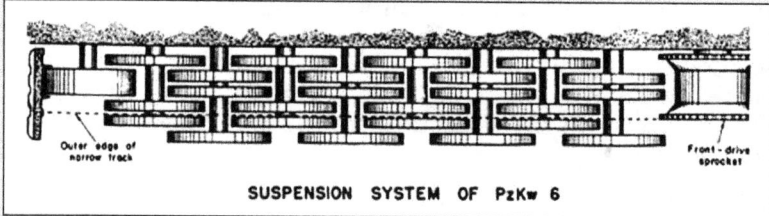

Outer edge of narrow track   Front-drive sprocket

SUSPENSION SYSTEM OF PzKw 6

The suspension system, which has only very briefly been described in Tactical and Technical Trends, is shown in the sketch The track is made of metal. To the far right in the sketch is the front-drive sprocket and to the far left, the rear Idler. There are no return rollers since the track rides on top of the Christie-type wheels, which are rubber rimmed. It will be noted that there are eight axles, each with three wheels to a side, or each with one single and one double wheel to a side. There are thus 24 wheels, or 8 single wheels and 8 double wheels, on each side of the tank. The system of overlapping is similar to the suspension system used on German half-tracks.

The tank is provided with two tracks, a wide one (2 ft, 4.5 in) and a narrow one (just under 2 ft). The wide track is the one used in battle, the narrow being for administrative marches and where manoeuvrability and economy of operation take precedence over ground pressure. The dotted line in the sketch of the suspension system indicates the outer edge of the narrow track. When the narrow track is used, the eight wheels outside the dotted line can be removed.

THE CONTEMPORARY VIEW NO.9
USE OF Pz. Kw. VI (TIGER)

(a) Information obtained from PW indicates that the Pz. Kw. VI was chiefly used in Tunisia to support other armoured units, and mention was made of its employment as mobile artillery. As a support tank it was always used in rear of lighter units. In one reported skirmish however, the lighter Pz. Kw. IIIs and IVs formed the spearhead of the advance; as soon as our tanks came within range the German 'spearhead' tanks deployed to the flanks, leaving the heavier Pz. Kw. VI tanks to engage.

(b) A PW who was with RHQ7 Pz. Regiment in Tunisia for sometime states that there were some 20 Pz. Lw. Vis in the regiment. When on the march ten of these moved with the main column, the others moving on the flanks. According to this PW, the tactics in the attack were to seek to engage enemy tanks from hull-down positions at short ranges, even down to 250 yards. On the other hand, this prisoner also reports an engagement in which two Pz. Kw. Vis brought indirect fire to bear, observation being carried out by an artillery FOO, each tank opening with one round of smoke. In confirmation of this there is another A.F.HQ. report which speaks of this exploitation by Pz. Kw. VI gunners of the great range of their 8.8 cm guns.

(c) 30 Military Mission also reports the use of Pz. Kw. VI in squadron strength on various parts of the Russian Front, especially the South-West.

(d) In conversation with Gerneral Martel, Marshal Stalin stated that in Russia, as in the desert, the Pz. Kw. VI went into battle in rear of a protective screen of lighter tanks.

(e) An A.F.HQ. training instruction states that the size and weight of the Pz. Kw. VI present many problems. PW indicated that extensive reconnaissance of terrain, bridges etc., was necessary before operations with this tank could be undertaken. Bridges had to be reinforced in many cases, and it was necessary for the 'going' to be good for the effective employment of the Pz. Kw. VI.

TIGERS BOLDLY USED

This is a standard Tiger tank - or, as the Germans designate it, Pz. Kpfw. Tiger. (The Roman numeral "VI" has been dropped.)

At first his Tigers were very boldly used and, once they were sure that their flanks were secured, they drove straight on. After several of these tanks had been knocked out, however, the crews appeared to be less enterprising and were inclined to use their tanks as mobile pillboxes. The fact remains, however, that in an armoured attack the Tiger tank must be regarded as a very formidable fighting component and, given adequate flank protection, will add very effective weight to the enemy firepower.

In the defensive the Pz. Kw. VI, usually well sited in a covered and defiladed position, was a particular danger. Despite the comparatively slow traversing rate of its turret, the Pz. Kw. VI proved an extremely good defensive weapon and could effectively cover a wide area with anti-tank fire. It was often used in good hull-down positions over very difficult ground, which made it hard for the Sherman to deal with it, and no amount of artillery fire could force it out.

Pz. Kw. VIIIs and IVs rarely took up good defensive positions on their own, but were used to watch the flanks of positions occupied by Pz. Kw. VIs. They were often used in small groups to counter-attack from concealed positions on the flank, from a cactus or olive grove or down a wadi. The terrain forced the enemy to employ rush tactics in close formation, and resulted in these counter-attacks being suitably dealt with.

Tank recovery requires a special note. It was often affected on the spot with speed and courage by attaching tow ropes to the casualties and towing them away by other tanks. Special trips at night were made by tanks to recover casualties (20 Jan BOU ARADA, and 1 Feb ROBAA). Where the enemy held the battlefield, tractors were brought up and the whole area cleared of recoverable casualties, both theirs and ours, in a very short time. The speed with which the recovery plan was made and carried out made action by our demolition squads very difficult, and where tank casualties were in no-man's land and unapproachable by day, the enemy would get out to them the moment darkness fell. Sometimes (eg ROBAA, BOU ARADA) as much as a company of infantry was used to hold off our patrols or stage a diversion while recovery was in progress. The enemy used tanks against our Churchills and was quick to take advantage of an unprotected flank

A broken down Tiger I being towed by two Sd.Kfz. 9. The convolutd arrangement was the only means by which a broken donw Tiger I could be officially recovered.

THE CONTEMPORARY VIEW NO. II
GEAR BOX TROUBLE

If a Tiger tank has gearbox trouble, it is customary to dismantle the flexible couplings in the half-shaft drives and to tow it out of the immediate battle area by another Tiger, using two tow ropes secured in 'X' formation to correct the tendency of the towed tank to sway.

Should, however, the track on a Tiger have ridden up over the sprocket teeth, the tractive effort required to move it is so great that two Tigers pull in tandem, each towing with crossed tow ropes.

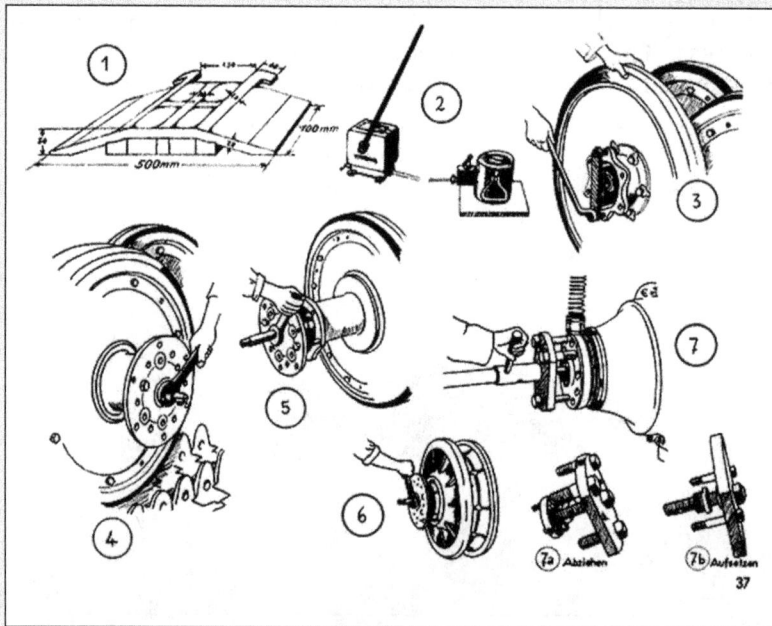

Illustration showing the tools and methods of running gear maintenance from Tigerfibel. Although the need to change road wheels was a frequent and frustrating occurrance, by far the largest share of the mechanical problems resulted from the gear box, the repair of which necessitated the removal of the turret by a mobile crane.

MOBILITY

Despite its drawbacks the Tiger was relatively manoeuvrable for its weight and size, and as it generated less ground pressure, it proved to be superior to the Sherman in muddy terrain,. The Tiger tank however was plainly too heavy to cross small bridges with certainty, so it was purpose designed with the built in mechanism to enable the tank to ford four-meter deep water while fully submerged. This required unusual mechanisms for ventilation and cooling when underwater. At least 30 minutes of set-up was required, with the turret and gun being locked in the forward position, and a large snorkel tube raised at the rear. Only the first 495 Tigers were fitted with this expensive and rarely used deep fording system; all later models were capable of fording only two meters.

The main source of mechanical breakdown of the Tiger I appears to have been the gearbox which is a recurring theme in relation to the numerous breakdowns suffered by these vehicles. Towing a Tiger was an enormous problem and frequently resulted in the breakdown of other Tigers assigned to tow broken down vehicle. The procedure was described in an R.A.C. liaison letter dated August 1944.

The real Achilles heel of the Tiger was the extent to which it was prone to mechanical breakdowns. Even when the vehicle was running smoothly vigilance and extreme care was required as the Tiger was exceptionally liable to becoming bogged down while moving across the difficult terrain which was particularly prevalent in Italy. It was here that the British discovered an inordinately large number of disabled Tigers. Initially these 12 machines were all thought to be victims of combat, but it was later discovered, through examination and prisoner interrogation, that the casualties were all as a result of either mechanical or terrain difficulties. This astonishing revelation was published in August 1944 in a report by the British Army's Technical Branch entitled *"Who Killed Tiger ?"*

THE CONTEMPORARY VIEW NO.12
WHO KILLED TIGER?

This Tiger of the 502nd overturned in the act of crossing a bridge in Russia, during November 1943. The tank commander was killed but the tank was recovered.

As a fairly large number of Tiger tanks were reported to have been knocked out in the breakout from the Anzio bridgehead and the advance on Rome we thought it might be educational to try and find out what weapon or what tactics had been responsible, so that the dose might be repeated on other occasions.

Hearing that there was somewhat of a concentration of bodies in a certain area we made a reconnaissance on the 5th August in an area between Velletri and Cori some 30 miles S.E. of Rome.

In all during this reconnaissance 12 Tigers were found either on the road, by the roadside or within easy sight of the road. The following is what we found:

(1) On the Via Tuscolana. Pulled up at the side of the road near a bridge diversion. No sign of battle damage but both tracks were off and each had been cut with a gas torch. Blown up and burnt out so the cause of the casualty could not be determined.

(2) On the village green of Giulianello. No sign of battle damage other than a penetration of the hull back plate by Bazooka. This is thought to have been done by following troops after the tank had been abandoned, because the engine cooling fan had been penetrated by the shot but was obviously not rotating at the time and, furthermore, several unused rounds of U.S. Bazooka ammunition were found lying near the machine. This tank had not been demolished by the crew and there was no indication of the cause of stoppage.

(3) By the side of the road one mile from Giulianello. Signs of two H.E. strikes on the turret and one on the cupola. A further H.E. had struck the upper side plate about track level and may have broken the track which was off on this side.

On the opposite side the three rear bogie spindles were bent upwards and the bogies were riding the track guides. A tow-rope was found in place and the tank had been demolished. If the right hand track had in fact been cut by H.E. it is possible that a recovery crew had been caught while extricating the tank which had become a casualty due to the suspension trouble on the other side.

(4) Halfway down a steep bank on the Guilianello-Cori road. No sign of any battle damage or suspension trouble. Tank had been demolished. In this case it is possible that the machine had either become ditched down the bank or had some internal mechanical trouble which could not be rectified.

An interesting point is that this tank had rubber bogie wheels on one side and steel on the other.

A Tiger I undergoing engine repair.

(5) Found in a small copse about 100 yards off the road. No sign of battle damage but tank appeared to have become ditched in a sunken lane where it had been trying to turn. Broken tow-ropes found in place. No important suspension defects so that the casualty must have been due to internal mechanical trouble possibly caused by trying to extricate itself from the lane. Blown up.

(6) Found off the road down a bank where it had been pushed to clear the road. Deep A.P. scoops on front of manlet and side of turret. Penetration by unknown weapon through 3rd bogie from rear on left hand side. Tracks off, blown up and burnt out. Not enough evidence to deduce the cause of the casualty except that it was certainly not due to the A.P. strikes which were probably sustained in an earlier engagement.

Two Tigers of the 504th Schwere Abteilung irrecoverably stuck in a steep valley. This battalion suffered six total write-offs in four days while on a road march in Italy in September 1944.

(7) Off the road at the edge of an olive grove. Definite evidence of track trouble. Several track guide lugs broken. R.H. sprocket ring cracked in one place and L.H. ring in two places. Attempts to tow had been made. Demolished. Possibly on tow because of mechanical trouble and abandoned when tracks rode the sprockets and damaged them.

(8) On the level in an olive grove. There were signs of the area having been used by a workshop detachment. No apparent battle damage other than penetrations of bogie wheels by H.E. splinters. Casualty probably due to internal mechanical trouble. One demolition charge had been blown.

The task of extricating a stricken Tiger from difficult terrain was beyond every vehicle except another Tiger. Activities of this nature placed a huge strain on the engine and could often result in both vehicles being lost and was officially against orders. However this type of activity, although frowned upon, was a daily occurrence for the men of the Panzerwaffe as there was simply no alternative.

(9) Found up against a house in Cori where it would appear to have been left by a recovery team. Two H.E. scoops on front plate. Tracks off and obvious signs of suspension trouble. R.H. front bogie bent and out of line. Tracks found near. These showed fractures of several links. Demolished.

(10) Off the road in Cori within 10 yards of No.9 above. One bogie wheel missing and others damaged. Sprockets cracked in three places. Tracks off and lying nearby showed evidence of trouble – cracked link and broken guide lug. Demolished.

(11) On the bridge at Cori. Within 50 yards of Nos 9/10. Tank had fallen through damaged arch of bridge. Both tracks off and laid out on the road behind. No battle damage to be seen. Demolished. The presence of Nos 9,10 and 11 tanks so close together suggests that Cori may have been a recovery point for tanks with mechanical trouble which were blown up when it was found impossible to repair them.

(12) Found on the road from Giulianello to Valmontone in a field by a stream some 300 yards off the road. No battle damage but two bogie wheels on one side were bent and out of line. Tracks were still on. There was evidence in the shrubs nearby that the crew of a recovery section had camped by the tank and had been attempting some mechanical repairs

which could not be completed in time so that the tank had to be left and demolished.

NOTES

Since the above examination was made some information has been received from a P.O.W. which suggests that these 12 tanks were the remnant of 3 Sqn, 506 Heavy Tank Battalion, which was given the job of resisting the Allied break-out from Anzio with 16 tanks.

Some were lost in the engagement while others suffered gearbox trouble and had to be towed out of action. The squadron was ordered to retreat on Cori and during this retreat so much trouble was experienced with the gearboxes and suspensions of towing tanks that attempts at extrication beyond Cori had to be abandoned.

CONCLUSION

Tiger is not yet sufficiently developed to be considered a reliable vehicle for long marches. He suffers from frequent suspension defects and probably also gearbox trouble. When pushed, as in a retreat, these troubles are too frequent and serious for the German maintenance and recovery organization to deal with.

TIGER RECOVERY

Due to its size and weight the high number of breakdowns and the recovery of battle damaged vehicles was to prove a real headache for the engineers. The tanks were immensely valuable and had to be recovered if at all possible. However, the infrastructure and, in particular the recovery vehicles, to support the easy recovery of such a heavy machine as the Tiger I was found to be severely wanting.

Three famo 18t tractors were needed to drag this Tiger I into the workshop during the assault on Kharkov, 1943.

The main problem was that the standard German heavy Famo recovery half-track tractor could not actually tow the tank; up to three Famo tractors were usually the only way to tow just one Tiger. It was the case therefore that another Tiger was needed to tow a disabled machine, but on such occasions, the engine of the towing vehicle often overheated and sometimes resulted in an engine breakdown or fire. Tiger tanks were therefore forbidden by regulations to tow crippled comrades.

In practice this order was routinely disobeyed as the alternative was the total loss of a large number of tanks that could otherwise have been saved. It was also discovered too late that the low-mounted sprocket limited the obstacle-clearing height. The wide Tiger tracks also had a bad tendency to override the sprocket, resulting in immobilisation. If a track overrode and jammed, two Tigers were normally needed to tow the tank. The jammed track was also a big problem itself, since due to high tension, it was often impossible to disassemble the track by removing the track pins. It was sometimes simply blown apart with an explosive charge.

The illustration from the driver section from Tigerfibel.

THE CONTEMPORARY VIEW NO.13
USE OF Pz. Kw. VI (TIGER)

A section of Tiger I tanks rolls into position prior to the battle of Kursk .

(a) Information obtained from POW indicates that the Pz. Kw. VI was chiefly used in Tunisia to support other armoured units, and mention was made of its employment as mobile artillery. As a support tank it was always used in rear of lighter units. In one reported skirmish however, the lighter Pz. Kw. IIIs and IVs formed the spearhead of the advance; as soon as our tanks came within range the German 'spearhead' tanks deployed to the flanks, leaving the heavier Pz. Kw. VI tanks to engage.

(b) A POW who was with RHQ7 Pz. Regiment in Tunisia for sometime states that there were some 20 Pz. Lw. Vis in the regiment. When on the march ten of these moved with the main column, the others moving on the flanks. According to this PW, the tactics in the attack were to seek to engage enemy tanks from hull-down positions at short ranges, even down to 250 yards. On the other hand, this prisoner also reports an engagement in which two Pz. Kw. VIs brought indirect fire to bear, observation being carried out by an artillery FOO, each tank opening with one round of smoke. In confirmation of this there is another

A rare shot of a Tiger engaged in combat during the battle of Kursk.

A.F.HQ. report which speaks of this exploitation by Pz. Kw. VI gunners of the great range of their 8.8 cm guns.

(c) 30 Military Mission also reports the use of Pz. Kw. VI in squadron strength on various parts of the Russian Front, especially the South-West.

(d) In conversation with General Martel, Marshal Stalin stated that in Russia, as in the desert, the Pz. Kw. VI went into battle in rear of a protective screen of lighter tanks.

(e) An A.F.HQ. training instruction states that the size and weight of the Pz. Kw. VI present many problems. PW indicated that extensive reconnaissance of terrain, bridges etc., was necessary before operations with this tank could be undertaken. Bridges had to be reinforced in many cases, and it was necessary for the 'going' to be good for the effective employment of the Pz. Kw. VI.

(f) It would seem that the employment of this tank in a support role is not however invariable, because a German press report of the fighting round Kharkov in March seems to indicate that the Pz. Kw. VI were used offensively in an independent role.

(g) Another German press report states that during the German withdrawal from Schusselburg, 'a few' Pz. Kw. VI formed the most rearward element of the German rearguard, a role in which they were most successful.

(h) An interesting and detailed newspaper article, written towards the end of May, on events on the Leningrad Front, points towards the use of the Tiger as a mobile defensive front and as having been in action 'for days' (i.e. by inference, that they had been in the same area). These operations were carried out in close co-operation with the infantry manning the defensive positions.

In one particular operation a troop of tanks is described as taking up a defensive position forward of the infantry positions from which (presumably hull-down) advancing Soviet tanks and the following infantry were engaged. All this defensive fire was put down at the halt including the fire from the MGs in the tanks. In order to move to an alternative position because of enemy arty fire it was necessary for the tank commander to obtain permission from the CO Battle Group, under whose command he was operating.

CONCLUSION

The use of Pz. Kw. VI tanks in both attack and defence seems, from all available information to hand, to be in a support role. The use of this type of tank in an independent thrusting role, even when supported by tanks of lighter types, would seem to be discouraged.

Distant Tigers moving up to engage Russian forces during the Kursk offensive. The millions of anti-tank mines were the greatest danger facing the Tigers during the assault phase of the battle.

TIGER COLOUR SCHEMES

In June of 1940 a general order was issued that stipulated all Panzers were to be painted *Dunkelgrau* (dark grey). This order was still in effect when the Tigers were initially deployed in August 1942. The very first Tiger I's were painted dark grey and as such are usually easy to identify in photographs.

In areas where winter camouflage was needed, the crews applied whitewash. When spring arrived, the crews had to scrub the whitewash off, which was a tedious, labour intensive chore.

In February 1943, a general order came down to change the base coat from dark grey to tan (Dunkelgelb nach Muster). Crews were issued cans of red brown (Rotbraun) and dark olive green (Olivgruen) to use in creating camouflage patterns over the basic tan colouration.

Some tigers were coated with the Zimmerit anti-magnetic mine coating starting in July 1943. This paste was applied in recognizable grooved patterns and the paint was applied over the top of the coating. Vehicles coated with Zimmerit have a distinctive rough look to their surface.

Camouflage patterns varied from unit to unit, as did the placement and colouring of the vehicle numbers. In addition to good camouflage the tanks themselves required close protection from infantry squads at all times.

A Tiger I painted in the original factory Dunkelgrau deployed on the Northern sector in January 1943.

THE CONTEMPORARY VIEW NO.14
USE OF A F Vs IN NORTH AFRICA

(a) A POW has described how riflemen with MGs were employed for the protection of tanks when in harbour. On the following morning they were withdrawn from this task for rest and in preparation for other duties.

(b) A POW reports that German tanks were always able to intercept Allied radio traffic, on one occasion obtaining in this way an exact location. Pz. Kw. VI were immediately detailed to engage.

(c) Voluntary destruction of tanks. On 5th December 1942 the following orders were issued by OC 8 Pz. Regiment: "Tanks may be blown up in the following circumstances only:

(i) If the tank cannot be moved

(ii) If the enemy is attacking, and then only,

(iii) If the tank has defended itself to its last round.

The Commander responsible for issuing the order to blow up the tank must make a report to R H Q detailing the circumstances".

(d) Another report describes as 'typical' a case in which a large concentration of tanks was observed opposite one area on our front, small parties of which were observed 'tapping' along our front, halting to fire from about 2,000 yards.

(e) On another occasion another report describes how an estimated total of 50 German tanks put in a counter-attack in the early evening in two groups, each under smoke cover.

The radio operator from the Tigerfibel.

DESIGN REVIEW

As the war wore on into 1944 the increasing volume of captured Tigers continued to yield invaluable intelligence information. With a number of complete machines now in the hands of the western allies it was possible to conduct increasingly scientific examinations. Practical testing of weapon systems and armour was soon undertaken to identify the strengths and weaknesses of the Tiger I. In November 1944 a series of gunnery trials was conducted by Major W. de L. Messenger and his report is summarized overleaf.

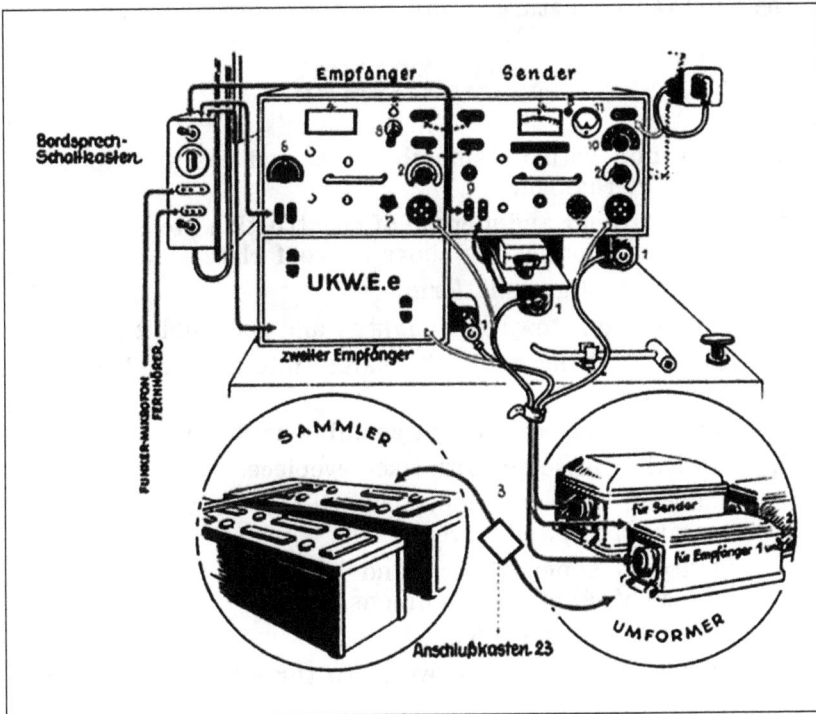

The Tiger radio set up from Tigerfibel which was split into a receiver and a transmitter.

THE CONTEMPORARY VIEW NO.15
DESIGN REVIEW

The design has been well thought out and it embodies a number of distinctly original features such as the heavy armament and armour, turret and hull construction, powered traverse layout and facilities for total submersion.

It appears that the user has not had the same influence on it as on British tanks since so many of the items, whilst basically good, are unsatisfactory and could well be improved from the user aspect by slight modification.

The outstanding features would appear to be:

GOOD POINTS

1. 8.8cm gun with its smooth action and easily stripped breech mechanism.
2. Heavy armour and method of construction (welding and front plates projecting above the roof plates).
3. Stability as a gun platform.
4. Ammunition stowage – quantity and accessibility.
5. Electrical firing gear with safety interlocks and novel trigger switch.
6. Flush turret floor without coaming or shields.
7. Binocular telescope with fixed eyepiece.
8. Mounting for periscopic binoculars in cupola and commander's hand traverse.
9. Ability to superimpose hand on power traverse and absence of oil pipes and unions.
10. Ample space for loader.
11. Method of attaching stowage to turret walls (flexible strips).
12. Spring assisted hatches.
13. S-mine dischargers.
14. 2-position commander's seat and backrest
15. Electrically fired smoke generator dischargers.
16. Handholds on roof to assist gunner.

BAD POINTS

1. Out-of-balance of gun and turret.
2. Obscuration by smoke from flashless propellent.
3. Ventilation of gun fumes
4. Lack of intercommunication for loader.
5. Cramped positions of gunner and commander.
6. Powered traverse control – Lack of definite neutral position and awkward range of movement
7. No armouring on bins.
8. Small gun deflector bag.
9. Awkward re-arming of co-axial M.G.
10. Gunner's exit via commander's cupola.
11. Head pad on auxiliary M.G.

The Pz. Kpfw. VI with its heavy armour, dual purpose armament and fighting ability is basically an excellent tank, and, in spite of the defects noted, constitutes a considerable advance on any tank that we have tried.

Its greatest weakness is probably the limit imposed on mobility owing to its weight, width and limited range of action. Taking it all round, it presents a very formidable fighting machine which should not be under-rated.

The Tiger was a prized target and was as vulnerable as any other tank to strongly motivated tank hunting teams. Close support from well trained infantry was therefore crucial to the survival of the Tigers on the battlefield. The Tiger on the right is carrying its own close support team.

PRODUCTION RUN MODIFICATIONS

During the production run of the Tiger I a number of modifications were introduced in order to correct imperfections to improve automotive performance, firepower and protection. Any good measure which led to the simplification of the design was also implemented, along with forced adjustments as a result of shortages of war materials. Due to a rigid production flow policy at the Henschel factory, incorporation of the new modifications could take several months. In 1942 alone, at least six revisions were made, starting with the removal of the *Vorpanzer* (frontal armour shield) from the pre-production models in April 1942. In May, mudguards bolted onto the side of the pre-production run were added, while removable mudguards saw full incorporation in September. Smoke discharge canisters, three on each side of the turret, were added in August 1942. In later years, similar changes and updates were added, such as the addition of Zimmerit in late 1943.

Modifications continued as a result of combat experiences in Italy at a comparatively late stage in the life of the Tiger I. The RAC liaison letter for August 1944 revealed that POW integration sources were still providing valuable information regarding the on-going modification programme, which mentioned modifications in the Model E over its predecessors including the following:-

THE CONTEMPORARY VIEW NO. 16
TURRET TOP ARMOUR

In early March '44 on the beachhead, a number of Tiger tanks were spotted from the air by an artillery recce aircraft and shortly afterwards a concentration of artillery fire was put down, during which the turret top of one Tiger was pieced by a direct hit from what appears to be an American "Long Tom."

This incident, which cost two dead of the crew, was duly reported and is considered to have been the reason for the thickening of the turret top armour back and front from 25mm to 40mm on the Model E Tigers which came down from Paderborn in late May 1944.

COMBAT HISTORY

As we have see the Tiger was first used in action on 28th September 1942 in marshy terrain near Leningrad. The action was a direct result of Hitler's desperation to see the Tiger in action. This resulted in the tank, which was still very much a prototype, being forced into action prematurely.

Unfortunately, on 22nd September 1942, as they entered the combat arena for the first time the Tigers were deployed single file over marshy terrain with the inevitable result that the machines began to bog down. It was to prove an ominous portent when, in their first day of combat, all four were knocked out. It is interesting to note however that the armour of the vehicles was not penetrated. Three of the Tigers which had been abandoned by their crews were later recovered.

In spite of this atrocious start the Tiger I was to become a fixture of a number of heavy units serving on the eastern front. Better tactics involving close co-operation with supporting infantry units were soon developed and other Panzer crews were quickly trained at Paderborn so that they too could be equipped with the Tiger I as the machines rolled off the production lines. The deployment of The Tiger I happened at a fairly rapid pace and by the end of 1942 the first Tiger formations had been deployed in Russia,

An interesting study of two Tigers passing on a narrow forest track in northern Russia during the summer of 1943.

A Grenadier standing in front of a trio of captured Russian anti-tank guns scans the skies as a Tiger I in summer camouflage paint scheme rolls on towards the enemy.

Tunisia, and Italy. A further training centre was soon established in France. Tigers would eventually be in service with ten Heer heavy tank battalions and one training battalion as well as and the Grossdeutschland Panzer Grenadier Division.

In addition to the regular army units three Waffen-SS heavy tank battalions were also equipped with the Tiger I. A number of additional Heer formations received a smattering of Tigers though the numbers were generally very limited. The 14 Tiger equipped units were the backbone of the fighting force and were issued with the bulk of the available machines.

In the North African theatre, the Tiger first saw action near Robaa Tunisia. In the ensuing battle, a battery belonging to the 72nd Anti-tank Regiment of the British Army equipped with six-pounder managed to knock out three enemy Tigers and rout the remaining forces. The action soon found its way into the British and US intelligence reports reprinted elsewhere in this book. The next theatre in which the allies encountered the Tiger was to be Italy where Tigers were encountered both in Sicily and on the mainland. Following the D-Day landings the Tiger I was encountered during the Normandy battles where it was fielded by the Leibstandarte division.

ROAD MARCHES

The Tiger's extreme weight limited which bridges it could cross. It also made driving through buildings something of a lottery as basements were liable to collapse trapping the tank in the rubble. Another weakness was the slow traverse of the hydraulically-operated turret. The turret could also be traversed manually, but this option was laborious and rarely used, except for very small adjustments.

Early Tigers had a top speed of about 45 kilometres per hour (28mph) over optimal terrain. This was not recommended for normal operation, and was discouraged in training. Crews were ordered not to exceed 2600rpm due to reliability problems of the early Maybach engines with their maximum 3000rpm output. To combat this, the Tiger's top speed was reduced to about 38 kilometres per hour (24mph) through the installation of an engine governor, capping the rpm of the Maybach HL 230 to 2600rpm (HL 210s were used on early models). Despite being slower than medium tanks of the time, which averaged a top speed of about 45 kilometres per hour (28mph), the Tiger still had a very respectable speed for a tank of its size and weight, especially if one considers the fact that the Tiger I was nearly twice as heavy as a Sherman or T-34.

Another shot of a Tiger I encountering difficult terrain and insurmountable obstacles in the Army Group North sector.

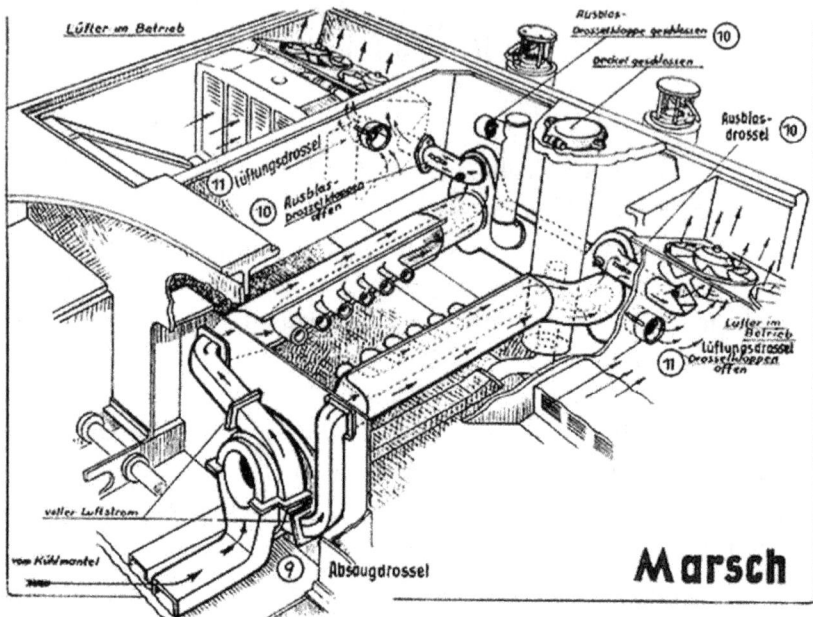

Labels in the diagram:
- Lüfter im Betrieb
- Lüftungsdrossel (11)
- Ausblas-drosselklappe offen (10)
- Ausblas-Drosselklappe geschlossen (10)
- Deckel geschlossen
- Ausblas-drossel (10)
- Lüfter im Betrieb
- Lüftungsdrossel Drosselklappen offen (11)
- voller Luftstrom
- vom Kühlmantel
- Absaugdrossel (9)
- **Marsch**

This diagram from Tigerfibel shows throttle and vent flap positions when the Tiger is moving on a road march.

The Tiger had reliability problems throughout its service life; Tiger units almost invariably entered combat under strength due to various mechanical breakdowns. It was rare for any Tiger unit to complete a road march without losing vehicles due to breakdowns. The tank also had poor radius of action ie the distance which a combat vehicle can travel and return to the battlefield without refuelling. Although the Tigerfibel gave the figure of 42.5km in each direction (see page 27) the reality was much lower - 35km across country was considered to be the maximum on a full tank. However, the Tiger I was a remarkably efficient cross-country vehicle. Due to its very wide tracks however, the Tiger did produce a lower ground pressure bearing than many smaller tanks, the most notable exception being the Soviet T-34 which also ran on comparatively wide tracks.

NOTES ON TANK TACTICS
USE OF PZ KW VI (TIGER)

Information obtained from PW indicates that the Pz Kw VI was chiefly used in Tunisia to support other armoured units, and mention was made of its employment as mobile artillery. As a support tank it was always used in rear of

lighter units. In one reported skirmish however, the lighter Pz Kw IIIs and IVs formed the spearhead of the advance; as soon as our tanks came within range the German 'spearhead' tanks deployed to the flanks, leaving the heavier Pz Kw VI tanks to engage.

A PW who was with RHQ7 Pz Regiment in Tunisia for some time states that there were some 20 Pz Kw Vis in the regiment. When on the march ten of these moved with the main column, the others moving on the flanks. According to this PW, the tactics in the attack were to seek to engage enemy tanks from hull-down positions at short ranges, even down to 250 yards. On the other hand, this prisoner also reports an engagement in which two Pz Kw Vis brought indirect fire to bear, observation being carried out by an artillery F O O, each tank opening with one round of smoke. In confirmation of this there is another A.F.HQ report which speaks of this exploitation by Pz Kw VI gunners of the great range of their 8.8 cm guns.

30 Military Mission also reports the use of Pz Kw VI in squadron strength on various parts of the Russian Front, especially the South-West.

In conversation with General Martel, Marshal Stalin stated that in Russia, as in the desert, the Pz Kw VI went into battle in rear of a protective screen of lighter tanks.

An A.F.HQ. training instruction states that the size and weight of the Pz Kw VI present many problems. PW indicated that extensive reconnaissance of terrain, bridges etc., was necessary before operations with this tank could be undertaken. Bridges had to be reinforced in many cases, and it was necessary for the 'going' to be good for the effective employment of the Pz Kw VI.

It would seem that the employment of this tank in a support role is not however invariable, because a German press report of the fighting round Kharkov in March seems to indicate that the Pz Kw VI were used offensively in an independent role.

Another German press report states that during the German withdrawal from Schusselburg, a "few" Pz Kw VI formed the most rearward element of the German rearguard, a role in which they were most successful.

An interesting and detailed newspaper article, written towards the end of May, on events on the Leningrad Front, points towards the use of the Tiher as a mobile defensive pillbox. The tanks are described as operation on a defensive front and as having been in action 'for days' (i.e. by inference, that they had been in the same area). These operations were carried out in close co-operation with the infantry manning the defensive positions.

In one particular operation a troop of tanks is described as taking up a defensive position forward of the infantry positions from which (presumably hull-down) advancing Soviet tanks and the following infantry were engaged. All this defensive fire was put down at the halt including the fire from the MGs in the tanks. In order to move to an alternative position because of enemy arty fire it was necessary for the tank commander to obtain permission from the CO Battle Group, under whose command he was operating.

The use of Pz Kw VI tanks in both attack and defence seems, from all available information to hand, to be in a support role. The use of this type of tank in an independent thrusting role, even when supported by tanks of lighter types, would seem to be discouraged.

The loader from Tigerfibel.

TACTICAL ORGANISATION

The Tiger I was usually employed in separate heavy tank battalions known as schwere-Panzer-Abteilung, and were so precious they were generally placed under army command. The heavy battalions would normally be deployed to critical sectors, for use either in breakthrough operations or, as the war wore on, more typically in local counter-attacks. A few favoured divisions, such as the Grossdeutschland and the 1st SS Leibstandarte Adolf Hitler, 2nd SS Das Reich, and 3rd SS Totenkopf Panzergrenadier Divisions at Kursk had a Tiger company in their tank regiments. The Grossdeutschland Division had its Tiger company increased to a battalion as the III Panzer Battalion in Panzer Regiment Grossdeutschland. 3rd SS Totenkopf retained its Tiger I company through the remainder of the war. 1st SS and 2nd SS tank regiments lost their Tiger Companies which were incorporated into a SS Tiger Battalion, the 101st SS Tiger Battalion, which was part of 1st SS Panzer Korps.

The commanders chosen to be granted command of a Tiger I represented the very best of the candidates who passed through the gates of the tank training facility at Paderborn.

The Tiger was originally designed to be an offensive breakthrough weapon, but by the time they went into action, the military situation had changed dramatically, and their main use was on the defensive, as mobile gun batteries known as "the mobile fire brigade". Unfortunately, this also meant rushing the Tigers constantly from location to location causing excessive mechanical issues. As a result, there are almost no instances where a Tiger battalion went into combat at anything close to full strength. Furthermore, against the Soviet and Western Allied production numbers, even a 10:1 kill ratio would not have been sufficient to turn the tactical tide. Some Tiger units did actually exceed the 10:1 kill ratio, including 13. Kompanie/Panzer-Regiment Grossdeutschland with a ratio of 16:1, schwere SS-Panzer-Abteilung 103 with a ratio of 12:1 and schwere Panzer-Abteilung 502 with a ratio of 13:1. These numbers must be set against the opportunity cost of the expensive Tiger. Every Tiger cost as much as four Sturmgeschütz III assault guns to build.

An English translation of a contemporary article from the Soviet Artillery Journal giving detailed instructions for the use of anti-tank weapons against the German Tiger tank, appeared in the U.S. intelligence periodical *Tactical and Technical Trends*, No. 40, December 16th, 1943. Vulnerability of various parts of the tank was cited in connection with directions for attack. At the time of publication, U.S. forces had only sporadically encountered the Tiger tank in Tunisia, Sicily, and Italy. The accompanying sketch shows vulnerable points and indicates weapons to be used against them. Material concerning the vulnerability of German tanks was published in Tactical and Technical Trends No. 8, p. 46 and No. 11, p.28. Detailed information about the Tiger tank was published in Tactical and Technical Trends No. 34, p.13. A translation of the Soviet Artillery Journal article follows overleaf:

THE RUSSIAN VIEW

VULNERABILITY OF TIGER TANKS

Fire at the gun   Fire at the gas-tank

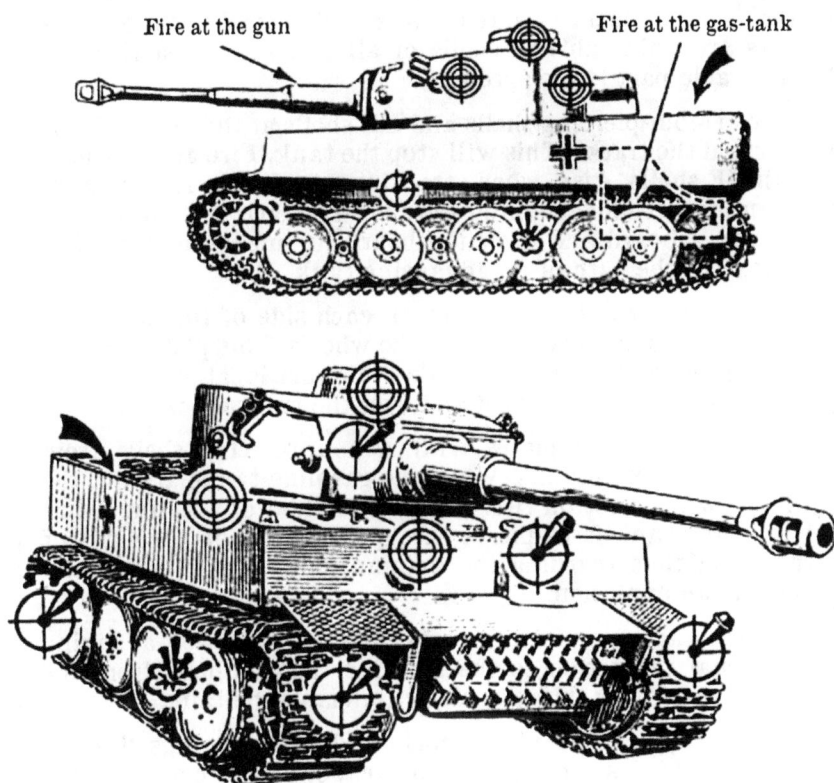

Условные обозначения:

Стреляй из всех видов оружия.
(Use all weapons)

Стреляй из пушек всех калибров.
(Use guns of all calibers)

Забрасывай бутылками с горючей жидкостью.
(Throw incendiary bottles)

Бей противотанковой гранатой.
(Use AT grenades)

The Russian view on how to attack the Tiger was reproduced for the benefit of western Allied soldiers in the December 1943 version of Tactical and Technical Trends.

THE CONTEMPORARY VIEW NO. 18
VULNERABILITY OF TIGER TANKS

"The mobility of tanks depends upon the proper functioning of the suspension parts - sprocket (small driving wheel), idler (small wheel in the rear), wheels and tracks. All of these parts are vulnerable to shells of all calibres. A particularly vulnerable part is the sprocket.

"Fire armour-piercing shells and HE shells at the sprocket, the idler and the tracks. This will stop the tank. Fire at the wheels with HE shells. Also, when attacking a tank, use AT grenades and mines. If movable mines are used, attach three or four of them to a board and draw the board, by means of a cord or cable, into the path of an advancing tank.

"There are two armour plates on each side of the tank. The lower plate is partly covered by the wheels. This plate protects the engine and the gasoline tanks which are located in the rear of the hull, directly beyond and over the two rear wheels.

"Fire at the lower plates with armour-piercing shells from 76-, 57- and 45mm guns. When the gasoline tanks are hit, the vehicle will be set on fire. Another method of starting a fire within the tank is to pierce the upper plates on the sides of the tank, thus reaching the ammunition compartments and causing an explosion.

"The rear armour plate protects the engine as well as giving additional protection to the gasoline tanks. Shells from AT guns, penetrating this armour, will disable the tank.

"The turret has two vision ports and two openings through which the tank's crew fire their weapons. The commander's small turret has five observation slits. There are two sighting devices on the roof of the front of the tank, one for the driver, the other for the gunner. Also, in the front of the tank there is a port with a sliding cover.

"The turret is a particularly important and vulnerable target. Attack it with HE and armour-piercing shells of all calibres. When it is damaged, use AT grenades and incendiary bottles (Molotov cocktails).

"There is a 10mm slit all around the base of the turret. AT gun and heavy machine-gun fire, effectively directed at this slit, will prevent the turret from revolving and thus seriously impair the tank's field of fire. Furthermore, hits by HE shell at the base of the turret may wreck the roof of the hull and put the tank out of action.

"The tank's air vents and ventilators are under the perforations in the roof of the hull, directly behind the turret. Another air vent is in the front part of the roof, between the two observation ports used by the radio operator and the driver. Use AT grenades and incendiary bottles against these vents.

"Explode antitank mines under the tank to smash the floor and put the tank out of action."

A Tiger I camouflaged in a static defensive position.

TIGER ACES

The Tiger is particularly associated with SS-Hauptsturmführer Michael Wittmann of schwere SS-Panzerabteilung 101. He worked his way up, commanding various vehicles and finally a Tiger I. In the Battle of Villers-Bocage, his platoon destroyed over two dozen Allied vehicles, including several tanks.

Astonishingly given his enduring reputation Wittmann was not the highest scoring tank commander. Over ten Tiger tank commanders claimed over 100 vehicle kills each, including Kurt Knispel with 168, Walter Schroif with 161, Otto Carius with 150+, Johannes Bölter with 139+, and Michael Wittmann with 138.

Name	Tank Kills	Unit
Kurt Knispel	168	s.Pz.Abt. 503
Martin Schroif	161	s.SS-Pz.Abt. 102
Otto Carius	150+	s.Pz.Abt. 502
Hans Bolter	139+	s.Pz.Abt. 502
Michael Wittmann	138	s.SS-Pz.Abt. 101
Paul Egger	113	s.SS-Pz.Abt. 102
Arno Giesen	111	8./SS-Pz.Rgt. 2
Heinz Rondorf	106	s.Pz.Abt. 503
Heinz Gartner	103	s.Pz.Abt. 503
Wilhelm Knauth	101+	s.Pz.Abt. 505
Albert Kerscher	100+	s.Pz.Abt. 502
Balthazar Woll	100+	s.SS-Pz.Abt. 101
Karl Mobius	100+	s.SS-Pz.Abt. 101
Helmut Wendorff	95	s.SS-Pz.Abt. 101
Will Fey	80+	s.SS-Pz.Abt. 102
Eric Litztke	76	s.Pz.Abt. 509
Emil Seibold	69	s.SS-Pz.Abt. 502
Karl Brommann	66	s.SS-Pz.Abt. 503

D 656/27

Tigerfibel

...sooo'ne schnelle Sache!

*The cover illustration
from Tigerfibel*

**Kurt
Knispel**

**Martin
Schroif**

**Otto
Carius**

**Hans
Bolter**

**Michael
Wittmann**

**Paul
Egger**

**Heinz
Rondorf**

**Heinz
Gartner**

**Wilhelm
Knauth**

**Albert
Kerscher**

**Bobby
Woll**

**Karl
Mobius**

Helmut
Wendorff

Will
Fey

Eric
Litztke

Emil
Seibold

Karl
Brommann

Alfred
Rubbel

Konrad
Weinert

Walter
Junge

Bobby
Warmbrunn

Jurgen
Brandt

Heinz
Kling

Heinz
Kramer

Alfredo
Carpaneto

Heinz
Mausberg

Franz
Staudegger

Alfred Rubbel	60+	s.Pz.Abt. 503
Konrad Weinert	59	s.Pz.Abt. 503
Walter Junge	57+	s.Pz.Abt. 503
Bobby Warmbrunn	57	s.SS-Pz.Abt. 101
Jurgen Brandt	57	s.SS-Pz.Abt. 101
Heinz Kling	51+	s.SS-Pz.Abt. 101
Heinz Kramer	50+	s.Pz.Abt. 502
Alfredo Carpaneto	50+	s.Pz.Abt. 502
Heinz Mausberg	50+	s.Pz.Abt. 505
Oskar Geiner	50+	s.SS-Pz.Abt. 103
Johann Muller	50+	s.Pz.Abt. 502
Joachim Scholl	42	s.SS-Pz.Abt. 102
Franz Staudegger	35+	s.SS-Pz.Abt. 101

The Tiger I has been estimated to have an overall ratio of 5.74 kills to each loss, with 9,850 enemy tanks destroyed for a loss of 1,715 Tigers. It is important to note that the number of Tiger Is lost is higher than those produced (1,347), as the Wehrmacht included tanks that had undergone heavy repair and brought back into combat in the total of new machines.

A powerful study of Tigers in action near Orel.

Tiger tank ace Michael Wittmann. Despite all of the reports, it comes as a surprise to many to discover that the highest scoring Tiger I ace was actually Kurt Knispel who survived the war with 168 tank kills to his credit.

The chart below demonstrates the estimated Tiger I kills to losses ratio:

Unit	Losses	Kills	Kill/Loss Ratio
schwere Panzer-Abteilung 501	120	450	3.75
schwere Panzer-Abteilung 502	107	1,400	13.08
schwere Panzer-Abteilung 503	252	1,700	6.75
schwere Panzer-Abteilung 504	109	250	2.29
schwere Panzer-Abteilung 505	126	900	7.14
schwere Panzer-Abteilung 506	179	400	2.23
schwere Panzer-Abteilung 507	104	600	5.77
schwere Panzer-Abteilung 508	78	100	1.28
schwere Panzer-Abteilung 509	120	500	4.17
schwere Panzer-Abteilung 510	65	200	3.08
13./Panzer-Regiment Grossdeutschland	6	100	16.67
III./Panzer-Regiment Grossdeutschland	98	500	5.10
13./SS-Panzerregiment 1	42	400	9.52
8./SS-Panzerregiment 2	31	250	8.06
9./SS-Panzerregiment 3	56	500	8.93
schwere SS-Panzer-Abteilung 101 (501)	107	500	4.67
schwere SS-Panzer-Abteilung 102 (502)	76	600	7.89
schwere SS-Panzer-Abteilung 103 (503)	39	500	12.82
Total	1,715	9,850	5.74

A Tiger I engages in action during the battle of Kursk.

TIGERPHOBIA

The Tigers forged an impressive combat record in Russia during 1943 and 1944. They destroyed tremendous amounts of enemy equipment especially anti-tank guns. Eventually it was held that often the mere sight of a Tiger was enough to cause Russian tank crews to withdraw from the battlefield. The Tiger enjoyed a similar psychological success in North Africa and Italy, creating a powerful negative effect on the morale of both British and US troops. The mere rumour that the troops were up against Tigers was often enough to spread panic.

The debilitating influence of the Tiger on allied morale was so widespread the condition was given its own name and was widely known as *Tigerphobia*. The grip which the Tiger held on the popular imaginations of allied soldiers was so severe that British Field Marshall Montgomery banned all reports of the Tiger which made any reference to its prowess in battle. There were times when even Monty couldn't prevail over the cold facts. In the right hands the Tiger was a ferociously weapon system. The Tiger's greatest moment of fame was one such moment. Michael Wittmann gained lasting notoriety with his amazing exploits in a single action on 13th

This impactful study of a Tiger I on the move creates a strong impression of the power of the Tiger I. Faced with the prospect of engaging with a fast moving and strongly equipped monster such as this it is easy to understand how the Tigerphobia condition grew and spread.

Panzer crewmen inspect the combat damage inflicted by enemy rounds which have just failed to pierce the strong side armour of the Tiger.

June 1944 in Normandy where the famous commander destroyed an entire column of 25 tanks, 14 half-tracks and 14 bren-gun carriers in a few short minutes with one Tiger I handled with deadly efficiency.

This press photo does a great job of conveying the strength of the frontal armour of a Tiger I which, although not efficiently sloped, was strong and robust enough to deal with the direct hit from a large calibre shell, the evidence of which can be seen on the front mantlet to the right of the figure in the helmet.

THE CONTEMPORARY VIEW NO.19
NOTES ON TIGER TANKS
IN THE BATTLE FOR FLORENCE

A field conference in the summer of 1943 , the half hearted camouflage and relaxed attitude suggest that soviet air cover was not percievd to be a threat by these tank men.

In the battle for Florence, a New Zealand division had its first experience with standard Tiger tanks on a fairly large scale, and noted several useful points about the ways in which the Germans employed these vehicles.

As a rule, the Tigers were well sited and well camouflaged with natural foliage. To delay the New Zealand infantry and to pick off tanks, the Tigers were used in hull-down positions. Another enemy method was to send Tigers by covered routes to previously selected positions. From these positions the Germans would fire a few harassing rounds, withdraw, and move to alternate positions. Tigers also were used to provide close support for German infantry, to lend additional fire power to artillery concentrations, and to engage buildings occupied by the New Zealanders. These troops noted that almost invariably a Tiger would be sited with at least one other tank or a self-propelled gun in support. The supporting tank or gun would remain silent unless its fire was absolutely needed. Sometimes a Tiger would be accompanied by infantrymen -

often only 6 to 12 of them - deployed on the flanks as far as 50 yards away from the tank.

The New Zealanders were of the opinion that the Tiger's heavy front and rear armour made it unlikely that the tank would be knocked out by hits on these parts. Simultaneous frontal and flank attacks were considered desirable. The New Zealanders found the Tigers' side armour definitely vulnerable to fire from 17-pounders. Other weak spots, it was reported, were the rear of the tank, just over the engines, and the large exhaust hole, also in the rear and just over the left of centre. Some commanders found high explosives the most effective ammunition against these rear parts.

As a rule, the Tigers were placed in position so skillfully that the New Zealanders found it difficult to employ a sniping anti-tank gun or a towed gun for stalking purposes. Unless very careful reconnaissance was carried out to site the gun to the best advantage, and so as to detect German supporting tanks or self-propelled guns, the effort was likely to be fruitless. For this reason, the New Zealanders concluded that maximum time for reconnaissance, and the maximum amount of information, were essential for a battery commander who was called upon to engage a Tiger. The German tank-and-gun combination seemed to be slow at manoeuvring and firing, and also very susceptible to blinding by U.S. 75mm smoke ammunition. On one occasion, two smoke rounds, followed by armour-piercing projectiles, were enough to force a Tiger to withdraw.

Sometimes the Germans used their Tigers with marked recklessness, the crews taking risks to an extent which indicated their extreme confidence in their vehicles. This rendered the latter vulnerable to New Zealand tank-hunting squads armed with close-range antitank weapons. When Tigers were closed down, and were attacking on their own at some distance from their supporting guns, the tanks' vulnerability to those close-range weapons was increased correspondingly.

Tigers were effectively knocked out, or were forced to withdraw, by concentrations of field artillery. It was clear that German tank crews feared the damaging effect of shell fire against such vital parts as tracks, suspension, bogie wheels, radio aerials, electrical equipment, and so on. The New Zealanders incorporated medium artillery in several of their artillery concentrations, and decided that medium pieces were suitable when a sufficiently large concentration could be brought to bear. However, owing to a dispersion of rounds, it was considered preferable to include a good concentration of field guns, to "thicken up" the fire. The division in question had no experience in using heavy artillery against Tigers.

It was admittedly difficult to locate stationary, well camouflaged Tigers which had been sited for defensive firing. Worth mentioning, however, is the performance of an artillery observation post, which was notified by Allied tanks that a Tiger was believed to be in a certain area. The observation post began to range. A round falling in the vicinity of the suspected tank blasted away the vehicle's camouflage, and the Tiger promptly retreated.

Several of the New Zealand antitank gunners' experiences in combating Tigers will be of special interest:

(1) A Tiger was observed about 3,000 yards away, engaging three Shermans. When it set one of the Shermans afire, the other two withdrew over a crest. A 17-pounder was brought up to within 2400 yards of the Tiger, and engaged it from a flank. When the Tiger realized that it was being engaged by a high-velocity gun, it swung around 90 degrees so that its heavy frontal armour was toward the gun. In the ensuing duel, one round hit the turret, another round hit the suspension, and two near-short rounds probably ricocheted into the tank. The tank was not put out of action. The range

A tank man inspects the combat damage inflicted by enemy rounds which have failed to pierce the strong side armour of the Tiger tank turret.

was too great to expect a kill; hence the New Zealanders' tactics were to make the Tiger expose its flank to the Shermans at a range of almost 500 yards, by swinging around onto the antitank gun. The Tiger did just this, and, when it was engaged by the Shermans, it withdrew. The enemy infantry protection of half a dozen to a dozen men was engaged by machine guns.

(2) At the junction of a main road and a side road, a Tiger was just off the road, engaging forward troops in buildings. Another Tiger, about 50 yards up the side road, was supporting the first. A field-artillery concentration was called for. It appeared to come from one battery only. Although no hits were observed, both Tigers withdrew.

(3) A Tiger on a ridge was engaged by what appeared to be a battery of mediums. After the first few rounds had fallen, the crew bailed out. (It is not known why.) Shortly afterward, while the tank still was being shelled, a German soldier returned to the tank and drove it off. About 10 minutes later, the remainder of the crew made a dash along the same route their tank had taken.

(4) A tank hidden in the garage of a two-story house ventured out for about 20 yards, fired a few harassing rounds, and returned to its shelter. Many hits on the building were scored by 4.2-inch mortars firing cap-on, but little damage was visible. Each night the tank was withdrawn from the area, even though it was in an excellent concealed position and was protected by infantry. Later the house was examined. Although it had suffered appreciable damage — and there were several dead Germans about there was no evidence that damage had been done to the tank itself.

INSIDE THE TIGER

The internal layout was typical of German tanks. Forward was an open crew compartment, with the driver and radio-operator seated at the front on either side of the gearbox. Behind them the turret floor was surrounded by panels forming a continuous level surface. This helped the loader to retrieve the ammunition, which was mostly stowed above the tracks. Two men were seated in the turret; the gunner to the left of the gun, and the commander behind him. There was also a folding seat on the right for the loader. The turret had a full circular floor and 157cm headroom.

The crews of the Tiger tank gained a feeling of invincibility and this mood of superiority on behalf of the German tank crews survived defeat and captivity as revealed by the interrogation of an veteran German tank gunner who had served in The Afrika Korps and in Italy and therefore could boast practical experience of both the Tiger and captured allied Sherman tanks.

This photograph from a contemporary British report shows the driving position of the Tiger I.

THE CONTEMPORARY VIEW NO.20
THE TIGER VS THE SHERMAN

The gun layer- an experienced tank man- was inclined to be very boastful where German tanks were concerned. He had landed in Africa in May 1941 and stayed in the desert for nearly two years (no home leave and only the rarest visits to towns). His memories of the campaign are chiefly a record of the numbers of British AFVs knocked out by the invincible Mk IIIs and IVs, tinged with a reluctant admission that the same tanks were matched in October 43 at Alamein by General Grants and General Shermans. He was critical of the fact that the employment of these AFVs had not been appreciated by the Germans and that the launching of the British push came as a surprise to the armoured Divs.

His confidence has been fully restored since he transferred to Tiger Tanks. On every occasion he stresses the great feeling of security which a crew has inside an AFV with such armour. Crews feel very certain of their ability to engage and destroy any target. He claims that he once ran into fire from the flank from seven 17 pdr A/Tk guns at close range and, having turned the hull of his tank so that a three quarter view was presented to the fire; proceeded to destroy five out of seven A/Tk guns with HE rounds. Several hits were registered on the frontal armour of the flaking from shell splinters.

The only situation in which he felt uncomfortable was to receive A/Tk gun fire from the flank and, having engaged the gun after having turned his AFV into the optimum position, to receive fire at right angles from an undetected A/Tk position in his rear. His reaction would then be to swing his turret as fast as possible and engage the more dangerous of the two targets.

The only time when a General Sherman stands a chance of knocking out a Tiger (in his opinion)is when it can close to less than 800 metres. He has observed that, even granted great superiority in numbers, Sherman tank crews do not venture willingly to close in, even on sides away from the principal preoccupation of the Tiger's fire. He claims that 3 Sqn has accounted for 63 Shermans since arrival in this theatre, 17 of which fall to his account.

The general opinion of the Sherman for its class was high. PW was instrumental in capturing two on the beachhead (one with a radial engine and one with twin Diesel engines) and the Bn had ample time to acquaint itself with these **AFVs** before removing the turrets and passing them back to 4 (workshops) Sqn for use as recovery vehicles, less turrets. His biggest criticism of the Sherman is of the visibility afforded to the commander when his hatch is closed down. He regarded the periscope as extremely poor.

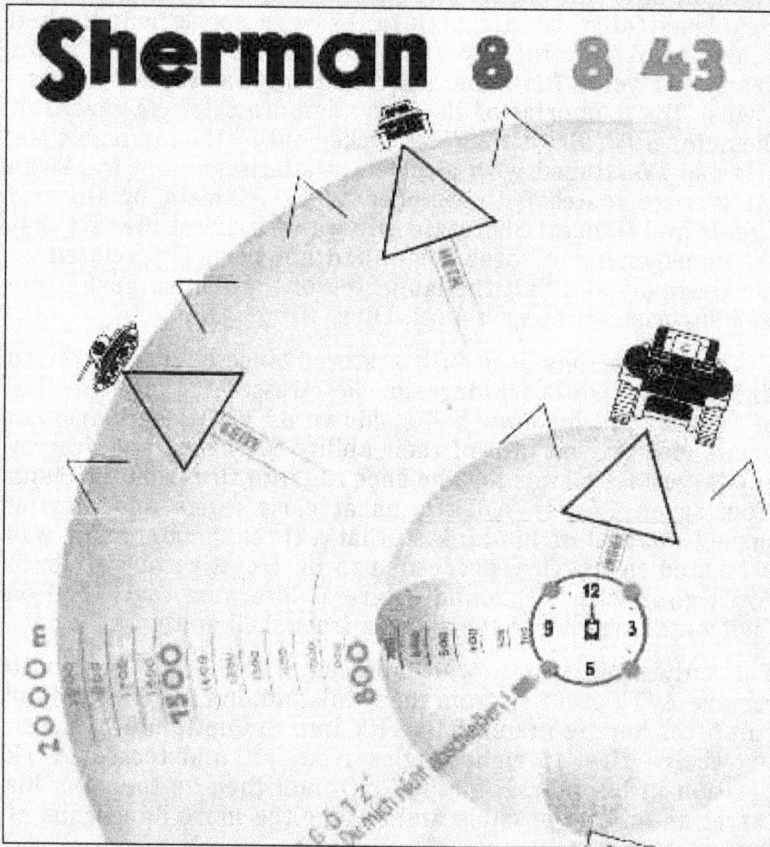

From Tigerfibel

"YANK" MAGAZINE

The following is an article on enemy vehicles tested at the Aberdeen Ordnance Research Centre from the January 21st, 1944 issue of Yank. The cover is an image of German Tiger I tank from the 1.Ko. of s.Pz.Abt. 504 which was captured by Allied forces in Tunisia.

The US Army did little to prepare for combat against the Tiger despite their assessment that the newly-encountered German tank was superior to their own. This conclusion was partly based on the correct estimate that the Tiger would be encountered in relatively small numbers. Later in the war, the Tiger could be penetrated at short range by tanks and tank destroyers equipped with the 76mm gun M1 when firing HVAP rounds, and at long range with the M2/M3 90mm AA/AT gun firing HVAP, and the M36 tank destroyer and M26 Pershing by the end of the war.

A Tiger I laden with grenadiers moves up towards the front, January 1944.

THE CONTEMPORARY VIEW NO.21
ENEMY VEHICLES FROM YANK

At Aberdeen's Ordnance Research Centre, inquisitive experts finds what makes an Axis vehicle tick, and their tests produce facts worth remembering.

By Sgt. MACK MORRISS and Sgt. RALPH STEIN,
YANK Staff Correspondents

ABERDEEN, MD.

This extract is taken from Yank magazine

The first thing you learn at the Foreign Material outfit here is never, ever, to call a Nazi tank a "Mark Six" or a "Mark Four." The correct designation is Pz. Kw. VI or Pz. Kw. IV. "Mark" is a British way of saying model, whereas Pz. Kw. means what it says: Panzer Kampfwagen, or armoured battlewagon.

For more than a year captured enemy vehicles have been arriving here from every battle front on earth. The first was a half-track prime mover that came in sections and required three months of trial-and-error tinkering to be completely reconstructed. Missing parts, which were requisitioned from North Africa, never arrived; mechanics in the Base Shop section made their own.

The worst headache for repair crews here is the difference in measurement caused by the European metric system. Nothing manufactured in the U.S. will fit anything in a Nazi machine unless it is made to fit. In reconstructing the captured stuff, it has sometimes been necessary to combine the salvaged parts of two or three vehicles in order to put one in running order. The mechanics have made their own pistons or recut foreign pistons to take American piston rings; they've cut new gears; they've had to retap holes so that American screws will fit them.

Specially assigned recovery crews, ordnance men trained to know and work with enemy material, roam the battlefields of the world to collect the captured rolling stock, which is being accumulated here. It arrives with the dust of its respective

Changing the huge front sprocket on the Tiger I was a regular job as the sprocket itself was set too low to the ground without much clearance and as a result was frequently damaged by obstacles.

theatre still on it, plus the names and addresses of GIs who scratch "Bizerte" or "Attu" or "Buna Mission" in big letters on the paint.

Generally speaking, ordnance experts here have found German stuff exceptionally well made in its vital mechanisms, whereas the less essential parts are comparatively cheap. The motor of a Nazi personnel carrier, for example, is a well-built affair, while the body of the vehicle is little more than scrap tin. Japanese pieces of equipment for the most part are cheap imitations of American or British counterparts.

The engineers, who judge by the mass of detail employed in all German-built machines, are convinced that the Nazi idea has been to sacrifice speed for over-all performance and manoeuvrability. The German equipment, from the sleek motorcycle to the massive Pz. Kw. VI, is rugged.

The famous Tiger is the largest and heaviest German tank. Weighing 61 1/2 tons, it is propelled at a speed of from 15 to 18 miles an hour by a 600-to-650 horsepower Maybach V-12 cylinder engine. Maybach engines are used in many of the Nazi Panzer wagonen and in submarines. The Pz. Kw. VI has an armour thickness which ranges from 3 1/4 to 4 inches. An additional slab of steel mounted in conjunction with its 88mm forms frontal armour for the turret. Besides the long-barreled 88, it carries two MG34 (Model 1934) machine guns. Largest tank used in combat by any nation today, the Tiger is more than 20 feet long, about 11 3/4 feet wide and 9 3/4 feet high. It has a crew of five.

Tigers training in perfect conditions in Normandy during May 1944.

The reconnaissance element of a Tiger company had an equally difficult and dangerous job. This evocative study was taken in Russia during March 1944.

TIGER I TANKS IN SICILY

In total 17 Tiger I tanks from schwere Panzer Abteilung 504 (s.Pz.Abt. 504) fought in Sicily in 1943 against the Allied invasion forces. All but one were lost in combat in the period from July 11th to August 10th 1943 when the German forces were finally forced to withdraw.

When the first elements of s.Pz.Abt. 504 with 20 Tiger I were sent to North Africa, the 2nd Kompanie remained behind in Sicily with nine Tiger I tanks. As a result of the surrender of German forces in North Africa, the nine Tigers of s.Pz.Abt. 504 were never actually shipped to Tunisia, but stayed behind on Sicily where they were soon called into action to repel the Allied assault which took place in July 1943. Prior to the Allied invasion eight additional Tiger I were shipped to the unit arriving early in the summer. By the time of the Allied invasion of Sicily, s.Pz.Abt. 504 with 17 Tiger I was attached to the Panzer Division Hermann Göring.

During the ill fated attack on the Allied beachhead near Gela, s.Pz. Abt. 504 was heavily engaged and lost ten Tigers in just two days of fierce fighting between 11th July and 12th July. Further Tigers were lost in action

A Tiger rolls through a Sicilian town in July 1943. These machines had been destined to serve with the Afrika Korps but arrived too late to take part in the campaign. All but one of the 17 Tigers deployed in Sicily were lost in action.

or abandoned during July and August as German forces slowly retreated across the island. In August, the unit's last surviving Tiger I bearing the tactical number 222 from managed to escape from the wreckage and was ferried across the Straits of Messina to Italy.

The following is an article on German tank trends, Panzer tactics, and how to fight the German heavy tanks from the October 1944 issue of the *Intelligence Bulletin*. The article includes suggestions from the Soviet Artillery Journal on combating the Tiger tank.

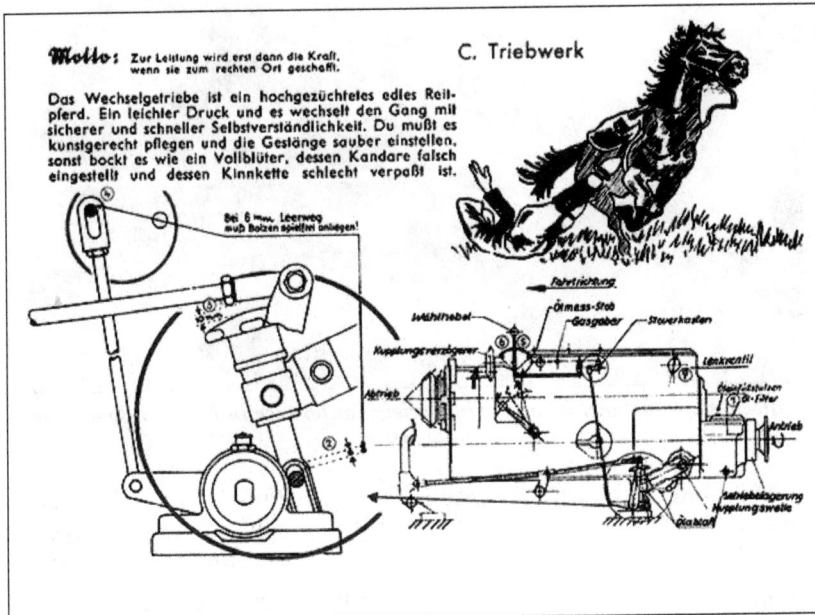

This page from the driver's section in Tigerfibel explains the workings of the drive train.

THE CONTEMPORARY VIEW NO.22
GERMAN TANK TRENDS

Officers plan the next move during a field conference in Normandy during June 1944.

Just what can be expected from German tanks in the near future? Which models are most likely to be employed extensively? Are present models undergoing much alteration?

A brief summary of the German tank situation at the moment should serve to answer these and other pertinent questions.

There is good reason to believe that the German tanks which will be encountered most frequently in the near future will be the Pz. Kpfw. V (Panther), the Pz. Kpfw. VI (Tiger), and the Pz. Kpfw. IV. However, the Germans have a new 88mm (346-inch) tank gun, the Kw. K. 43, which is capable of an armour-piercing performance greatly superior to that of the 88mm Kw. K. 36. According to reliable information, the Kw. K. 43 is superseding the Kw. K. 36 as the main armament of the Tiger. A new heavy tank, which has been encountered on a small scale in northwestern France, also is armed with the Kw. K. 43. This new tank looks like a scaled-up Panther, with the wide Tiger tracks. (Further information regarding this tank will appear in an early issue of the Intelligence Bulletin.)

During recent months both the Tiger and the Panther have been fitted with a slightly more powerful 690-horsepower engine in place of the 642-horsepower model. The principal benefit from this slight increase will be a better margin of power and improved engine life. The maximum speed will be increased by no more than 2 or 3 miles per hour.

Face-hardened armour, which was not used on the early Tiger tanks, has reappeared in certain plate of at least one Panther. On other Panthers which have been encountered, only machine-quality armour is used. There is no reason to believe that face-hardening would substantially improve the armour's resistance to penetration by the capped projectiles now in use against it.

It would not have been surprising if the Pz. Kpfw. IV had slowly disappeared from the picture as increased quantities of Panther tanks became available, but actually there was a sharp rise in the rate of production of Pz. Kpfw. IV's during 1943. Moreover, the, front armour of the Pz. Kpfw. IV has been reinforced from 50mm (1.97 inches) to 80mm (3.15 inches) by the bolting of additional armour to the nose and front vertical plates. And the 75mm (2.95-inch) tank gun, Kw. K. 40, has been lengthened by about 14 3/4 inches.

All these developments seem to indicate that the Pz. Kpfw. IV probably will be kept in service for many months. Recent organization evidence reflects this, certainly. In the autumn of 1943, evidence regarding provisional organization for the German tank regiment in the armoured division indicated that the aim was a ratio of approximately four Panther tanks for each Pz. Kpfw. IV. Now, however, the standard tank regiment has these two types in approximately equal numbers.

The possibility that Tiger production may have been discontinued has been considered. Although discontinuing the Tiger would relieve the pressure on German industry, it is believed that a sufficient number of these tanks to meet the needs of units equipped with them still is being produced.

Tiger tanks constitute an integral part of division tank regiments only in SS armoured divisions. However, armoured divisions of an army may receive an allotment of Tigers for special operations.

Early in 1944 a number of Pz. Kpfw. III's converted into flame-throwing tanks appeared in Italy. Nevertheless, it is believed that production of this tank ceased some time ago. Some of the firms which in the past produced Pz. Kpfw. III's now are making assault guns; others are believed to be turning out Panthers. It is extremely unlikely that production of Pz. Kpfw. III's as fighting tanks will ever be resumed, no matter how serious the German tank situation may become.

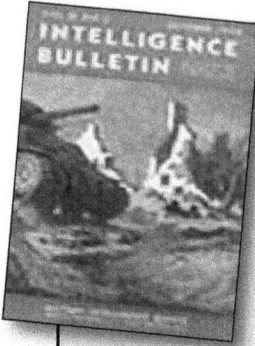

In an effort to combat attacks by tank hunters, the Germans have fitted the Tiger with S-mine dischargers, which are fired electrically from the interior of the tank. These dischargers are mounted on the turret, and are designed to project a shrapnel antipersonnel mine which bursts in the air a few yards away from the tank. Thus far these dischargers have been noted only on the Tiger, but the Germans quite possibly may decide to use them on still other tanks.

The Germans take additional precautions, as well. For protection against hollow-charge projectiles and the Soviet antitank rifle's armour-piercing bullet with a tungsten carbide core, they fit a skirting of mild steel plates, about 1/4- inch thick, on the sides of the hull. In the case of the Pz. Kpfw. IV, the skirting is suitably spaced from the sides and also from the rear of the turret. Finally, the skirting plates, as well as the hulls and turrets of the tanks themselves, are, coated with a sufficient thickness of non-magnetic plaster to prevent magnetic demolition charges from adhering to the metal underneath.

Despite the recent introduction of the new heavy tank which resembles the Panther and mounts a Kw. K. 43, it is believed that circumstances will force the Germans to concentrate on the manufacture and improvement of current types, particularly the Pz. Kpfw. IV and the familiar version of the Panther.

Evidence suggests that a modified Pz. Kpfw. II will shortly appear as a reconnaissance vehicle. Official German documents sometimes refer to it as an armoured car and sometimes as a tank.

ARMOUR AND ARMAMENT

The overwhelming advantage of the Tiger I lay in the quality of its main armament. From a 30 degree angle depending on the wind and weather conditions the Tiger's 88mm gun was capable of penetrating the well sloped front glacis plate of an American M4 Sherman at ranges up to 2,100m (1.3 miles). The better armoured British Churchill IV became vulnerable at a closer range of 1,700m (1.1 mile), the hardy Soviet T-34 could be destroyed at 1,400m (0.87 mile), and the Soviet IS-2 could only be destroyed at ranges between 100 and 300m.

The Soviet T-34 equipped with the 76.2mm gun could not penetrate the Tiger frontally at any range, but could achieve a side penetration at approximately 500 m firing BR-350P APCR ammunition. The T34-85's 85mm gun could penetrate the front of a Tiger between 200 and 500 m (0.12 and 0.31 mi), the IS-2's 122mm gun could penetrate the front between 500 and 1,500 m (0.31 and 0.93 mi).

A Tiger I rolls through the open countryside in Normandy in June 1944. The tank is obviously some distance from the combat zone as the crew have not taken any form of anti-aircraft precautions.

From a 30 degree angle of attack, the M4 Sherman's 75mm gun could not penetrate the Tiger frontally at any range, and actually needed to be within 100 m to achieve a side penetration shot against the 80mm upper hull superstructure. However, the British 17-pounder as used on the Sherman Firefly, firing its normal APCBC ammunition, could penetrate the front armour of the Tiger I out to 1000m. The US 76mm gun, if firing the APCBC M62 ammunition, could penetrate the Tiger side armour up to a range of 500m, and could penetrate the upper hull superstructure at ranges up to 200m. Using HVAP ammunition, which was in constant short supply and primarily issued to tank destroyers, frontal penetrations were possible at ranges of up to 500m. The M3 90mm cannon used in the late-war M36 Jackson, M26 Pershing, and M2 AA/AT mount could penetrate its front plate at a range of 1000 m, and from beyond 2000m when using HVAP.

As range decreases in combat, all guns can penetrate more armour. HEAT ammunition was the most effective round but this projectile was rare and in short supply. The great penetrating power of the Tiger's gun meant that it could destroy many of its opponents at ranges at which they could not respond. The issue which was compounding the Allied tank crew's problem was the superiority of German optics. This advantage increased the chances of a hit on the first shot and in tank to tank battles one shot was frequently all that mattered. In open terrain, this was a major tactical advantage as opposing tanks were often forced to change position in order to make a flanking attack in an attempt to knock out a Tiger.

GERMAN TANKS IN ACTION

A German prisoner observes that the following are standard training principles in the German tank arm:

(1) Surprise.

(2) Prompt decisions and prompt execution of these decisions.

(3) The fullest possible exploitation of the terrain for firing. However, fields of fire come before cover.

(4) Do not fire while moving except when absolutely essential.

(5) Face the attacker head-on; do not offer a broadside target.

(6) When attacked by hostile tanks, concentrate solely on these.

(7) If surprised without hope of favourable defence, scatter and reassemble in favourable terrain. Try to draw the attacker into a position which will give you the advantage.

(8) If smoke is to be used, keep wind direction in mind. A good procedure is to leave a few tanks in position as decoys,

A section of Tiger's deploying for combat operations in Russia in January 1943. The vehicle on the left still has the cover on the muzzle break which suggests this tank is not anticipating being forced into combat.

and, when the hostile force is approaching them, to direct a smoke screen toward the hostile force and blind it.

(9) If hostile tanks are sighted, German tanks should halt and prepare to engage them by surprise, holding fire as long as possible. The reaction of the hostile force must be estimated before the attack is launched.

A German Army document entitled "How the Tiger Can Aid the Infantry" contains a number of interesting points. The following are outstanding:

(1) The tank expert must have a chance to submit his opinion before any combined tank-infantry attack.

(2) If the ground will support a man standing on one leg and carrying another man on his shoulders, it will support a tank.

(3) When mud is very deep, corduroy roads must be built ahead of time. Since this requires manpower, material, and time, the work should be undertaken only near the point where the main effort is to be made.

(4) Tanks must be deployed to conduct their fire fight.

(5) The Tiger, built to fight tanks and antitank guns, must function as offensive weapon, even in the defence. This is its best means of defence against hostile tanks. Give it a chance to use its unique capabilities for fire and movement.

(6) The Tiger must keep moving. At the halt it is an easy target.

(7) The Tiger must not be used singly. (Obviously, this does not apply to the Tiger used as roving artillery in the defence. On numerous occasions the Germans have been using single Tigers for this purpose.) The more mass you can assemble, the greater your success will be. Protect your Tigers with infantry.

A Tiger which has received a coating of anti-magnetic Zimmermit coating designed to prevent the application of magnetic mines by tank hunting teams.

THE TWO EXTREMES

The Tiger I enjoyed some spectacular triumphs on the battlefield, but it also endured its fair share of ignominious set backs. These two contrasting combat reports demonstrate the two extremes of the Tiger I experience.

On 21st April 1943, a Tiger I of the 504th German heavy tank battalion, with turret number 131, was captured after being knocked out on a hill called Djebel Djaffa in Tunisia. A round from a Churchill tank of the British 48th Royal Tank Regiment hit the Tiger's gun barrel and ricocheted into its turret ring. The round jammed the turret traverse mechanism and wounded the commander. Although the vehicle was still in a driveable condition the crew flew into a panic and bailed out. The complete tank was captured by the British. The tank was repaired and displayed in Tunisia before being sent to England for a thorough inspection.

In complete contrast to the dismal performance of Tiger 131 the Tiger I commanded by Franz Staudegger enjoyed an amazing string of successes. On 7th July 1943, this single Tiger tank commanded by SS-Oberscharführer Franz Staudegger from the 2nd Platoon, 13th Panzer Company, 1st SS Division Leibstandarte SS Adolf Hitler engaged a group of about 50 T-34s around Psyolknee in the southern sector of the German thrust into the Soviet salient known as the Battle of Kursk. Staudegger used all his ammunition and claimed the destruction of 22 Soviet tanks, forcing the rest to retreat. For this amazing feat of arms he was understandably awarded the Knight's Cross.

The Tigerfibel emphasized the smooth ride of the Tiger I comparing it to a sports car.

THE CONTEMPORARY VIEW NO.24
HOW TO FIGHT PANZERS: A GERMAN VIEW

An anti-Nazi prisoner of war, discussing the various methods of combating German tanks, makes some useful comments. Although they are neither new nor startling, they are well worth studying since they are observations made by a tank man who fought the United Nations forces in Italy.

German tanks undoubtedly are formidable weapons against a soft-shelled opposition, but become a less difficult proposition when confronted with resolution combined with a knowledge not only of their potentialities but also of their weaknesses.

When dealing with German heavy tanks, your most effective weapon is your ability to keep still and wait for them to come within effective range. The next most important thing is to camouflage your position with the best available resources so that the German tanks won't spot you from any angle.

Two Tigers pictured just before they were to go into combat at Villers Bocage in June 1944.

If these two factors are constantly kept in mind, the battle is half won. Movement of any kind is a mistake which certainly will betray you, yet I saw many instances of this self-betrayal by the British in Italy. Allow the enemy tank to approach as close as possible before engaging it — this is one of the fundamental secrets of antitank success. In Italy I often felt that the British opened fire on tanks much too soon. Their aim was good, but the ranges were too great, and the rounds failed to penetrate. My own case is a good illustration: if the opposition had held its fire for only a few moments longer, I should not be alive to tell this tale.

By letting the German tank approach as close as possible, you gain a big advantage. When it is on the move, it is bound to betray its presence from afar. Whereas you yourself can prepare to fire on it without giving your own position away. The tank will spot you only after you have fired your first round.

A tank in motion cannot fire effectively with its cannon; the gunner can place fire accurately only when the vehicle is stationary. Therefore, there is no need to be unduly nervous because an approaching tank swivels its turret this way and that. Every tank commander will do this in an attempt to upset his opponents' tank recognition. If the tank fires nothing but its machine guns, you can be pretty sure that you have not yet been spotted.

Consider the advantages of firing on a tank at close range:

(1) In most cases the leading tank is a reconnaissance vehicle. Survivors of the crew, when such a short distance away from you, have little chance of escape. This is a big advantage, inasmuch as they cannot rejoin their outfit and describe the location of your position to the main body.

(2) Another tank following its leader on a road cannot run you down. In order to bypass the leading tank, it has to slow down. Then, long before the gunner can place fire on you, you can destroy the tank and block the road effectively. Earlier in the war, a German tank man I knew destroyed 11 hostile tanks in one day by using this method.

THE BRITISH RESPONSE

In contrast to the laissez-faire attitude of the Americans, who correctly assumed that there would never be enough Tigers in the field to present a potent threat, the more experienced British had observed the gradual increase in German AFV armour and firepower since 1940 and had anticipated the need for more powerful anti-tank guns. As a result of the lessons learned in France work on the Ordnance QF 17 pounder had begun in late 1940 and in 1942 100 early-production guns were rushed to North Africa to help counter the new Tiger threat. So great was the haste that they were sent before proper carriages had been designed and constructed, and the guns had to be mounted in the carriages designed for 25-pounder howitzers.

Hasty efforts were also made to get Cruiser tanks armed with 17 pounder guns into operation as soon as possible. The A30 Challenger was already at the prototype stage in 1942 and was pressed into service, but this tank was poorly protected, having a front hull thickness of only 64mm. It was unreliable, and was fielded in only limited numbers - only around 200 were ever built although crews liked it for its high speed. The Sherman Firefly, armed with the 17-pounder, was a notable success even though it was only intended to be a stopgap design. Fireflies were successfully used against Tigers. In one famous engagement, a single Firefly destroyed three Tigers in 12 minutes with five shots and as a result of the superior Allied product capability over 2,000 Fireflies were built during the war. Five different 17-pounder-armed British tanks and self-propelled guns saw combat during the war. These were the A30 Challenger, the A34 Comet, the Sherman Firefly, the 17-pounder SP Achilles and the 17-pounder SP Archer.

The gunner from Tigerfibel.

TIGER I TANKS IN NORMANDY

Something like 130 Tiger Is were deployed in Normandy during June and July 19944. The machines were chiefly deployed by the three schwere Panzer Abteilung equipped with Tiger I tanks which fought in Normandy against the Allied invasion forces. In addition, a small number of Tiger I tanks also fought in Normandy serving with the Panzer Lehr Division.

s.Pz.Abt. 503 was a particularly formidable unit and was transferred to Normandy with a full complement of 33 Tiger I and 12 of the new Tiger II tanks. The unit went into action in early July 1944. The 33 Tiger Is were all shipped to the unit in June 1944. Photographs of the unit's Tigers are very limited. Technical features are, of course, identical to late Tigers shipped to the other units. However one possible distinguishing features is the fact that spare tracks do not appear to have been mounted on front plate as was customary elsewhere. Camouflage patterning was similar to other units, but on at least some vehicles, the Balkankreuz appear to have been unusually large in size. Tactical numbers were relatively thin, neatly stencilled with a white outline and a very dark, probably black, interior.

s.SS-Pz.Abt. 101 received 45 Tiger I in deliveries in total beginning with 10 in October 1943, nine additional late model machines were delivered in January 1944, and 25 in April 1944. The unit reached Normandy in early June and Michael Wittmann and the 1st and 2nd Kompanie fought in the celebrated battle of Villers-Bocage on 13th June 1944. The Tigers issued to this unit included both the rubber-wheel and steel-wheel variants. Unlike s.Pz.Abt. 503 spare track appears to have been mounted on the front plate of most, but it seems not all of the unit's Tigers. Each Kompanie carried the distinctive unit marking of crossed keys in a shield, on the front and rear. In addition, the 1st Kompanie also carried a Panzer lozenge with an "S" and a small "1" on the front and rear plates. Tactical numbers were fairly large and dark with white outline, except for the command tanks.

s.SS-Pz.Abt. 102 was transferred to Normandy with a full complement of 45 Tiger I and went into action for the first time in early July. The unit was originally issued with a mere six Tiger I in April 1944 but received a further batch of 39 Tiger I in May 1944. Photographs of this unit's Tigers are very rare. However, the unit appears not to have mounted spare track on the front plate. Camouflage was large patches of colour which on some vehicles leads to the appearance of lines of the original dunkelgelb. Tactical

A knocked out Tiger I of s.SS-PzAbt.101 abandoned at Villers Bocage.

numbers were thin, neatly stencilled with white outline and dark interior. Tactical numbers on the turret sides were often sloped, being aligned with the slope of the turret roof. Some Tigers carried a single underlined "S" rune painted on the zimmerit on the front and/or rear plates.

Panzer Lehr Division was issued 10 Tiger I in September-October 1943 and five Tiger II in February-March 1944. Of the ten Tiger I, three Tiger were listed as still with the division in summer 1944. The division reported six of eight Tigers operational on June 1 and three Tigers operational on July 1st.

THE CONTEMPORARY VIEW NO.25
VULNERABILITY OF THE PZ. KPFW. VI

A late model Tiger I lies abandoned after being knocked out in action.

A tank is such a complicated weapon, with its many movable parts and its elaborate mechanism, that it is particularly valuable to know its points of greatest vulnerability. Recently the Soviet Artillery Journal published a number of practical suggestions, based on extensive combat experience, regarding the vulnerability of the Tiger.

All weapons now used for destroying German tanks - antitank guns and rifles, caliber.50 heavy machine guns, antitank grenades, and Molotov cocktails - are effective against the Pz. Kpfw. VI.

(1) Suspension System - The mobility of tanks depends upon the proper functioning of the suspension parts: the sprocket (small driving wheel), the idler (small wheel in the rear), the wheels, and the tracks. All these parts are vulnerable to shells of all calibres. The sprocket is especially vulnerable.

Fire armour-piercing shells and high-explosive shells at the sprocket, idler, and tracks.

Fire at the wheels with high-explosive shells. Use antitank grenades, antitank mines, and movable antitank mines against the suspension parts. Attach three or four mines to a board. Place the board wherever tanks are expected to pass. Camouflage the board and yourself. As a tank passes by, pull the board in the proper direction and place it under the track of the tank.

(A German source states that this method was successfully used on roads and road crossings in Russia, and that it still is taught in tank combat courses for infantry. The mine is called the Scharniermine (pivot mine). It consists of a stout length of board, 8 inches wide by 2 inches thick, and cut to a length dependent on the width of the road to be blocked. A hole is bored at one end, through which a spike or bayonet can be driven into the ground, thus providing a pivot for the board. A hook is fastened to the other end of the board, and a rope is tied to the hook, as shown in Figure 3. Tellermines are secured to the top of the board.

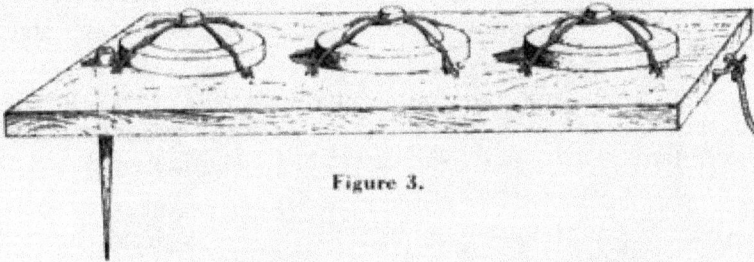

Figure 3.

One man can operate this mine. After the board has been fastened down at one end with the spike (in emergencies, a bayonet) and a rope tied to the hook at the other end, the board is laid along the side of the road. On the opposite side of the road, a man is posted in a narrow slit trench. He holds the other end of the rope. When a tank approaches, the tank hunter waits until it is close enough to the pivoted board, and, at the very last moment, he pulls the free end of the board across the road. The rope and slit trench must be well camouflaged. A good deal of emphasis is placed on this point.)

(2) Side Armour Plates - There are two armour plates on each side of the tank. The lower plate is partly covered by the wheels. This plate protects the engine and the gasoline tanks, which are located in the rear of the hull — directly beyond and over the two rear wheels. Ammunition is kept in special compartments along the sides of the tank. These compartments are protected by the upper armour plate.

Fire armour-piercing shells from 76-, 57-, and 45mm guns at the upper and lower armour plate. When the gas tanks or ammunition compartments are hit, the vehicle will be set on fire.

(3) Rear Armour Plate - The rear armour plate protects the engine, the gasoline tank, and the radiators.

Use antitank guns. Aim at the rear armour plate. When the engine or the gasoline tanks are hit, the tank will halt and will begin to burn.

(4) Peepholes, Vision Ports, and Slits - The main turret has two openings for firing small-arms weapons, and two vision ports. The turret has five observation slits. There are two sighting devices on the roof of the front part of the tank - one for the driver, the other for the gunner. There is also a port with sliding covers in the front armour plate.

Use all available weapons for firing at the peepholes, observation ports, vision slits, and the ports for small-arms weapons.

5. Turrets - The commander's turret is an important and vulnerable target.

Fire high-explosive and armour-piercing shells of all calibres at the commander's turret. Throw antitank grenades and incendiary bottles after the turret has been damaged.

The Tiger I that knocked out the first M26 Pershing in combat. The victorious Tiger then backed into a demolished building and became immobile. The crew then abandoned the tank which fell into Allied hands.

The tank commander, the turret commander, and the gunner ride in the turret. The tank gun and many mechanical devices are found in the turret.

Fire at the turret with 76-, 57-, and 45mm shells at ranges of 500 yards or less.

(6) Tank Armament - The turret is armed with a gun and a machine gun mounted coaxially. Another machine gun is found in the front part of the hull. It protrudes through the front armour plate, on a ball mount, and is manned by, the radio operator.

Concentrate the fire of all weapons on the armament of the tank. Fire with antitank rifles at the ball mount of the hull machine gun.

(7) Air Vents and Ventilators - The air vents and the ventilators are found under the slit-shaped perforations of the roof of the hull, directly behind the turret. Another air vent is located in the front part of the roof, between the two observation ports used by the radio operator and the driver.

Use incendiary bottles and antitank grenades to damage the ventilating system.

(8) Tank Floor - When an antitank mine explodes under the tank, the floor of the tank is smashed, and the tank is knocked out of action.

(9) Base of Turret - There is a 10mm slit going all around the turret, between the base of the turret and the roof of the hull.

Fire at the base of the turret with heavy machine guns and antitank guns, to destroy the turret mechanism, and disrupt the field of fire. Fire with high-explosive shells at the base of the turret in order to wreck the roof of the hull and put the tank out of action.

THE SOVIET RESPONSE

The initial Soviet response to the Tiger I was to restart the production of the 57mm ZiS-2 anti-tank gun, which had been halted in 1941 in favour of smaller and cheaper alternatives. The 76mm F-34 tank gun which was then in use by most Red Army tanks, proved to be all but inadequate when faced with the Tiger I. The ZiS-2 had better armour penetration.

A 2.52 firing APCR rounds could usually be relied upon to penetrate the Tiger's frontal armour. A small number of T-34s were fitted with a tank version of the ZiS-2, but the drawback was that as an anti-tank weapon the ZiS-2 could not fire a strong high-explosive round, thus making it an unsatisfactory tank gun. The Russians had no inhibitions about following the German lead and accordingly the 85mm 52-K anti-aircraft gun was modified for tank use. This gun was initially incorporated into the SU-85 self-propelled gun which was based on a T-34 chassis and saw action from August 1943. By the spring of 1944, the T-34/85 appeared, this up-gunned T-34 matched the SU-85's firepower, but had the additional advantage of mounting the gun with a much better HE firing capability in a revolving turret. The redundant SU-85 was replaced by the SU-100, mounting a 100mm D-10 tank gun which could penetrate 185mm of vertical armour plate at 1,000m, and was therefore able to defeat the Tiger's frontal armour at normal combat ranges.

In May 1943, the Red Army deployed the SU-152, replaced in 1944 by the ISU-152. These self-propelled guns both mounted the large, 152mm howitzer-gun. The SU-152 was intended to be a close-support gun for use against German fortifications rather than armour; but, both it and the later ISU-152 were found to be very effective against German heavy tanks, and were nicknamed Zveroboy which is commonly rendered as "beast killer" or "animal hunter". The 152mm armour-piercing shells weighed over 45 kilograms (99lb) and could penetrate a Tiger's frontal armour from 1,000 metres. Even the high-explosive rounds were powerful enough to cause significant damage to a tank. However, the size and weight of the ammunition meant both vehicles had a low rate of fire and each could carry only 20 rounds.

The tide was definitely turning against the Tiger I and the Tiger II was introduced as a replacement in mid 1944. In order to shore up the crumbling morale, the German School of Tank Technology released re-assuring combat reports such as the detailed example opposite.

THE CONTEMPORARY VIEW NO. 26
THE JOSEF STALIN

A column of German infantry, captured during the destruction of Army Group Centre, file past an intact Tiger I which is now also in the hands of the Russians.

The new Soviet heavy tank, 'Josef Stalin', has caused the German tank experts no little worry. It is, therefore, of interest that the following unconvincing description of a 'Tiger' versus 'Stalin' engagement is printed in the official 'Notes for Panzer Troops' of September 1944, presumably as an encouragement to the German tank arm.

A 'Tiger' squadron reports one of a number of engagements in which it knocked out 'Stalin' tanks.

The squadron had been given the task of counter-attacking an enemy penetration into a wood and exploiting success.

At 1215 hours the squadron moved off together with a rifle battalion. The squadron was formed to move in file by reason of the thick forest, bad visibility (50 yards) and narrow path. The Soviet infantry withdrew as soon as the 'Tigers' appeared. The A/tk guns which the enemy had brought up only three-quarters of an hour after initial penetration were quickly knocked out, partly by fire, partly by crushing.

The point troop having penetrated a further 2,000 yards in to the forest, the troop commander suddenly heard the sound of falling trees and observed, right ahead, the large muzzle brake of the 'Stalin'. E immediately ordered: 'AP fixed sights-fire' but was hit at the same time by two rounds from a 4.7 cm A/tk gun which obscured his vision completely. Meanwhile the second tank in the troop had come up level with the troop commanders's tank. The latter, firing blind, was continuing the fire fight at a range of 35 yards and the 'Stalin' withdrew behind a hillock. The second 'Tiger' had in the meantime taken the lead and fired three rounds at the enemy tank. It was hit by a round from the enemy's 122mm tank gun on the hull below the wireless operator's seat but no penetration was effected, probably because the 'Tiger' was oblique to the enemy. The 'Stalin', however, had been hit in the gun by the 'Tiger's' last round and put out of action. A second 'Stalin' attempted to cover the first tank's withdrawal but was also hit by one of the leading 'Tigers' just below the gun and brewed up.

The rate of fire of the 'Stalin' was comparatively slow. The squadron commander has drawn the following conclusions from all the engagements his squadron has had with 'Stalin' tanks:

(1) Most 'Stalin' tanks will withdraw on encountering 'Tigers' without attempting to engage in a fire-fight.

(2) 'Stalin' tanks generally only open fire at ranges over 2,200 yards and then only if standing oblique to the target.

(3) Enemy crews tend to abandon tanks as soon as hit.

(4) The Russians make great efforts to prevent 'Stalin' tanks falling into our hands and particularly strive to recover or blow up such of them as have been immobilized.

(5) 'Stalin' tanks can be brewed up although penetration is by no means easy against the frontal armour at long ranges (another 'Tiger' battalion reports that 'Stalin' tanks can only be penetrated by 'Tigers frontally under 550 yards).

(6) 'Stalin' tanks should, wherever possible, be engaged in flanks or rear and destroyed by concentrated fire.

(7) 'Stalin' tanks should not be engaged under any circumstances by 'Tigers' in less than troop strength. To use single 'Tigers' is to invite their destruction.

(8) It is useful practice to follow up the first hit with AP on the 'Stalin' tank with HE, to continue blinding the occupants.

The Inspector-General of Panzer Troops (who is responsible for this official publication) commented as follows on the above remarks:

(1) These experiences agree with those of other 'Tiger' units and are correct.

(2) Reference para. (4), it would be desirable for the enemy to observe the same keenness in all our 'Tiger' crews. No 'Tiger' should ever be allowed to fall into the enemy's hands intact.

(3) Reference paras (5) and (6), faced as we are now with the 122mm tank gun and 57mm A/tk gun in Russia and the 92mm AA/Atk gun in Western Europe and Italy. 'Tigers' can no longer afford to ignore the principles practiced by normal tank formations.

This means, inter alia, that 'Tigers' can no longer show themselves on crests 'to have a look round' but must behave like other tanks – behaviour of this kind caused the destruction by 'Stalin' tanks of three 'Tigers' recently, all crews being killed with the exception of two men.

This battalion was surely not unacquainted with the basic principle of tank tactics that tanks should only cross crests in a body and by rapid bounds, covered by fire – or else detour round the crest. The legend of the 'thick hide', the 'invulnerability' and the 'safety' of the 'Tiger', which has sprung up in other arms of the service, as well as within the tank arm, must now be destroyed and dissipated.

Hence, instruction in the usual principles of tank versus tank action becomes of specific importance to 'Tiger' units.

(4) Reference para (7), though this train of thought is correct, 3 'Tigers' do not form a proper troop. Particularly with conditions as they are at the moment, circumstances may

Marshal Georgy Zhukov inspecting a captured Tiger

well arise where full troops will not be readily available. And it is precisely the tank versus tank action which is decided more by superior tactics than superior numbers. However it is still true to say that single tanks invite destruction.

(5) It may be added that the 'Stalin' tank will not only be penetrated in flanks and rear by 'Tigers' and 'Panthers' but also by Pz. Kpfw. IV and assault guns.

TIGERS IN ITALY

Due to Allied air superiority, the Tigers in Normandy and France were frequently employed mainly in a static defensive role. This conserved fuel as the Tiger normally consumed huge amounts of petrol. It also kept the mechanical breakdowns to a minimum. In other theatres such as Italy, Allied air cover was less comprehensive and the Tigers still enjoyed some freedom of action. This was not always a good thing however.

Although the Tiger was a formidable design and recognized as being such in a number of allied studies although the high fuel consumption and frequent mechanical breakdowns occasionally rendered its battlefield performance all but worthless. This was certainly the case with the 508 schwere Abteilung in May 1944 which the British report of which from August 1944 makes sobering reading and further deflates the myth of the invincible Tiger.

TIGER TANK IN ACTION
FIRST MAJOR REVERSE OF
3 SQN 508 HY TK BN

As an illustration of the difficulties encountered in the employment of Tiger tanks it is interesting to reconstruct one of the two mobile engagements on a Sqn basis which the Bn fought in Italy, when it won a victory and yet lost almost all its tanks.

The action took place between 23 and 25 May 44 in the general area of Cisterna. 3 Sqn, which had brought down 14 Tiger tanks from France, lost two burnt out at the end of Feb 4 – one through carelessness on the part of the crew and another by Allied A/tk action. It had received four of the latest pattern AFVs during May 44 and was two tanks over war establishment strength on 23 May 44, i.e. 16 instead of 14.

The Sqn formed up behind a railway embankment between the Mussolini Canal and the level crossing at G 063299 and engaged troop concentrations with HE. It then crossed the embankment and put three AFVs out of action in the attempt (one with gearbox trouble and two with tracks riding over the sprocket teeth). The remaining thirteen crews had all to stop on open ground because the guns had dug into the earth as the tanks came down the embankment and needed pulling through.

The Allied troops were driven back about three kms and a number of Sherman tanks surprised and knocked out.

The first loss sustained in action was a Tiger which had one radiator destroyed by an artillery round and had to limp back towards Cori in stages.

Twelve Tigers were thus left in action during the night 23/24 May 44. On the morning of 24 May 44 a retreat was ordered to everyone's surprise and A/tk fire accounted for one Tiger (hit on the right reduction gear and subsequently blown up by its crew).

Eleven Tigers withdrew to the embankment and the OC Sqn ordered five to continue to hold the enemy whilst the six were to tow away the tree tanks which had failed to cross.

Four of the six towing tanks experienced gearbox trouble and the OC then ordered the three towed tanks to be destroyed and tow out of the five fighting tanks to assist in towing away the breakdowns.

These eight AFVs were got back to an assembly point near Cori, leaving four Tigers only in fighting order. Of these four, one was hit by A/Tk gun fire and two more experienced gearbox trouble (all three were blown up), so that only one runner was left.

Two converted Sherman tanks came down from Rome during the night 24/25 May 44 and extricated the one runner which had also become u/s meanwhile, by towing it in tandem along the railway tracks.

By 25 May 44, the situation had so deteriorated that it was manifestly impossible to get towing vehicles through and the OC ordered the blowing up of the nine Tigers which had reached the assembly area.

Although a good many of the crews had gone back to Rome with the one runner, the OC and about 45 men were left near Cori. They had to march back to Rome and came under fire several times in the process, arriving in an exhausted condition.

PW states categorically that this action had a profound effect upon the Sqn's morale and also decided against the mass use of Tiger tanks. Of sixteen AFVs put into action, not one would have been lost, had adequate recovery facilities been provided.

Although the OC Sqn's personal courage was not in doubt, it was generally thought that he had not appreciated the situation and had created the disaster by attempting to salvage the three AFVs that jibbed at the embankment. Had he not done so, he might have saved about ten out of the original sixteen.

'Penny wise, pound foolish' was the criticism made of him. 3 Sqn also took a poor view of the fact that almost at once a new troop was formed from tanks drawn from 1 and 2 Sqn crews put in, the former crews going back to their Sqn pools.

The citizens of the liberated French town of Marle clamber around this Tiger I which was abandoned in the main street.

TANK LOSSES

With such an important range of industries in operation the city of Kassel was targeted for destruction and was bombed around 40 times by the Allies during the course of the war. These unwelcome intrusions severely disrupted Tiger production. The most notable occasion took place in late 1943. During the night of October 22nd/23rd the RAF dropped an amazing 1800 tons of bombs which obviously causing severe damage at the Henschel facilities. In addition to the damage caused to the infrastructure of the factory itself and the local transport system the RAF bombers also killed or injuring a high proportion of its workforce.

Despite these set backs and the huge difficulties which had to be overcome Tiger production continued right up until almost the end of the war. The U.S. Third Army began the battle to capture Kassel on April 1st, 1945. The Henschel works continued working to the bitter end and, as US forces approached, the Henschel factory completed work on the final batch of 13 Tiger II tanks which were handed directly over from the factory to two companies of schwere Panzer-Abteilung 510 and 511. Three days later at 1200 hours on April 4th, 1945 the city was surrendered and Tiger tank production was ended forever.

Tank losses on the eastern front by year:

Year	German Losses	Russian Losses	Kill/Loss Ratio
1941	2,758	20,500	7.43
1942	2,648	15,000	5.66
1943	6,362	22,400	3.52
1944	6,434	16,900	2.63
1945	7,382	8,700	1.18
Total	25,584	83,500	3.26

NOTABLE VARIANTS

In Italy, a field version of a demolition carrier version of the Tiger I was built by maintenance crews in an effort to find a way to clear minefields. It is often misidentified as a Berge Tiger recovery vehicle. As many as three may have been built. It carried a demolition charge on a small crane mounted on the turret in lieu of the main gun. It was to move up to a minefield and drop the charge, back away, and then set the charge off to clear the minefield. There is no verification any were used in combat although such a vehicle would have been of great value at Kursk.

During 1942, anticipating orders for his version of the Tiger tank, Ferdinand Porsche had actually gone as far as to build 100 chassis based on his Tiger prototypes. On losing the contract, the Porsche vehicles were used as the basis for a new heavy assault gun/tank hunter. In the spring 1943, ninety-one hulls were converted into the Panzerjäger Tiger (P), also known as Ferdinand. After Hitler's orders of 1st and 27th February 1944, the Elefant.

The Ferdinand represents a fascinating glimpse into what the Tiger might have been the Tiger had Porsche won the competition for the Tiger contract. This heavily armoured tank destroyer variant utilised all of the

The Elefant was deployed in Russia and also saw action during the Warsaw uprising in 1943, and finally ended its career in Italy.

The Sturmtiger with its 15in howitzer protuding. This calibre was as great as many a battleship's big guns.

The Ferdinand or Elefant, shown here in Italy in 1944, actually performed far better in combat than is generally perceived.

remaining redundant chassis which Ferdinand Porsche had ordered to be produced in anticipation of receiving the order for the Tiger I. These vehicles were a scratch built solution introduced into combat in 1943. The Ferdinand has an unfair reputation as a complete failure and is widely held to have floundered then disappeared following an unsuccessful showing at Kursk where the poor performance has been ascribed as being due to the lack of a close defence machine gun. The reality is that the Ferdinand was a highly effective tank destroyer which performed very creditably in Russia and Italy. Mechanically the Ferdinand was to prove remarkably reliable and in many respects may actually have been a better machine than the Tiger I.

Among other factory variants of the Tiger I was the fearsome Jagdtiger which was one of the most formidable tank destroyers of the war however production was very low and only 160 machines were built. Also of note was the compact, armoured self-propelled rocket projector, today commonly known as Sturmtiger, only 16 of these machines built and when the first of these was captured by the Americans a great deal of attention was focused on this remarkably powerful weapon.

The end for the Tiger I came in May 1945, almost three years to the day from its birth.

TIGER I

OFFICIAL WARTIME CREW MANUAL
(THE TIGERFIBEL)

INTRODUCTION & TRANSLATION NOTES

Tiger I was the most famous heavy tank produced in World War II. It was developed in great haste during 1942 by the Henschel & Sohn company in order to combat the Russian T-34 and the KV-1.

The Tiger was envisaged as being as the answer to the unexpectedly formidable Soviet armor encountered in the initial months of Operation Barbarossa, during 1941. This radical new breed of tank was designed to house a new type of Kampfwagenkanone (or tank gun) based on the German high velocity 88mm Flugzeugabwehr-Kanone the famous Flak 36 anti-aircraft gun, which had been forced into action in an anti-tank role in Russia and the western desert. This was the only German gun on the battlefield which had demonstrated its effectiveness against heavily armored ground targets such as the KV1 and which was portable enough to be adapted in order to fit into the turret of a tank. It was rapidly redesigned for conversion into the Kwk 36 / L56 which was a parallel development designed to produce a gun which could be mounted into the 11 ton turret of the Tiger I.

Rushed into service in August 1942 the Tiger I design had many flaws and design faults. It was essentially still at prototype stage, but at least it gave the Panzerwaffe its first tank capable of mounting the fearsome 88 mm gun as its main armament .

The Roman numeral I was only officially added in 1944 when the later Tiger II entered production. The initial official German designation was Panzerkampfwagen VI Ausführung H ('Panzer VI version H', abbreviated to PzKpfw VI Ausf. H), but somewhat confusingly the tank was redesignated as PzKpfw VI Tiger Ausf. E in March 1943. It also had the ordnance inventory designation SdKfz 181.

The Tiger was first saw action on 22nd September 1942 near Leningrad. It was not an instant success. Under pressure from Hitler, the tank was driven into action in unfavourable terrain months earlier than planned. The early models, not surprisingly, proved to be mechanically unreliable; in this first action there were breakdowns. More worryingly three others were easily knocked out by dug-in Soviet anti-tank guns aiming at the running gear although there was some comfort in the fact that none suffered a hit that actually managed to pierce the armor of the tank.

Just as there was a great need of haste in producing the Tiger I, so too was there a need to train effective crews. The very best of the existing tank crews were soon creamed off to form the cadre of the Tiger tank crews - the elite of the Panzerwaffe.

A prospective Tiger crew member went through, as rapidly as possible, long hours of essential classroom study. This was coupled with extensive and hands-on training at the Panzer School located in Paderborn.

The head of training for the Inspectorate of the Panzerwaffe and also based at Paderborn was

Hans Christern.

Oberstleutnant Hans Christern, an experienced tank commander who could provide proof to his own practical experience as evidenced by his possession of the Knight's Cross awarded to him for bravery in the field.

With the introduction of the Tiger I (Ausf H) in late 1942, Christern found himself faced with the need to rapidly instruct crews in the operation of a very different type of vehicle. For the first time Germany possessed a heavy tank worthy of the name. Tactically this tank had to be handled very differently; mechanically it needed far more care and attention than any other machine so far delivered to the Panzewaffe.

The situation dictated that everything needed to be done in a hurry and Christern therefore decided it would help to move matters along if he were to replace the usual dusty tank instruction manual with a special training booklet for the Tiger students which was simple yet memorable. The end result was certainly a success on both counts. The simplistic but effective style recalled a children's school book, and it was therefore given the name Tigerfibel, which means Tiger primer. This booklet was assigned the official publication number of D656/27.

The task of actually writing the new training manual was assigned to Leutnant Josef von Glatter-Goetz. Glatter-Goetz took the assignment to heart and gave serious consideration to the need to impart such a large amount of information quickly and make it stick in the minds of bored young tank men. He therefore developed the idea of writing a humorous and highly risqué manual that would hold fast in the memories of the young men training on the Tiger. To do this he used humorous and risqué cartoon illustrations along with slang and the everyday situations which it was hoped the target audience would identify with.

The illustrations in the Tigerfibel were completed by two serving soldiers named Obergrenadier Gessinger and Unteroffizier Wagner. This wide range of images included the usual technical drawings and photographs, supplemented by a range of cartoons. Wherever possible the cartoons featured an attractive and curvaceous blonde named Elvira. She was depicted naked as often as possible and somewhat predictably was the romantic target for the affections of a Tiger crewman who gets the girl in the end.

The Tigerfibel also contains some short verses and rhyming couplets which do not lend themselves readily to an exact translation from German and English, but have been rendered as closely as possible to the produce essence of what was intended.

Each of the five fictitious crew-members appearing in the Tigerfibel was given a memorable name connected with his function. The commander was Speedy "the right timer" which might better be rendered in English as Speedy Quickthinker. His driver was Gustav "the land rover", the radio operator was Funker Piepmatz "the decrypter", the gun loader was Hulsensacke der hemmungslose which is probably best translated as the "the indefatigable" and Gunner Holzauge "the infallible" was the man responsible for the effective use of the main weapon system.

The manual covered a wide range of subjects and besides the obvious information concerning the Tiger I and its basic maintenance requirements and peculiarities, there was also important advice on gunnery and ammunition drill as well as a comprehensive run down on the type of enemy targets likely to be encountered. There was also advice on driving techniques, fuel conservation, how to deal with enemy infantry at close quarters and target spotting.

Although it was quite unconventional when compared to any other manual hitherto produced, the Tigerfibel was actually authorized by Guderian himself and it proved to be very effective training aid.

Each Tigerfibel also came with a set of fold out supplements that were contained in a pocket on the inside of the back cover. One of these supplements was an enemy vehicle recognition chart, which folded out to reveal good black and white photos and diagrammatic representations of the various Allied tanks which the Tiger I crew could be expected to encounter in the field. Another particularly interesting supplement was the graphic demonstration of the range the Tiger could be penetrated by or itself penetrate enemy tanks such as the Sherman M4, T-34 or KV1.

In addition to the advice on fighting and maintaining the machine, the Tigerfibel also affords a fascinating insight into the deteriorating supply situation in the form of exhortations to conserve ammunition and to overrun targets rather than use precious shells. The Tigerfibel is also noteworthy for the fact that no Nazi iconography appears anywhere in the booklet. For a vehicle which has become synonymous with Hitler and the Third Reich it is ironic that there is not a single swastika to be found on any of its pages.

Bob Carruthers

THE TIGERFIBEL

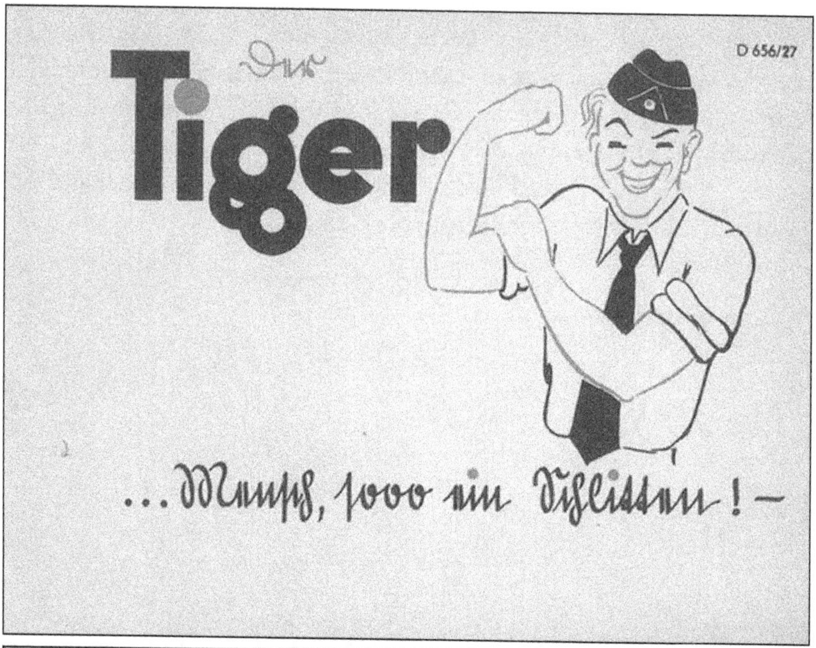

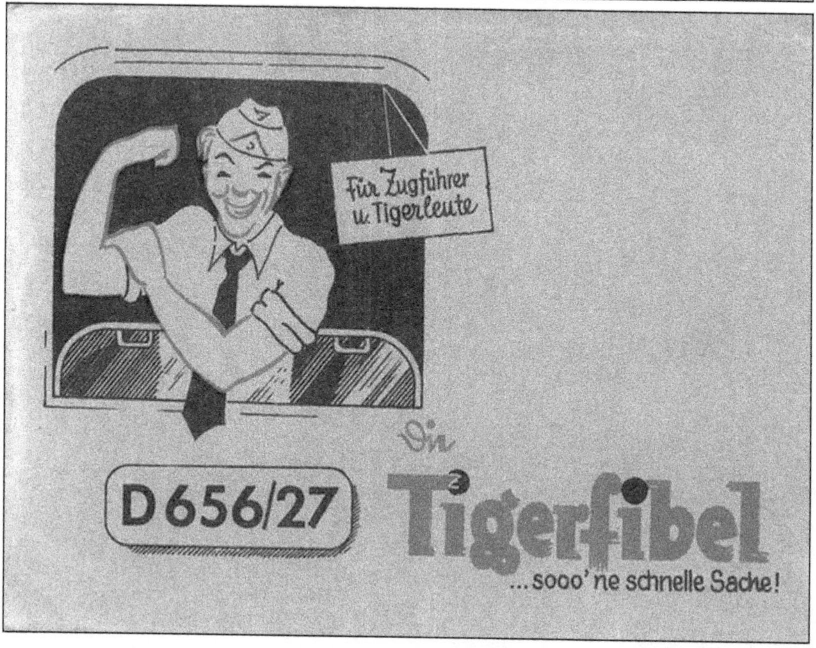

Original front cover translation

Man – what a machine!

Original page 1 translation

**For Commanders and Tiger men.
Tiger primer...what a quick thing!**

Er fährt sich wie ein Pkw

Mit zwei Fingern kannst Du
700 PS schalten,
60 Tonnen lenken,
45 Sachen Straße,
20 Sachen Gelände und
4 m unter Wasser fahren.

2

Original page 2 translation

Handles like a car!

With two fingertips you can steer
- 700 horsepower
- 60 tons of steel
- 45 km per hour top speed on surfaced roads
- 20 km per hour in rough terrain
- Travel 4 m under water

Er schießt alles zu Klumpen

Leutnant M. schoß im Nordabschnitt an einem Tage mit seinem Tiger

38 T 34 ab

und erhielt dafür das Ritterkreuz

Original page 3 translation

Will blast anything to pieces!

On the northern front in the course of one day Lieutenant M. destroyed 38 T-34 tanks. In recognition he was awarded the Knights Cross.

Er hält alles aus....

Dieser Tiger erhielt im Südabschnitt in 6 Stunden:

227 Treffer Panzerbüchse,
14 Treffer 5,2 cm und
11 Treffer 7,62 cm.

Keiner ging durch.

Laufrollen und Verbindungsstücke waren zerschossen,

2 Schwingarme arbeiteten nicht mehr,

mehrere Pak-Treffer saßen genau auf der Kette, und

auf 3 Minen war er gefahren.

Er fuhr mit eigener Kraft noch 60 km Gelände.

Original page 4 translation

Will withstand anything!

This Tiger tank serving on the southern sector endured these hits within a period of six hours:

- 227 hits by anti-tank rounds
- 14 hits by 52mm shells
- 11 hits by 76.2mm shells

Not one of the above penetrated its armor!

Inside the tracks, the rollers and links had been heavily damaged.

Two crank arms were no longer operating.

Several shots from anti-tank guns hit directly on the tracks. The tank had rolled over three mines.

This tank negotiated a further 60 km of rough terrain under its own power.

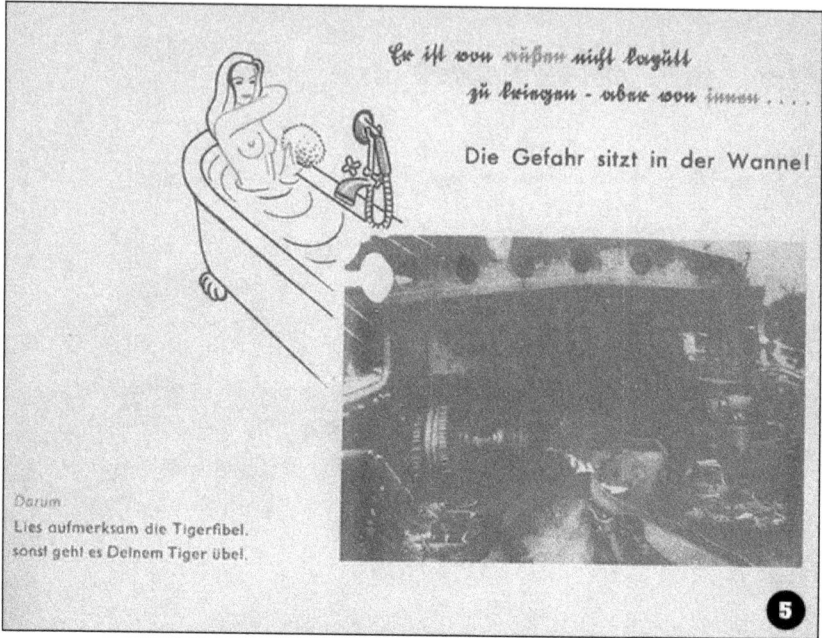

Original page 5 translation

Never conquered by external forces, but single-handedly beaten from within...

DANGER lurks in the sump!

Remember then:
Study your Tiger primer well, or your Tiger goes to hell!

Motto: Griesgrämig plagt sich nur der Tor
Der Tigermann lernt mit Humor

Moral: Selbst Moralisten und Moral
sind unmoralisch manches Mal!

Die Tiger-Fibel

HERAUSGEGEBEN AM 1. 8. 1943 VOM
GENERALINSPEKTEUR DER PANZERTRUPPEN

7

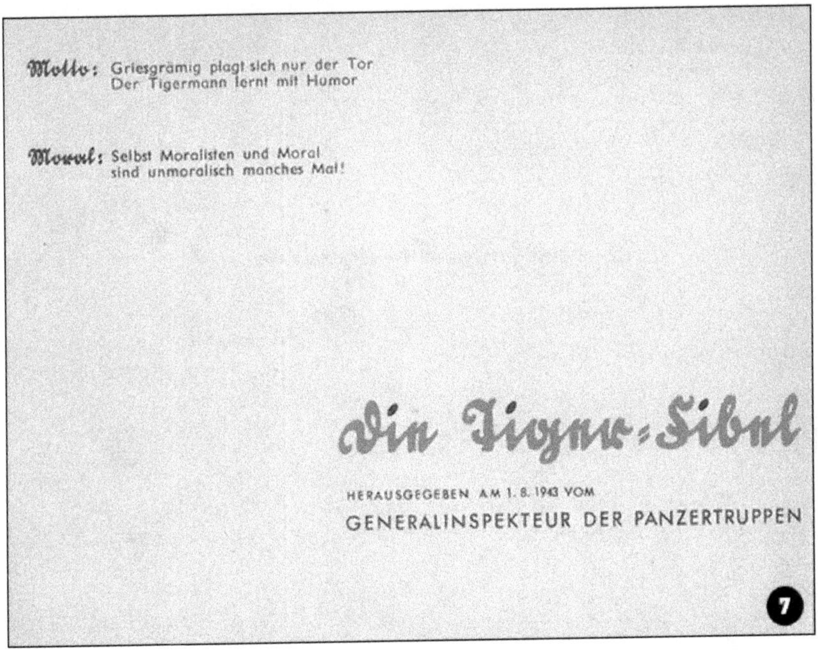

Original page 7 translation

Motto: A morose attitude won't reach the goal
The Tigerman learns with humour

Moral: Even moralists for their preachings
Are sometimes immoral, despite their teachings

The Tiger Tank Manual

Published on 8/1/1943 by
THE CHIEF OF STAFF OF THE TANK CORPS

Ich genehmige die Tigerfibel

Guderian

8

Original page 8 translation

CHIEF OF STAFF
TANK CORPS
Headquarters, 8/1/1943

I authorize the Tiger Tank Manual
Guderian

THE DRIVER

Original page 11 translation

"Gustav the land rover"

You drive a tank which has few opponents worthy of note, but also very few brothers. It is up to you whether the Tiger is transformed into a predator waiting to pounce or into a heap of scrap metal.
Driver

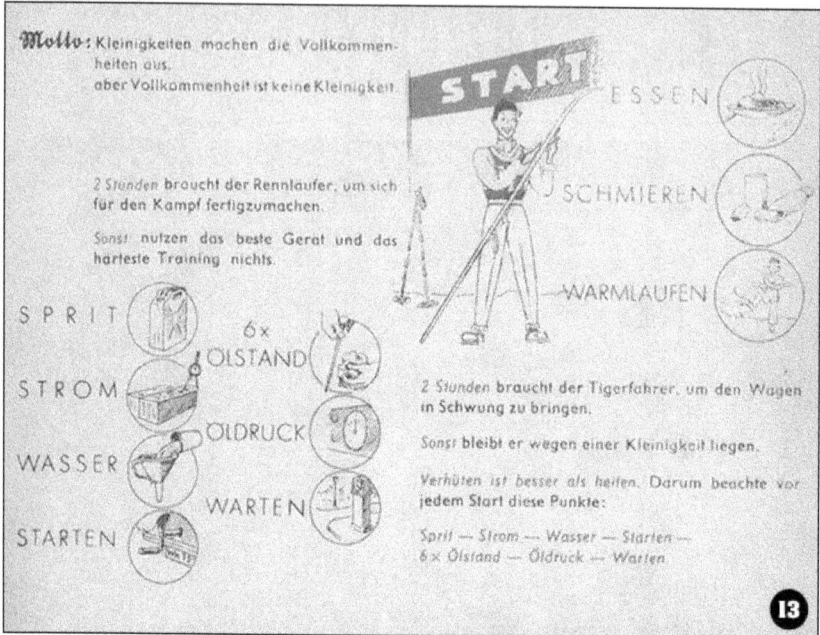

Original page 13 translation

**Motto: Attention to detail makes a good job perfect;
a good job is no minor detail.**

A runner will take two hours to warm up for the competition. If he does not, the best equipment and the most vigorous training are valueless.

**FUEL
POWER
WATER
STARTER
6 x OIL CHECK
OIL PRESSURE
IDLING**

The driver of a Tiger tank needs two hours to get his vehicle moving.

Otherwise it will break down because of a minor problem.

Prevention is easier than cure. Therefore, before starting, pay attention to:

**FUEL - POWER - WATER - STARTING
6 X CHECK OIL - OIL PRESSURE - WAITING**

Motto: Oh Freund, zwei Seiten hat der Sprit.
Mal fährst Du und mal fliegst Du mit.

Sprit ist ein Kraftstoff

Wenn er vergast und mit Luft gemischt in kleinen
Mengen entzündet wird, treibt er den Tiger mit seinen
60 Tonnen durch lauter kleine Explosionen über die
Straße, wie ein Kind einen Reifen durch lauter kleine
Puffe.
Mit 1 Liter im Tank kannst Du 200 m weit fahren. Es
steckt die Schlagkraft eines Riesen darin, aber sie
wirkt über eine halbe Minute verteilt wie eine Massage,
und das hat der Tiger gern.

Sprit

Sprit ist ein Sprengstoff

Fließt derselbe Liter aber, statt in den Vergaser,
in die Wanne, dann vergast er durch die Motor-
wärme, das Gas mischt sich mit der wirbelnden
Luft und wird durch einen Funken oder Hitze auf
einmal gezündet.
Dieser Liter sprengt Deinen Tiger so, daß die
Motorklappe mit Deinem Hausdach höher davon-
wirbelt, als Du einen Stein werfen kannst. Die
Riesenkraft ballt sich in einen einzigen k. o. zusammen und den hält auch ein Tiger nicht aus.

Darum.

Original page 14 translation

Motto: Oh friend, fuel has two sides, on the one hand it propels you, on the other you fly with it!

Fuel is a propellant: If fuel evaporates and is then mixed with air and ignited in small quantities it will move all 60 tons of the Tiger along the road. It does so by repeated small explosions, in the same way that a child might roll a wheel using a stick, by continuously striking the wheel.

One litre in the fuel tank will propel the Tiger a distance of 200 meters. The strength of a giant is harnessed in that portion, but it is spread over half a minute just like a massage. And the Tiger likes that.

Fuel is an explosive: If that same litre of fuel flows into the sump and not through the carburetor, then the fuel will evaporate by way of engine heat, mix with the air circulating in the engine bay and suddenly ignite at a hot spot or through a spark.

In this way just this one litre will blow up your Tiger as if the giant's force is applied at once in a single knock out blow, which even your Tiger cannot withstand. The engine and your own roof will fly up higher in the air than you can throw a stone.

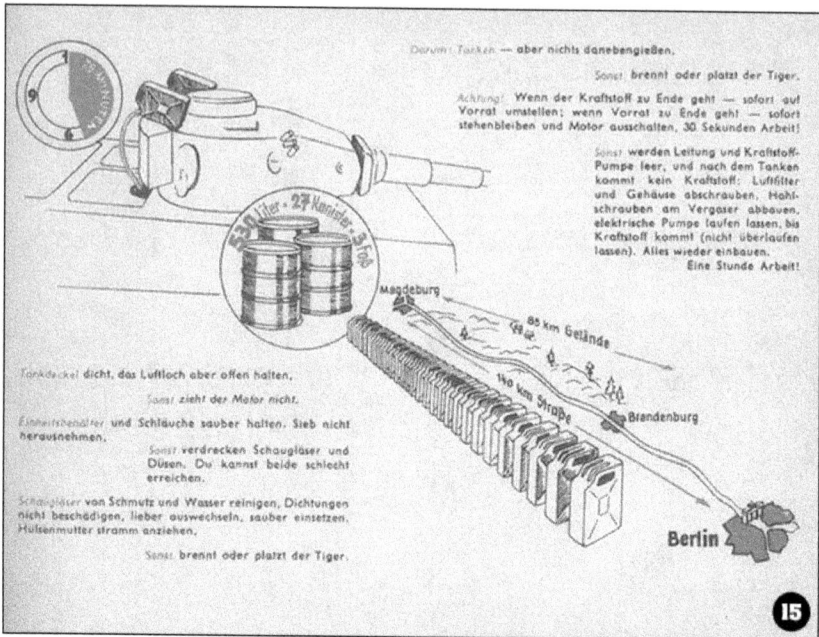

Original page 15 translation

Therefore: Refuel - but do not spill, otherwise the Tiger will burn or burst.

Attention! If fuel is running low - immediately switch to reserve, if the fuel reservoir is used up stop immediately and shut off the engine - *30 seconds worth of effort.*

However, if you do not maintain fuel in the lines and the fuel pump runs empty, after refueling no fuel will flow through it: You must then remove the air filter and housing, remove the access screws at the carburetor, prime with the electric fuel pump all of this without causing a spill! Then you must reinstall everything - *One hour of work.*

- Close the lid for the fuel tank, but keep the vent open.
  Otherwise the engine will have no pickup.

- Keep fuel canisters and hoses clean, do not remove the filter.
  Otherwise the sight glass and jets will get dirty, both of which can be reached only with great difficulty for repair.

- Clean sight glass of dirt and moisture, do not damage the seals, if in doubt replace seals, insert properly, tighten cap nut.
  Otherwise the Tiger will burn or burst.

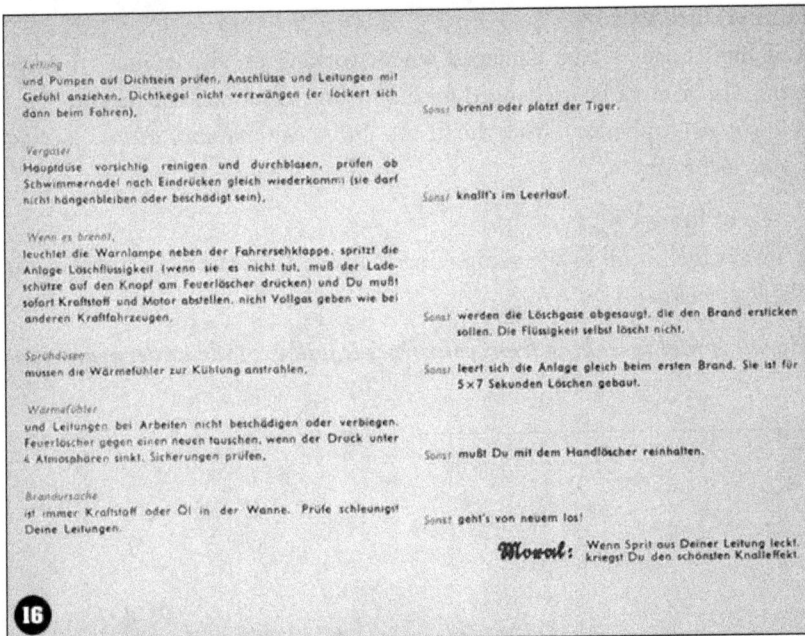

Original page 16 translation

Fuel lines and pumps must be checked for leaks. Fittings and lines must be tightened carefully. Do not cock the cone seal, it will work itself loose in the course of operation - *Otherwise the Tiger will burn or bust.*

Carburetor

The main jet must be cleaned with care. Blow air through the jet when finished. Check if the needle returns from the seat immediately. It must not stick or be damaged - *Otherwise, the engine backfires at idle.*

In case of fire

The warning light next to the driver's lookout will illuminate and the fire control apparatus will spray liquid. If it does not, the gunner must press the button on the fire extinguisher. You must immediately shut off fuel supply to the engine. Do not open to full throttle position as with other vehicles - *Otherwise the gases intended to extinguish the flames will be removed by the blowers. The liquid dispensed by the fire extinguisher will not put out the flames except as a pressurised gas.*

Extinguisher jets

Must aim at the temperature sensors - *Otherwise, the apparatus will continue and dispense all liquid at the first outbreak of fire. It is designed to extinguish for seven seconds each time, on five different occasions.*

Temperature sensors

And lines must not be damaged when working on the engine. The fire extinguisher must be exchanged for a new one as soon as the pressure falls below 4 atmospheres. Check the fuses - *Otherwise you must use the manual fire extinguisher.*

Cause of fire

Is always fuel or oil in the sump. Check all the lines at once - *Otherwise it will happen again!*

Moral: If fuel is leaking from your lines it will explode underneath you.

Motto:

Wer seine Sammler pflegt und schont wird überreich dafür belohnt.

Das sind Deine besten Kameraden

Sie kurbeln Deinen Motor an, wenns draußen schießt, sie verfeuern Deine Granaten, sie saugen den Qualm ab! Du kannst im Dunkeln sehen, im Nebel Richtung halten, beim größten Lärm Dich verständigen, 10 km weit hören und sprechen!

Gib ihns eine Runde aus

damit sie sich richtig vollaufen lassen können!

Halt sie Dir warm

Ein geladener Sammler zerfriert erst bei —65°, ein entladener aber schon bei —10°. Das kommt sehr leicht vor, weil Spannung und Inhalt sehr schnell abnehmen, wenn es richtig kalt wird!

Gib ihnen Strom ab,

wenn Du welchen übrig hast, damit sie Dir aushelfen, wenn er Dir fehlt!

Destilliertes oder abgekochtes Wasser nachfüllen, im Winter zur Not geschmolzenen Schnee, bis die Platten 1 fingerbreit überspült sind. Klemmen säurefrei halten, gut anziehen, fetten. Sonst verschlammt oder verschlampt der Sammler.

Im Winter mit Schwunganlasser durchdrehen und starten, das ist billiger als Sammler ausbauen und aufladen! Sinkt die Spannung unter 11 Volt oder stellst Du den Tiger für längere Zeit ins Kalte — Sammler ausbauen und pflegen!

12 Volt! Nicht unter 11 Volt sinken lassen. Beim Prüfen Voltmeter mit einem Pol an Masse legen, den anderen an Fernlichtsicherung. Fernlicht einschalten. Prüfst Du mit dem Taucher, ist Marke 1,285 = geladen, Marke 1,15 = entladen. Keinen Kurzschluß machen, nicht umklemmen. Sonst verziehen sich die Platten.

Moral: Es ist schon eine alte Mär, wer richtig voll ist, friert nicht sehr!

17

Original page 17 translation

Motto: He who treats his batteries with great care, will receive benefit in return!

They are your best comrades.

They start your engine as the bullets fly outside. They fire off your shells, they clear the smoke! They light your way in the dark and in fog, they allow you to communicate despite the noise of battle, you broadcast and receive up to a distance of 10 km!

Give them an extra charge often!

So that they stay fully charged!

Keep them warm-hearted towards you!

A charged battery will freeze at -65°C, a discharged battery will freeze at just -10°C. Discharge can very easily happen. Voltage and charge decrease faster as the cold increases outside. Charge them with some electricity anytime you have a surplus, so they can support you when you are running short.

Use distilled water or boiled water. In the wintertime melted snow may be used in emergencies. Fill up until the plates are covered plus one finger's width. Keep the clamps free of acid, tighten them firmly and cover them with grease - *Otherwise the battery will gunk up or fail!*

In winter use the manual inertia starter to turn and start the engine. It is actually a lot less effort than taking out the batteries and recharging them! If the voltage falls below 11 volts or the Tiger has been parked in the cold for a long time - take the batteries out and look after them! Otherwise they may fail.

12 volts! Do not let the charge fall under 11 volts. To check connect voltmeter between the ground and the fuse for high beam. Turn on high beams. When checking with the hydrometer, if mark at 1.285 = charged, 1.15 = empty. *Do not create a short circuit, do not change battery polarity. Otherwise the plates will become distorted!*

Moral: So runs the old tale, he who is full will not freeze pale!

Original page 18 translation

Motto: Water is a benevolent power
as long as you remembered the antifreeze!

Water is a coolant, like a fresh shower, the water flushes through the case and removes the heat accrued by combustion and friction, and carrying it to the radiators. Additionally, in the winter time the hot water will preserve engine heat making it easier to start again, much like a battery holds a charge.

The Tiger needs 120 litres of water. He feels great at 85°C.

Anytime you are thirsty, give some water to the good animal too, and make it clean water. If you can get the coolant additive "Akorol", put it in, but be careful, Akorol can be a poison too. Like a vigilant hawk it will guard against rust and mineral deposits.

Water
Water is an explosive, when freezing to ice it expands by 10%. If the engine walls cannot flex, they are cracked under the enormous pressure. Ice is used to break iron and rock.

Those 120 litres will then turn to 132 litres, and they have no place to go. Not even in the Tiger's belly!

Therefore:

Fill up, until the water level touches the bottom of the filter, check the hose clamps and lines, check especially on the bottom connecting the radiators.

Wenn Du Durst hast, gib dem braven Tier auch was zu saufen, und zwar sauberes Wasser. Wenn Du das Kühlschutzmittel *Akorol* kriegen kannst, tu's rein, aber Vorsicht: Akorol ist giftig. Wie ein Steinhäger verhindert es Rost und Verkalkung.

95° — Achtung! Das ist schon zu heiß. Das Öl hört jetzt auf zu schmieren, und Du kannst Dich nach einem neuen Motor umsehen. Bleib lieber sofort stehen und prüfe:

Im Winter mischt man den Grog mit Vorteil etwas steifer. Mische Dein Kühlwasser bei Kälte mit Glysantin.

Hier das berühmte Rezept aus der Eisbar in Sa Ukalt:
2 Liter Glysantin auf 3 Liter Wasser.
Bis —20° also   48 Liter Glysantin
               +72 Liter Wasser einfüllen
              120 Liter
Bis —40° umgekehrt 72 Liter Glysantin
            +48 Liter Wasser
            120 Liter

Kühlanlage ständig nachsehen, weil Glysantin alle Ablagerungen löst. Aber Glysantin nicht mit Akorol mixen.

Darum: Nachfüllen, bis Siebboden benetzt ist, Schlauchbinder und Leitungen prüfen, vor allem die untersten, die die Kühler verbinden.

1. Hast Du genug Wasser im Kühler?
2. Sind die Lüfter eingeschaltet?
3. Arbeiten die Rutschkupplungen?
4. Ist der Ölkühler dicht?
Sonst: Frißt der Motor sich fest.

Sonst: platzt der Motor.
Dazu Einfüllkappe öffnen, Wasser über Gummischlauch durch Ablaßhahn heiß ablassen. Vor Neufüllen Kühlanlage durchspülen und Ablaßschraube mit Dichtung schließen. — Nach einer Woche heiß ablassen, drei Stunden stehenlassen, damit sich Rost und Schlamm absetzen, durch Leinenlappen wieder einfüllen; auch nach Arbeiten am Motor Wasser nachfüllen.
Sonst: Leckt der Kühler.

Moral: Der Tiger säuft das Wasser meist so gern wie Du den Himbeergeist.

19

Original page 19 translation

95°C - attention! That is too hot. The oil ceases to lubricate and you can start looking for a new engine. Stop immediately and check:

1. Is there enough water in the radiators?
2. Are the blowers working?
3. Are the sliding clutches operating?
4. The oil cooler must be sealing tight!

Otherwise the engine will seize up!

In the wintertime a hot toddy is best mixed a little more on the stiff side. When it is cold, mix the water with antifreeze. Otherwise the engine will crack!

Here is the infamous recipe from the ice bar:
2 Litres of antifreeze per 3 litres of water.

Down to -20°C that's:
48 Litres of antifreeze + 72 Litres of water = 120 Litres

Down to -40°C that's:

72 Litres of antifreeze + 48 Litres of water = 120 Litres

Constantly check the cooling system, because antifreeze loosens all deposits. But do not mix antifreeze with the additive "Akorol".

Open the filler cap cover. Drain the water hot, through a rubber hose attached to the drain cock. Before refilling flush the cooling system and tighten the drain cock with gasket installed.

- After a week again drain hot, let sit for three hours, so that rust and sludge can settle, refill using a rag as filter; check and water level each time after working on the engine.

Otherwise the radiator will leak.

Moral: The Tiger drinks the water most like you and spirits.

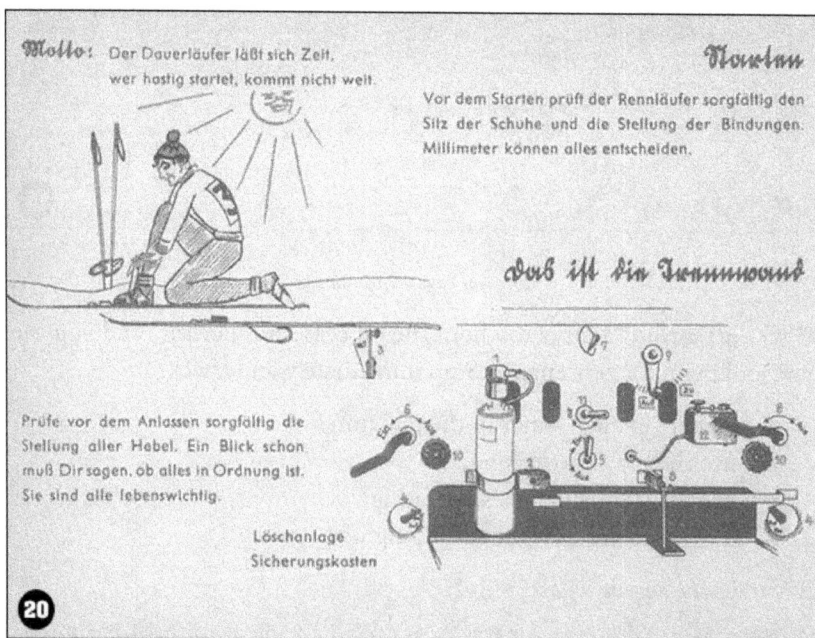

Original page 20 translation

**Motto: A cross-country skier takes his time to prepare,
if he starts hastily he won't make it there.**

Before the start the runner will check the soles of his shoes and laces with care. Even millimeters make a difference.

Before starting out, carefully check the position of all levers. One look must tell you if everything is okay. They are all essential for survival.

1. Fire extinguisher   2. Fusebox

3. Bodenluke	auf	damit die Gase abziehen können, gleichzeitig Heckhutze offen-halten, damit frische Luft von oben nachdrückt. Erst beim Waten, bei U-Fahrt, bei Schlamm und vor dem Gefecht schließen.	Sonst platzt der Tiger.
4. Kraftstoffhähne	auf	Kraftstoffbehälter hintereinander leerfahren. Geht Vorrat zu Ende, Motor sofort abstellen.	Sonst siehe „Sprit".
5. Sammlerhauptschalter	ein	er schaltet alle Verbraucher ab.	Sonst kannst Du nicht anlassen.
6. Lüfterschalter	auf „Land"	bei U-Fahrt werden die Lüfter abgestellt;	Sonst kocht der Motor.
7. Entlüfter	auf „Land"	bei U-Fahrt werden die Kraftstoffbehälter in den Motorraum entlüftet.	Sonst ins Freie.
8. Absaugdrossel	runter	sie drosselt die Luft im Absaugkanal zwischen Wechselgetriebe und Gebläse.	Sonst wird das Wechselgetriebe heiß.
9. Ausblasdrossel	auf „Land"	sie leitet die heiße Getriebeluft zu den Lüftern oder in den Motorraum.	Sonst wird der Motor heiß.
10. Lüftungsdrossel	auf	sie leitet die heiße Motorluft zu den Lüftern.	Sonst wird der Motor heiß.
11. Schieber	zu	nur gleichzeitig mit Fronthutze öffnen.	Sonst stinkt's im Kampfraum.
Kraftstoffpumpe	ein	damit der Vergaser schon Kraftstoff hat, wenn Du anläßt.	Sonst wird der Sammler leer.
Richtungshebel	auf 0	Hebel nach vorn = vorfahren, zurück = rückwärtsfahren.	Sonst fährt er an.
Zündschlüssel	rein	nicht umdrehen, andere Verbraucher abschalten.	Sonst wird der Sammler leer.
Hebel der Anlaßvorrichtung	vor	damit das Gemisch fett wird. Dabei Fuß weg vom Gas.	Sonst springt er nicht an.
Kupplung	treten	damit Anlasser nicht das Wechselgetriebe mitzuziehen braucht.	Sonst wird der Sammler leer.
Anlaßknopf	drücken	lieber länger und mit längerer Unterbrechung.	Sonst wird der Sammler leer.
Anlaßknopf	loslassen	sobald der Motor anspringt.	Sonst leidet der Anlasser.
Hebel der Anlaßvorrichtung	zurück	wenn der Motor gleichmäßig rundläuft.	Sonst verrußen die Zündkerzen.
Gashebel	antippen	5 Minuten so langsam laufen lassen, daß Prüflampe flackert. Motor nicht hochjagen.	Sonst stottert er.
Kupplung	kommenlassen	damit das Wechsel- und Lenk-Getriebe handwarm werden.	Sonst kannst Du nicht schalten.
Gas	geben	Warmlaufen lassen, auf 1000 bis 1500 U/min. steigern.	Sonst verrußen die Zündkerzen.

21

Original page 21 translation

Bottom plug - open - so that the gases can vent, at the same time keep rear cover open, so that fresh air can circulate. Close only when driving in or through water, mud or upon entering an engagement - *Otherwise the Tiger will blow up!*

Fuel valves - open - Fuel tanks must be empty one after the other. If fuel runs out, immediately turn off the engine. - *Otherwise, see "fuel".*

Main battery switch - on - It turns off all appliances - *Otherwise you cannot start!*

Blower switch - "land" - The blowers must be turned off under water - *Otherwise the engine overheats!*

Fuel vent - "land" - While under water the tanks are vented into the engine bay - *Otherwise to the outside.*

Throttle #1 - down - this regulates air flow in the duct between blower and transmission - *Otherwise the transmission overheats.*

151

Throttle #2 - "land" - It directs the hot air from the transmission to the blowers or into the engine bay - *Otherwise the engine overheats.*

Throttle #3 - open - It pushes the hot engine air to the blowers - *Otherwise the engine overheats.*

Vent flap - closed - Open only together with the front hatch - *Otherwise engine bay air enters the vehicle.*

Fuel pump - on - So that the carburetor has fuel as you start - *Otherwise the battery discharges.*

Directional lever - on "0" - forward = lever forward, reverse = lever back - *Otherwise the tank moves on starting.*

Ignition key - in - Do not turn, turn off other appliances - *Otherwise the battery discharges.*

Choke lever - forward - So that the mixture is enriched. Take your foot off the throttle when starting - *Otherwise it will not start.*

Clutch - depress - So that the starter motor does not break between attempts at starting the engine - *Otherwise the battery discharges.*

Starter button - push - Push longer, take longer breaks between attempts at starting the engine - *Otherwise the battery will discharge.*

Starter button - release - as soon as the engine starts - *Otherwise the starter motor suffers.*

Choke lever - reverse - As soon as the engine runs smoothly and evenly - *Otherwise the spark plugs foul.*

Throttle - touch lightly for five minutes, so that the warning lamp flickers. Do not race the engine - *Otherwise it will stall.*

Clutch - engage slowly, so that transmission and steering gear become warm to the touch - *Otherwise no gear change.*

Throttle - push in to warm up the engine. Increase engine speed to within 1000 and 1500 rpm - *Otherwise the spark plugs foul.*

Im Winter

wird das Öl zäh und steif. Die Wellen kleben in den Lagern,
die Kolben an den Zylinderwänden. Es gehört eine Bärenkraft
dazu, diese Teile zu trennen und so lange zu bewegen, bis das Öl
warm und flüssig wird. Obwohl der Tiger bis –20° auch mit dem
elektr. Anlasser sofort anspringt, mit dem Schwungkraftanlasser
durchdrehen und anwerfen. Schone die Sammler,

Sonst kannst Du nicht anlassen, wenn's draußen schießt.

Bei großer Kälte

kann ein Tiger den anderen anwärmen. Das heiße Kühlwasser des
einen Motors wird in den kalten Motor gepumpt und gleichzeitig
dessen kaltes Kühlwasser angewärmt. Hinterher sorgfältig prüfen,
ob der normale Betrieb wiederhergestellt ist.

Sonst fliegt der Tiger in die Luft.

Lüfter

abschalten, damit der Motor schneller warm wird, dabei scharf
das Thermometer beobachten,

Sonst kocht der Motor wie ein Suppentopf über.

Einspritzen

wenn es der Schwungkraftanlasser nicht schafft,

Sonst verlierst Du Vertrauen und Zeit.

In den Tropen

und im Hochsommer wird der Lüfter auf hohe Umdrehungen
gestellt.

Sonst kocht der Motor.

Schwungkraftanlasser

mit der Handkurbel im Uhrzeigersinn hochdrehen, Hebel rasch
einrücken und halten, bis Motor anspringt, dann loslassen!
Wenn das Ritzel nicht einspurt, Einrücken wiederholen. Nicht einrücken, wenn Motor läuft!

Kühlwasser übertragen:

A. Schläuche füllen.
   1. Motor abstellen.
   2. Schläuche an den roten Anschluß schrauben.
   3. Kühler durch die Leitungsdrosseln abschalten.
   4. Lüfter abschalten, Kühlerverschraubung abnehmen.
   5. Motor laufen lassen, Schlauch hochhalten, Stößel am freien
      Schlauchende so lange drücken, bis Wasser kommt.
   6. Fehlendes Wasser und Glysantin ergänzen.

B. Übertragen.
   1. Motor abstellen, wenn er 60° hat.
   2. Schläuche so anschließen, daß immer ein roter mit einem
      grünen Anschluß verbunden ist.
   3. Am wärmenden Motor wieder Drosseln zu, Lüfter aus,
      Kühlerverschraubung ab.
   4. Motor erst mit 2400, dann mit 2000 U/min laufen lassen, bis
      der andere Motor 50° warm geworden ist.
   5. Motor abstellen, Drosseln auf, Lüfter ein, Kühlerverschrau-
      bung zu.

Schalthebel

des Lüftergetriebes lösen und bei Stellung „erhöhte Kühlung"
wieder festschrauben.

Moral: Ein bißchen drehn, ein heißer Trunk
bringt selbst die Eisigste in Schwung.

22

Original page 22 translation

In the wintertime...

The oil gets thick, so much so that it can hardly be called a liquid. Shafts lock in their bearings, pistons clamp to the cylinder walls. It takes an enormous amount of force to separate these parts and move them until the engine oil gets warm and liquid. Although the Tiger can be started immediately at temperatures down to -20°C using the electric starter motor, use the manual inertia starter instead to crank over and start the engine. Save the batteries - *Otherwise you cannot start when the bullets fly outside.*

When it is very cold...

One Tiger can warm up the other. The hot engine coolant in one engine is pumped into a cold engine. At the same time the cold engine is warmed up. After this procedure, be sure to check that normal operation has been reinstated - *Otherwise the Tiger will explode.*

Blowers...

Must be shut off, so that the engine heats up faster. Watch the thermometer carefully - *Otherwise the engine will boil over like a pot full of soup.*

Inject...

If the manual inertia starter does not start the engine - *Otherwise you will lose faith and time.*

In the tropics...

And in high summer conditions the blowers must be set at high speed - Otherwise the engine overheats.

Manual inertia starter...

Swing with the hand crank in clockwise direction. Swiftly engage the crank and hold it until the engine starts, then immediately release the crank!

If the pinion does not mesh, repeat the engagement of the crank. Do not engage the crank when the engine is running!

To exchange engine coolant...

A. Fill the hoses.

1. Shut off the engine.
2. Attach the hoses to the red fittings.
3. Shut off radiators through the in line Valves.
4. Shut off blowers, remove the radiator cap.
5. Run the engine, hold up the hose, work the plunger at the open end until water flows out.
6. Replace lost water and antifreeze.

B. Exchange the coolant.

1. Shut off engine as soon as it reaches 60°C coolant temperature.
2. Connect the hoses so that each one connects a red and a green fitting.
3. Once more close the valves in the coolant lines of the warm engine. Turn off the blowers, remove the radiator caps.
4. Run the engine at 2400 rpm, then at 2000 rpm. Until the cold engine has reached a coolant temperature of 50°C.
5. Shut off the engine, open the coolant lines, turn on the blowers, close the radiator caps.

Selector...

on the blower transmission must be loosened and switched back to position "increased cooling", then tightened.

> *Moral: A little warm drink and after a while*
> *even a frigid one will cut a dash*

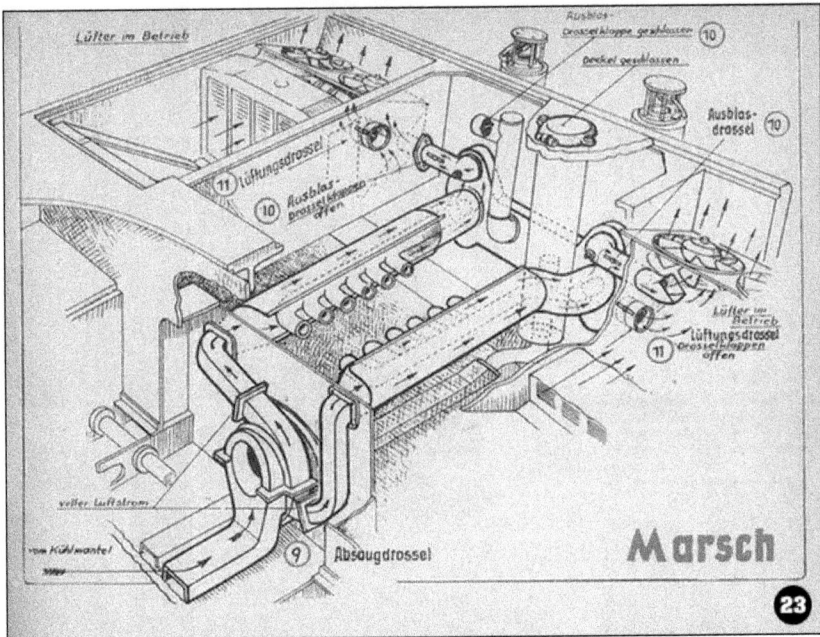

Lüfter im Betrieb

Ausblas-Drosselklappe geschlossen (10)

Deckel geschlossen

Ausblas-drossel (10)

(11) Lüftungsdrossel

(10) Ausblas Drosselklappen offen

Lüfter im Betrieb

(11) Lüftungsdrossel Drosselklappen offen

voller Luftstrom

vom Kühlmantel

(9) Absaugdrossel

Marsch

23

Motto: Das Öl ist hier der Feind der Sonne, dem Tiger ist es eine Wonne.

6 x Ölstand

Öl ist ein Schmiermittel

Schon wenn Du Deine Hände miteinander reibst, werden sie heiß. Du brauchst sie gar nicht schnell oder mit viel Kraft bewegen. Tust Du aber ordentlich Hautöl dazwischen, dann bleiben sie kühl.

Deine Maschine macht 3000 Umdrehungen in der Minute und 700 PS sitzen dahinter. Sie würde brennend heiß werden, alles Bewegliche würde sich festfressen. Du kämst keinen Kilometer weit, wenn nicht Öl die Hitze aufnähme und hinwegspülte. Zu wenig Öl ist gefährlich.

Öl ist ein Brennstoff

Wenn es aus den Leitungen leckt, durch Wellen ausgeworfen wird, aus schadhaften Dichtungen tropft und sich mit Sprit vermischt, brennt es lichterloh und steckt Spritlachen und den üblichen Wannensatz an.

Zuviel Öl ist gefährlich.

Darum:

24

Original page 24 translation

6 x Check Oil

Motto: Oil blocks the heat of the sun
For the Tiger it's bliss.

Oil is a lubricant

Even just rubbing your hands one against the other will cause them both to become hot. You need not even rub quickly or use much effort. But, if sufficient skin oil is placed between your hands, they stay cool. Your machine does 3000 rotations per minute with 700 horsepower behind it. It would get burning hot, all moving parts would size up before you had gone one kilometer, if the oil did not take up the heat and disperse it away.

A low oil level is dangerous.

Oil is a combustible

If it leaks from your lines, or is discharged from moving driveshafts, or drips from damaged seals and mixes with fuel, it will burn furiously and set other pools of fuel and the remaining sludge in the sump on fire»

Too much oil is dangerous.

Therefore:

Wo füllen?	Was füllen?	Wieviel füllen?	Sonst passiert was?
1. Motor	28 Liter Motoröl	höchstens obere Marke mindestens untere Marke	Sonst verölen die Zündkerzen, brauchst Du viel Öl und Motoren
2. Wechsel-Getriebe	30 Liter Getr. Öl	bis Meßstab gerade eben eintaucht	Sonst kannst Du weder schalten noch lenken
3. Vorgelege (rechts)	6 Liter Getr. Öl	kleine Prüfschraube (nicht die große Schraube) abschrauben	Sonst füllst Du zu viel oder zu wenig. Beides ist schlecht.
4. Vorgelege (links)	6 Liter Getr. Öl	nachfüllen bis Öl überläuft	
5. Turmantrieb	5 Liter Getr. Öl	füllen bis Spiegel 1 fingerbreit unter Füllöffnung steht	Sonst kannst Du den Turm nicht schwenken.
6. Lüftertrieb	7 Liter Getr. Öl	nur bis oberste Marke, bei stehender Maschine auffüllen.	Sonst wird es auf den Auspuffmantel geschleudert.

Ölstand
Zuviel Öl ist genau so schlecht, wie zu wenig! Bei laufendem Motor (1000 U/min) und mindestens 50° Wärme messen und ergänzen, am besten nochmals nach 5 km Fahrt. — Sonst stimmt die Ölmenge nicht

Kein Öl verlieren
Auf tadellose Dichtungen achten, Einfüll- und Ablaßschrauben festziehen, Leitungen verfolgen, jedem Ölklecks nachgehen, Auf Ölschaum und Schleuderöl achten. Wannenboden durch Bodenluke säubern. — Sonst brennt der Tiger.

Ölwechsel
vor und nach dem Winter, bei der vorgeschriebenen Kilometerzahl und nach Reparaturen ordentlich durchführen. — Sonst muß ein neuer Motor rein.

Im Winter
kannst Du mit dem Motorenöl der Wehrmacht (Winter) bis —30° tadellos fahren. Unter 30° mußt Du bei handwarmem Motor vom vorgeschriebenen Ölstand ablassen. Dafür 4 Liter Ottokraftstoff einfüllen und zum Durchmischen den Motor bei mittlerer Drehzahl kurze Zeit laufen lassen. — Sonst frierst Du fest.

Nach 3 Stunden Fahrt
ist der Sprit wieder verdampft, wenn der Motor über —60° warm ist. Du kannst zwar ruhig weiter fahren, mußt aber vor dem Abstellen die verdampften 4 Liter Ottokraftstoff bei laufendem Motor nachfüllen. Ist nicht alles verdampft, kannst Du den Grad der Verdunstung mit dem Luftblasenmesser messen.
Das Getriebeöl der Wehrmacht 8 E (grün) taugt bis minus 40°, es braucht also nicht verdünnt zu werden. — Sonst ist er am Morgen festgefroren.

Moral: Er brennt dir fest, wenn du nicht schmierst und er verbrennt, wenn du's verlierst.

25

Original page 25 translation

1. Fill the Engine - with 28 L engine oil - up to maximum level at upper mark, Minimum level at lower mark - *Otherwise the spark plugs foul. You will use lots of oil and maybe lose an engine.*

2. Fill the Transmission - with 30 L of transmission oil - until the measuring rod just touches the oil level - *Otherwise you can neither change gears nor steer.*

3. Fill the Right reduction gear - with 6 L transmission oil - remove small inspection bolt - *If you fill up too much or too little, both conditions are equally bad.*

4. Fill the Left reduction gear - with 6 L transmission oil - fill up until the oil flows over

5. Fill the Turret drive - with 5 L transmission oil - fill up until level is one finger's width under fill plug hole - *Otherwise you cannot traverse the turret!*

6. Fill the Blower drive - with 7 L transmission oil - only up to upper level with the engine turned off - *Otherwise the oil is thrown onto the exhaust manifold cover.*

Oil level:

Too much oil is just as bad as too little! With the engine running at 1000 rpm and warmed up, to 50°C coolant temperature measure the oil level and fill up to the proper level. Repeat the process after traveling 5 km, if possible - *Otherwise the amount of oil in the engine will be incorrect.*

Do not lose oil:

Check that the seals are in excellent shape. Tighten the fill- and drainplugs. Check all lines to discover leaks. Check the oil for signs of foaming and oil discharge at radial seals. Clean the bottom of the sump, drain through the bottom plug - *Otherwise the Tiger will burn.*

Oil change:

Change the oil before and after the winter, also within specified intervals. Change it especially after performing engine repairs - *Otherwise a new engine must be installed.*

In the winter time:

You can run the military engine oil labeled (winter) without a problem down to temperatures of -30°C. Below 30°C you must drain 4 Litres of engine oil while the engine is warm to the touch. Substitute 4 Litres of petrol for the oil drained off. Mix the oil and petrol by running the engine at fast idle for a short period - *Otherwise you will freeze up.*

After driving for three hours:

The petrol in the oil will have evaporated as long as the engine was above -60°C and warm. You can keep moving but must replenish the 4 Litres of petrol with the engine running, before shutting it off. Whether or not all the petrol has evaporated can be checked against the bubble meter. The transmission oil for the military is effective up to minus 40°C, therefore it need not be thinned out - *Otherwise the next morning the engine will be frozen up.*

Moral: It will seize up if you don't lubricate,
if you lose it, you will incinerate

Motto: Dem rechten Hochdruck seiner Säfte verdankt der Tiger erst die Kräfte.

Öldruck

Die richtige Ölmenge allein tut es auch nicht. Öl im Sumpf ist genau so unnütz wie Bier im Keller, wenn der Druck fehlt, um es nach oben zu den durstigen Verbrauchern in die heißen und trockenen Kehlen zu pumpen. Dann erst kommt Schwung in den Laden. Dann erst kannst Du rauf- und runterschalten, daß es nur so scheppert, lenken, daß es staubt, und den Turm schwenken wie einen Wetterhahn.

Der Öldruckmesser
muß bei leerlaufendem Motor mindestens einen Druck von 3 at anzeigen. 7 at ist beim Fahren das Richtige. Wenn eine Leitung geplatzt oder verstopft ist, oder das Lagerspiel zu groß geworden ist, fällt der Druck. Du mußt dann sofort den Motor abstellen. *Sonst frißt sich der Motor fest.*

Den Ölfilter für das Motoröl mußt Du bei jedem Ölwechsel, besser aber öfter reinigen.

1. Deckel abschrauben, Filterpaket herausnehmen.
2. Flügelschraube lösen, Filter- und Spannscheiben einzeln abstreifen.
3. Scheiben und Gehäuse mit Kraftstoff tadellos saubermachen. Achtung! Der Kraftstoff ist verbleit und tut der Haut nicht gut.
4. Erst eine Filterscheibe, dann abwechselnd Spann- und Filterscheibe aufstreifen und mit Endscheibe und Flügelschraube gut festpressen.
5. Paket einsetzen, Deckel aufschrauben, Druckfeder nicht vergessen!

Moral: Auch für das Leben gilt die Lehre: Der Druck erst macht die Atmosphäre.

26

Original page 26 translation

Oil Pressure

Motto: Only with his blood under full pressure will the Tiger show his strength to full measure.

The correct amount of oil alone is not sufficient. Oil in the reservoir is just as useless as beer in the cellar, if there is no pressure to pump it upstairs to the parched throats of the consumers. Only then will the place start swinging. Only then can you change gears up and down with a clatter, throw up the dust and swing your turret like a flag in the wind.

The oil pressure gauge:
With the engine running, the gauge must show a pressure of at least 3 atmospheres. When on the move 7 atmospheres is the right pressure. If a line bursts or gets clogged or if the bearing clearance has become too large, the pressure will fall. In that case you must immediately shut off the engine. - *Otherwise the engine will seize up.*

The oil filter for the engine oil must be cleaned with each oil change or, even better, more frequently.

1. Remove lid, remove filter pack.
2. Loosen the wing nut, remove the filter plates and separator plates one by one.
3. The housing and the separator plates must be cleaned in petrol. Caution! The petrol contains lead and will damage the skin.
4. To install, first slide one filter plate, then in alteration one separator- and one filter plate over the suction pipe. Then install the top plate and press the assembly in place with the wingnut.
5. Install the filter pack. Do not forget the top pressure spring!

Moral: As one learns in life,
a certain pressure produces the right atmosphere!

Moral: You'll find the fittings, even through the grime, by looking at the lube chart every time.

Before the race, a runner will run around the track a few times in order to warm up. If he starts cold he may tear tendons, but he will not break records.

Idling

Before moving off, the Tiger's driver will let his engine idle, in the summer for 5 minutes, in the winter for 15 minutes, until the engine coolant temperature reaches 50°C, the transmission is warm to the touch and the oil pressure has risen to 3 atmospheres - *Otherwise the bearings will be shot!*

Run at fast idle so that the engine turns between 1000 and 1500 rpm. Do not remain at base idle - *Otherwise the spark plugs foul.*

Do not be hasty, wait on the Tiger!

Regular service procedures: Lubrication

Those who take care of themselves are ahead of all others. Rather more often and thoroughly should the crème for day and night be applied. - *Otherwise you'll get in trouble with your supply sergeant.*

Moral: *The movie star powders and paints,*
the driver pays attention to the chassis.

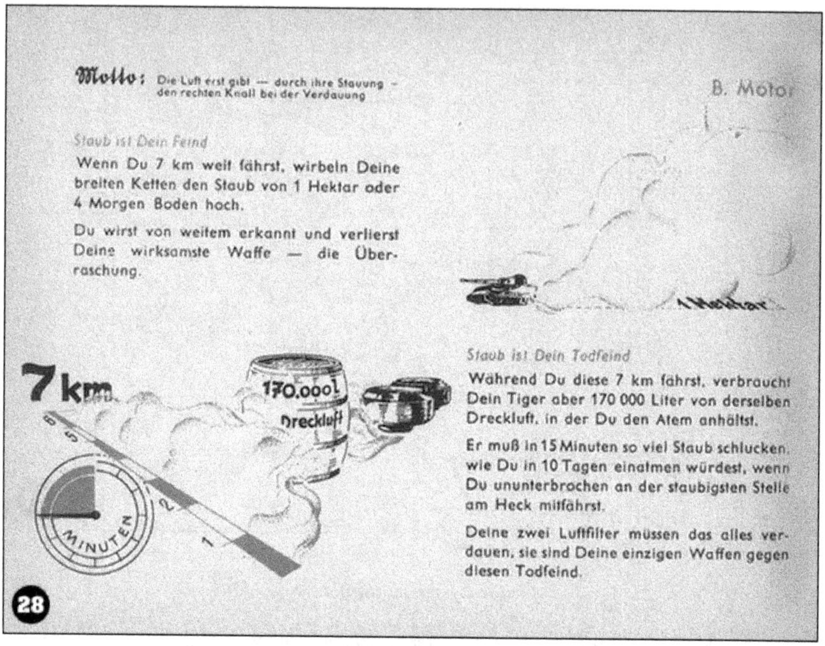

Original page 28 translation

B. Engine

Motto: Air will give - by compression
the proper explosion upon ingestion.

Dust is your enemy!

If you go a distance of 7 Km, your wide tracks will throw up the dust from
1 hectare of land. You will be spotted from far away and will lose your most
effective weapon - surprise.

Dust is your arch-enemy!

As you are traveling these 7 kilometers, your Tiger uses 170,000 litres of the
same dirty air against which you are holding your breath.

Within 15 minutes it must breathe in as much dust as you would breathe
in during a period of ten days spent riding on the back of the tank, where
the air contains the highest concentration of dust.

Both of your filters must digest all that dusty air. They are your only
weapons against this deadly foe.

Der Luftfilter fängt den Staub genau so ein wie der Fliegenfänger die Fliegen. Wenn er aber ganz besetzt ist, taugt er nicht mehr. Die Luft kommt dann fast ungefiltert in den Zylinder, der feine Staub wird zwischen Zylinderwand und Kolben zermahlen und schmirgelt unablässig. Mit dem Verschleiß steigt der Sprit- und Ölverbrauch, weil die Kolben in den Zylindern klappern.

Der Filter läßt außerdem zu wenig Luft durch, drum saugt der Motor mehr Sprit an, der dann von den Zylinderwänden das Öl abspült. Zum zweitenmal steigt mit dem Spritverbrauch der Verschleiß, diesmal wegen mangelnder Schmierung.

Die beiden steigern sich wechselseitig in die Höhe, bald bleibst Du liegen. Ein neuer Motor muß rein.

Mit Deinem Maybach fährst Du im Einsatz glatt 5000 km, wenn Du ihm saubere Luft zum Atmen gibst. Sonst keine 500 km.

Darum:

Nach jeder staubigen Fahrt Luftfilter reinigen! Flügelschraube lösen, Filter vom Saugrohr abheben, herunter vom Panzer, Verschlüsse auf, Deckel ab, Einsatz heraus. Einsatz und Gehäuse in Kraftstoff (Achtung Gift!) waschen und gut trocknen. Gebrauchtes Motoröl bis zur roten Marke einfüllen, Einsatz einbauen, auf gute Dichtung achten, Deckel anklemmen, Filter sauber und dicht auf Saugrohr setzen und mit Flügelschraube festziehen. . . . und die Vorfilter nicht vergessen!

Filterdecke!
Verschluß
Ölstandsmarke
Anschlußstutzen
Ölfangeinsatz

29

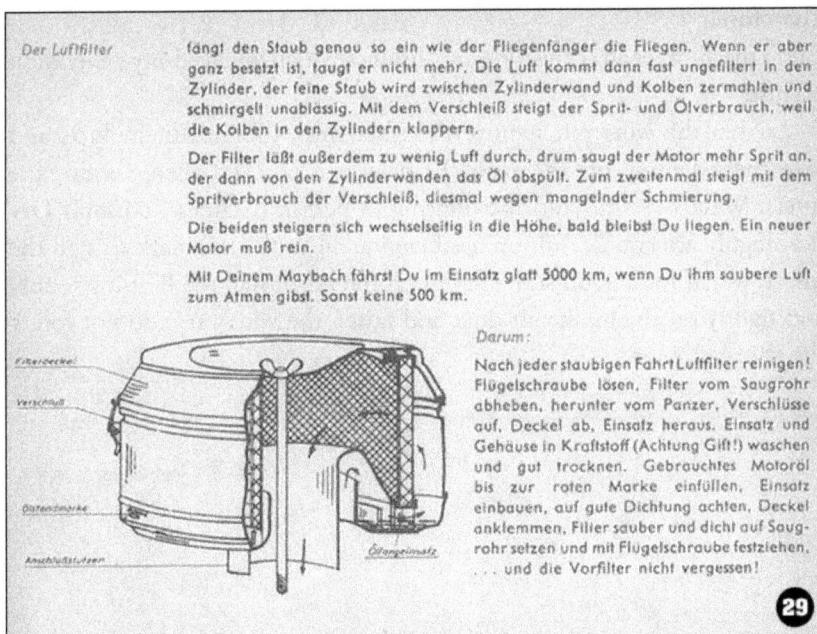

Original page 29 translation

The air filter

Catches dust like a flycatcher catches flies. But as soon as it is covered or saturated completely, it is useless. The air then enters the cylinders almost without having been filtered at all, the fine dust is ground between cylinder walls and pistons, constantly working like sand paper. With increasing wear the consumption of petrol and oil rises because the pistons are banging inside the cylinders.

In addition, a saturated filter allows insufficient air to go through. The engine now draws in an increasing amount of petrol, which in turn washes the lubricating oil off the cylinder walls. For the second time wear is increased together with fuel consumption, this time due to a lack of lubrication.

Both factors multiply each other, soon causing a breakdown. A new engine must be installed.

In action your Maybach engine will serve you for 5000 km, if you give it clean air. Otherwise it will not even last 500 km.

Therefore:

Clean the air filter after covering any distance which involved any generation of dust!

Loosen the wingnut, remove the filter from the intake air duct, and take the assembly off the tank. Remove the lid, and then remove the insert. Wash the filter and the housing in petrol. (Caution, poison!) Dry thoroughly afterwards. Fill up used engine oil to the red mark. Install the insert, watch for a good seal. Clamp on the lid. Install the housing evenly and tightly on the intake air duct and fasten the wingnut ...do not forget the wire gauze inserts.

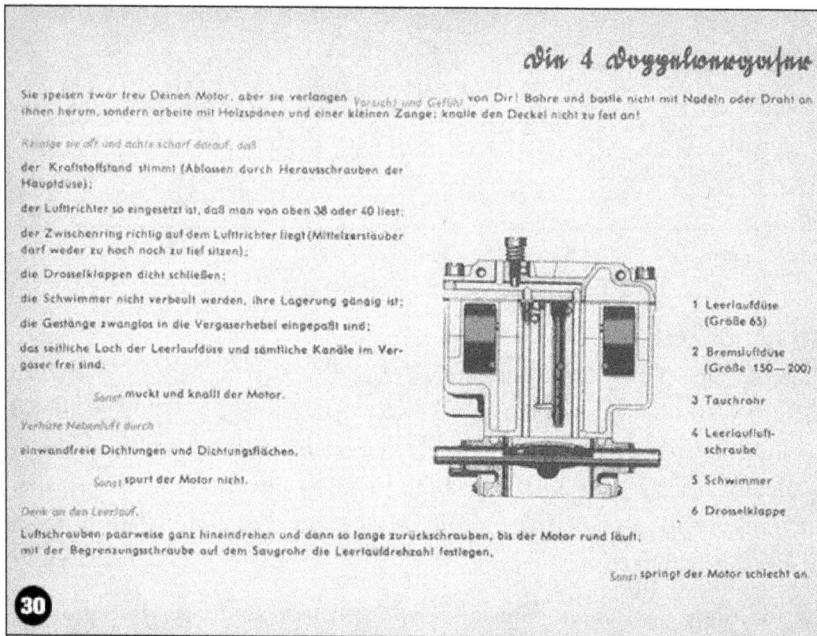

Original page 30 translation

Four two barrel carburetors

They faithfully feed your engine, but they demand care and attention from you! Do not drill or scrape with needles or wires, use pliers and a splinter of wood instead. Do not overtighten the lid!

Clean them often and pay special attention to:
- The fuel level (drain by unscrewing main jet).
- The main venturi, it must be installed so that "38" or "40"can be read from the top.

- The center ring, it must rest squarely on the main venturi. (The center atomizer must not be installed too high or too low).
- The throttle valves, they must close tightly.
- The floats, they must not be dented and they must hang free without binding.
- The linkage, it must fit into the throttle levers without binding.
- Also, that the side opening for the idle screw and all passages in the carburetor housing are free - *otherwise the engine jerks and backfires.*
- Avoid vacuum leaks by attending to immaculate gaskets and sealing surfaces - *otherwise the engine has no pickup.*

Think of the idle speed!

Turn the air screws in pairs all the way in then turn out until the engine runs smoothly, retain the idle speed setting by fastening the limiter screw on the air pipe - *otherwise the engine will only start with difficulty.*

Original page 31 translation

Correct fuel level in the fuel bowl.

Remove the air horn and lay the lower index finger on the edge of the float bowl, The finger tip must get wet when doing this - *otherwise, you will search forever for the defect.*

Your guardsman in the engine is the engine speed governor,

- He helps you when the Tiger needs better pickup.
- He warns you, should you be driving carelessly, not watching the oil pressure gauge.
- He checks your temper when you race the engine.

Because, up to 1900 rpm, you are running on only four carburetors, those of the first stage. The first stage forms the forward part of the carburetors two barrels. It is easily identified by the limiter on the throttle valve.

If the engine speed is increased over 1900 rpm, the second stage is opened by means of the centrifugal governor and oil pressure. The second stage is used for engine speeds between 1900 and 2800 rpm.

They close again as soon as 2800 rpm are exceeded.

If the engine has insufficient oil pressure, a bypass will prevent higher engine speeds - your ailing Tiger must only be driven into the repair shop.

Jet-limerick:

...The wrong idle jet will take its toll, remember, number sixty five is your friend! For the first stage, to learn you should strive one-five-zero, two-thirty-five: For the second remember without thinking: two-twenty-five and two-hundred!

1. main jets (size 235 - 225)
2. idle air jets (size 150 - 200)
3. emulsion tubes
4. main venturi (size 38 - 40)
5. center atomizer
6. float bowl
7. air horn
8. throttle valves

Moral: When the engine jerks and hisses,
it's the carburetor, without doubt.

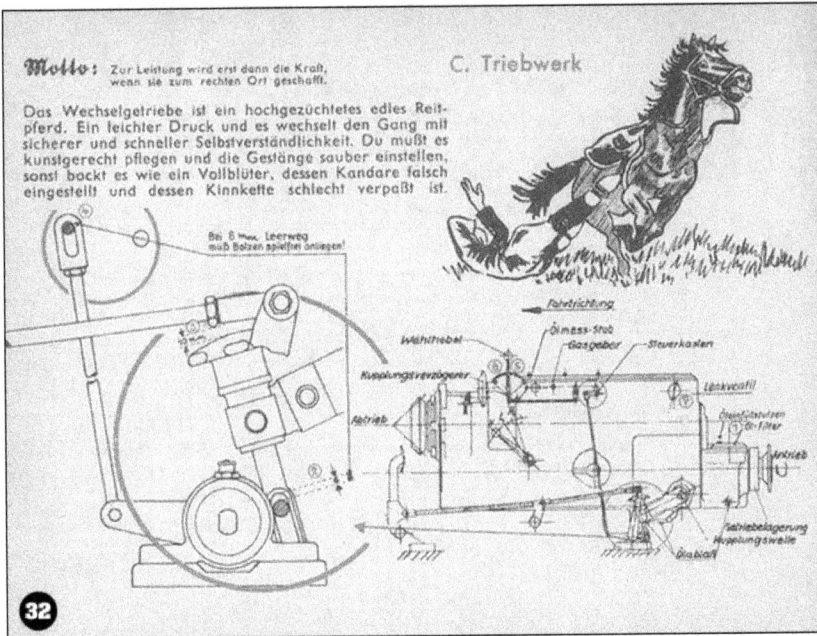

Original page 32 translation

C. Drive Train

Motto: Power will only come of applied force, when directed properly.

The sliding gear transmission is a thoroughbred race horse. It changes its pace with steady and natural swiftness after very little pressure is applied. You must care for it by the book and keep the linkages properly adjusted. Otherwise it will buck like a full blood whose reins are wrong and whose leash is not properly hung.

Original page 33 translation

Therefore, Transmission:

1. Check the oil level, frequently. Clean the oil filter.
2. Turn the wingnut by hand to the right until the clutch is released after a free travel of only 6 mm. Make a gauge from a twig for the 6 mm measurement.
3. Adjust the limiter on the foot-operated lever, so that the wingnut still travels upwards.
4. The connecting lever to the relay box must be seated without play once the foot-operated clutch lever has traveled through its free play of 6 mm. (See measurement #2).
5. Adjust the lever on the accelerator shaft so that the engine will reach maximum speed when the accelerator linkage is moved to the wide-open throttle position by hand.
6. The linkage on the selector lever must release securely for each gear.
7. Lubricate the linkages and keep them from binding, so that they may swiftly and securely return to the disengaged position.
8. There must always be some play in the cables to the steering rods.
9. Clean the steering valve, when steering trouble is encountered. The sealing surfaces must be cleaned of any dust particles once the valve plate is pressed in.

10. Retighten the mounting bolts for the sliding gear transmission. - *Otherwise you cannot shift gears.*

Drive shafts: Tighten the nuts fastening the drive shaft flanges frequently. - *Otherwise the drive shafts will come apart.*

Original page 34 translation

The friction surface on the brake itself cannot be replaced. It is glued on, not riveted. You must change the entire disc including the friction surface. To do so: Loosen the intermediate shaft and lever, remove the brake from the brake carrier, and loosen the screws on the lid together with the brake housing. Readjust them often with a special wrench (21 E 2799 U 15) and replace the radial seal as soon as oil enters through the brake retainer. - *Otherwise they heat up and produce smoke.*

Auxiliary transmission (steering gear), check the seals. If oil is being discharged, they must be replaced immediately.

When your Tiger is traveling 33 km/hour, it has the same thrust as your armor piercing shell#40 flying at the speed of 3300 km/hour.

If you step on the brake this thrust must be absorbed by the friction surface of the brake disc. The Tiger stops after traveling a distance of 12 meters.

If the grenade hits, the armor plate must absorb the whole impact, even 20 cm of steel do not offer sufficient resistance. A braking distance of 20 cm is not enough.

Therefore, the friction surface on the brake must sustain what 20 cm of armor plate cannot. Think of that every time you use the brakes.

Therefore: A free play of 13 mm must be adjusted on the brake. With the brake loose, you can insert a feeler gauge into the inspection cavity. If the free play is above specifications you must readjust the linkage by one further hole.

Motto: Man denkt sich bei geriss'ner Kette: Wenn ich bloß nachgesehen hätte.

D. Laufwerk

Kettenspannung ist außerordentlich wichtig!

Die Kette läuft oben mit doppelter Wagengeschwindigkeit nach vorn, bei 45 km/Stunde also mit 90 Sachen. Wenn Du die Kette nicht ordentlich spannst, knallt sie beim Bremsen und Lenken so an das Triebrad wie eine 18-Tonner-Zugmaschine, die aus 4 m Höhe drauffällt. 4 Finger breit soll sie über der ersten Laufrolle durchhängen. Beachte beim Spannen die Anschläge und überdrehe sie nicht.

Sonst muß der Motor raus.

Schrauben und Muttern von Triebrad, Leitrad und Laufrollen prüfen und nachziehen, Sicherungsbleche schonen oder wechseln.

Sonst laufen die Räder ab.

Im Winter müssen sich alle Laufrollen drehen. Taue sie mit der Lötlampe auf.

Sonst verlierst Du die Bandagen.

Achte auf gelockerte oder gerissene Bandagen, auf entsicherte Bolzen, gerissene Radscheiben, auf gebrochene Drehstäbe und Kurbeln, tausche sie beizeiten aus.

Sonst wird der Schaden immer größer.

Drehstäbe sind die Sprunggelenke des Tigers. Ihre polierte Oberfläche darfst Du nicht verletzen. Es ist mit ihnen wie mit einer Liebschaft. Hat sie erst einen winzig kleinen Riß, geht sie schnell zu Bruch. Werfe keine Werkzeuge darauf, ziehe keine schweren und scharfkantigen Teile darüber, steige nicht mit genagelten Stiefeln darauf herum.

Sonst mußt Du in die Werkstätte.

Geländekette auflegen: Flansche tadellos von Farbe, Rost, Schmutz und Eis säubern und hauchdünn fetten. Räder aufsetzen, Schrauben kreuzweise gut festziehen und sichern. Verladekette unter dem Leitrad auf einer Seite aufmachen. Panzer vorfahren, bis Kette abgespult ist, Geländekette davor auslegen, Panzer vorfahren, bis Kettenende dicht vor der ersten Laufrolle liegt. Seil 3mal um das Triebrad schlingen, Kette anseilen, das andere Triebrad mit dem Lenkhebel festbremsen, Kette aufziehen, Kette schließen und spannen, die andere Seite in gleicher Weise auflegen.

Die Verladekette wird genau so aufgelegt. Die äußeren Laufrollen können dann leicht abgenommen werden, weil sie frei hängen.

Bolzen und Keilmgglieder wechselt man unter dem Leit- oder Triebrad. Neue Glieder nicht zusammenhängend einbauen, sondern verteilen.

Zahnkränze der Triebräder wechseln, wenn die Vorwärtsflanken abgenutzt sind.

35

Original page 35 translation

D. Running Gear

Motto: One thinks, upon discovering a broken track:
I should have checked, now we must slink back.

Tension of the tracks is extremely important! On top, the track runs to the front with twice the vehicle speed, going 45 km/hour, that's 90! If you do not properly preload the track it will slam onto the drive wheels with a force of 18 tons when steering or braking. The track should hang four fingers' width over the top of the first roller adjacent to the drive wheel.

When adjusting the preload check the limiter stops and do not overtension them, - *Otherwise the engine must be removed.*

Check bolts and nuts on the drive wheel, also on the rollers and the guide wheel. Retighten as necessary. Take care not to damage the sheet-metal locks or replace the locks. - *Otherwise, the wheels fly off by themselves!*

In the winter time all the rollers must turn freely. Thaw them with a blow torch, - *Otherwise, you lose the rubber rims.*

Check for loose or broken rubber rims, unlocked bolts, fractured roller discs, broken torsion bars and trailing arms. Exchange them on time. - *Otherwise the faults will multiply!*

Torsion bars are the joints of the Tiger. You must not injure their polished surface. With them it's the same as a love affair. If there is a small fracture, it soon falls apart. Do not throw any tools onto them, drag heavy or sharp-edged objects on their surface or step on them with studded boots. - *Otherwise you need to go into the shop.*

All terrain track

To install the all-terrain track:
- Completely remove paint, rust, dirt and ice from the flanges.
- Apply a very thin coat of grease.
- Install the rollers.
- Tighten the bolts in a criss-cross pattern and secure.
- Open the transport track under the guide wheel on one side.
- Move the tank forward until the track is off the wheels.
- Lay out the all-terrain track in front of the tank.
- Drive the tank forward until the end of the track is close to the first roller.
- Tie a rope around the drive wheel threefold.
- Hook the rope into the track.
- Block the other drive wheel using the steering lever.
- Pull the track onto the rollers.
- Lock the track links and put tension on it.

The other side is installed in the same manner.

The transport track is installed in the same manner as the all-terrain track. In this way the rollers can be removed easily, because they hang freely.

Bolts and track links are replaced with the weak link under the drive wheel or the guide wheel.

New links must not be replaced close together, but distributed evenly over the length of the track.

Change the sprockets on the drive wheels as soon as the forward edge of the teeth has worn off.

Hier ist eine Übersicht über die Arbeiten, Schlüssel und Sonderwerkzeuge, die nötig sind, um eine Laufrolle, ein Triebrad, Leitrad oder einen Flansch zu wechseln.

Laufrolle Reihe	1	2	3	4	5
Wie bocke ich die Schwingarme hoch?	Auflaufbock vor innerstes Laufrad des zu hebenden Armes legen, Pz auffahren 1			Kette aufmachen. Mit Winden zahnhöhe hochheben	
	Am besten mit 2 soliden Stützplatten, 2 Ölhebern zu 30 t eine Längsseite hochbocken 2				
Wieviele Rollen müssen ab?	1	3	4	8	13
Welche Steckschlüssel, Sonderwerkzeuge brauche ich?	27	27	27	10 (2799/5) -70 50 C 2798 U5 4 Gew. Zapfen M 39×1,5 Schraube 18×35	15 (2799/5) 70 50 C 2798 U5 5 Gew. Zapfen M 39×1,5 Schraube 18×110

Wieviele Rollen müssen ab?	1	3	3	5	
	Außenflansch	Innenflansch	Leitrad	Triebrad	
Welche Steckschlüssel, Sonderwerkzeuge brauche ich?	27	27 2798 U10 Schraubenzieher 3	22 50 C 2798 U5 Schrauben M 16×90 Gew. Zapfen M 39×1,5 Rohr mit 15 mm Innen-Ø, 75 mm lang 6	Schlüsselweite 50, 46 Triebrad mittels Abdrückschraube abdrücken, Kolben mit Feder entfernen, Vorrichtung C 2798 U3 mit Spindel und Mutter, Steckschlüssel 27, 46, Kopfschraube 50, Mitnehmer abnehmen, geteilten Ring abnehmen, Filzring erneuern 7	

Moral: Wenn's finster wie in einer Kuh, kalt, naß und dreckig noch dazu, im Matsch versunken Bock und Winden, Hammer und Schlüssel nicht zu finden,

wenn Stäbe brechen, Arme hängen, drei Rollen fehlen, fünfe zwängen — dann denkt man sich bei dem Malör: „was tät hier wohl der Konstrukteur?"

36

1 2 3 4 5 6 7a Abziehen 7b Aufsetzen

37

This is not a centipede; it's a Tiger from underneath.

This is an assessment of the tasks, wrenches and special tools involved in order to change a roller, a drive wheel, a guide wheel or a flange.

Roller in row	1	2	3	4	5
How do I lift the trailing arms?	Lay ramp in front of innermost roller of the arm to be lifted, drive tank onto ramp. *See 1.*			Open the track, lift one side of the tank over teeth height, using winches.	
	Jack up one side of the tank using two solid support bases and two bottle jacks of 30 ton rating. *See 2.*				
How many rollers must be removed?	1	3	4	8	13
Which special tools and sockets are needed?	27	27	27	10 (2799/5) 70 50 C 2798 U5 *See 4* stud M39x1.5 bolt 18x35	15 (2799/5) 70 50 C 2798 U5 *See 5* stud M39x1.5 bolt 18x35
Meditr. 1942	4443	379	5/0	440	35
How many rollers must be removed?	1 Outer flange	3 Inner flange	3 Guide wheel	5 Drive wheel	
Which special tools and sockets are needed?	27	27 2798 U10 screw-driver *See 3.*	22 50 C 2798 U5 bolts M14x90 studs M39x1.5 pipe of 15mm ID 75mm long *See 6.*	Wrench size 50, 46 Remove drive wheel using screws to press off, remove piston with spring. Device C2798 U3 with spindle and nut, socket size 27 and 46, machine screw 50, remove link, remove split ring, replace flet washer. *See 7.*	

Moral: When it's dark likeas the inside of a cow,
cold wet and dirty, full of slime,
Jacks and winches stuck in the ground
hammer and wrenches nowhere to be found
When bars break, crank arms drag
three rollers missing, five of them snag,
If only the maker was here!

Original page 38 translation

Defensive Driving

Motto: The Tiger is easy to guide by a thinking man.

26 turns a minute in the three quarter step is that of a fine gentleman dancing the waltz. At this pace the music melts in your ear and harmonizes with the regularity of motion. Going slower is boring, but if you turn too fast you will get dizzy and your partner will melt from all the heat.

2600 rotations per minute in the four cycle is what the Tiger loves. At this speed he will perform best for the fuel consumed. Your instinct, your ears and your tachometer will tell you when you have brought your partner up to the perfect heat.

Do not race her over 3000 rpm ever, otherwise she will overheat. The water boils, the oil ceases to lubricate, the bearings, pistons and valves burn and freeze - the dance is over...

Therefore drive with your head, not with your behind!

- Constantly check the speed (1) coolant temperature (2) and oil pressure (3)
- Find the best way to go but hold the direction,

174

- Approach cautiously but keep on moving,
- Check what is ahead but scrutinise the gauges.
- Report on the intercom but listen to engine and transmission.

On the move
Turn the cannon to the 6 o'clock position and fasten it down.

Buildings and walls
Do not be run over! The rubble looks better in the weekly movie tone news than on the tail end of your Tiger. The blower will suck in all the dirt and dust, the radiator gets immersed in dust and no longer functions. The engine overheats and fails.

Tarp, leaves, rubble, luggage
Must not lay on the blower cover or disturb the cannon when rotating the turret.

Plane, Blätter, Schutt, Gepäck	dürfen das Luftgitter nicht verstopfen und die Kanone beim Schwenken nicht stören.
Morast, Sumpf	dunkle Stellen, hohes Gras meiden. Lieber weite Umwege machen. Boden zu Fuß erkunden. Nimm einen Mann huckepack und stell Dich auf ein Bein. Wenn der Boden trägt, trägt er auch den Panzer. Zügig durchfahren, nicht lenken, nicht schalten. Geht es nicht weiter, halt und sofort zurück. Nicht festmahlen. Ein anderer Tiger zieht Dich heraus. Seil verankern, Haken in die Gleiskette, selbst herausziehen!
Knüppeldamm	Er muß 3,5 m breit, und alle Knüppel 15 cm dick sein, sonst brechen sie durch oder reißen sich los.
Flüsse	Harter Grund, feste Ufer sind nötig. Wo andere Panzer waten, kommt der Tiger auch durch. Motor abstellen und U-Fahrt vorbereiten: Bodenventil zu, Lenz-Pumpe einschalten.
Brücken	Zu Fuß erkunden, Furten vorziehen. Vor Brücke halten, Tiger so einrichten, daß sie ohne Lenken überschritten werden kann, kleinen Gang wählen, nicht schalten, nicht halten, verkürztes Schrittempo fahren, erst Gas geben, wenn Du 5 m drüberweg bist.
Graben und Trichter	Gerade anfahren, nasse Stellen meiden.
Wald	Tiger wirft Bäume bis 80 cm Durchmesser mit der Bugkante um. Nicht auffahren. Bei zu schmaler Schneise Zick-Zackfahren, eine Seite fahrt frei.
Minen	Spurfahren, auf Spur zurückstoßen, nicht lenken, wenn möglich räumen.
Schnee	Trockener Neuschnee bis 70 cm ist unbedenklich. Papp und Harsch, Bruchharsch nur bis zur Bodenfreiheit — 50 cm.
Eis	Kettenglied vor die Kette werfen. Schwungfahren, nicht lenken, Konten senkrecht anfahren. Eine Kette im Graben oder an Rändern entlangschwindeln. Äste und Streuen hat wenig Zweck.

39

Original page 39 translation

Morass, swamps
Avoid dark areas and high grass. Prefer to make long detours. Investigate the ground on foot. Take another man piggyback and stand on one leg. If the ground supports you, it will support the tank. Go through swiftly, do not steer or change gears. If you get stuck, do not dig yourself in by

attempting to get out. Another Tiger will pull you out. Anchor the cable, hook into the tracks and pull yourself out.

Log dam
The dam must be 3.5 meters in width and the logs must be at least 15 cm in diameter. Otherwise they will break or work loose when passing over the dam.

Rivers
A solid riverbed and firm riverbanks are necessary. Where other tanks wade through the water, the Tiger can go too. Turn off the engine and prepare for under-water driving. Close the sump vent, turn on the bilge pump.

Bridges
Investigate on foot. Prefer to ford. Stop in front of the bridge. Position the Tiger so it can cross without the need to steer. Select low gear, do not change gears, do not stop, drive slower than walking pace. Accelerate only after 5 meters of having crossed the bridge.

Ditches and craters
Approach head on, avoid wet areas.

Wooded areas
The Tiger will smash down trees up to 80 cm in diameter using the edge of the front plate. If the clearance between trees is too narrow, drive in a zig-zag pattern, with one side running free.

Mines
Stay on the tracks, bump back on tracks, do not steer, and eliminate mines if possible.

Snow
New dry snow is no reason for concern below 70 cm in height. Compacted snow or sleet only up to the level of ground clearance - 50 cm.

Ice
Throw chainlink in front of the track, use inertia, do not steer, approach edges or ditches with one track. Using twigs or sand for traction makes little sense.

Dies ist Dein Sorgensitz. Du mußt Dich auf ihm gut auskennen, damit Du auch im Finstern und im Schlaf alle Hebel und Schalter findest, wie zu Hause den Lichtschalter oder die Türklinke, oder . . . na, Du weißt schon.

Fahrersehklappe

gängig halten! Im Winter und bei Beschuß klemmt sie manchmal. Löse die 4 versenkten Schrauben am Gehäuse, entferne den Deckel und drehe die außermittigen Buchsen so weit nach links, bis das Räderspiel groß genug ist.

Anfahren:
1.—4. Gang
(5.—8. Gang unmöglich)

4. Kupplung aurchtreten
5. Richtungshebel vor
6. Wähler vor Gangraste 1—4
   Wähler einrücken
7. Gas geben
   Kupplung langsam loslassen

Ein Gang ist immer drin.
Wenn er zum Anfahren paßt, brauchst Du nicht einzurücken.

Raufschalten:
8 Gänge

Wähler vor Gangraste
Wähler einrücken

Weder Gas wegnehmen noch Kuppeln nötig. 1—2 Gänge können bei warmem Wechselgetriebe übersprungen werden.   *Drehzahl!*

Runter-schalten:

8. Wähler vor Gangraste
   Handbremse nach Gefühl
   Wähler einrücken

Weder Zwischengas noch Kuppeln nötig. 1—2 Gänge können bei warmem Wechselgetriebe übersprungen werden.   *Drehzahl!*

40

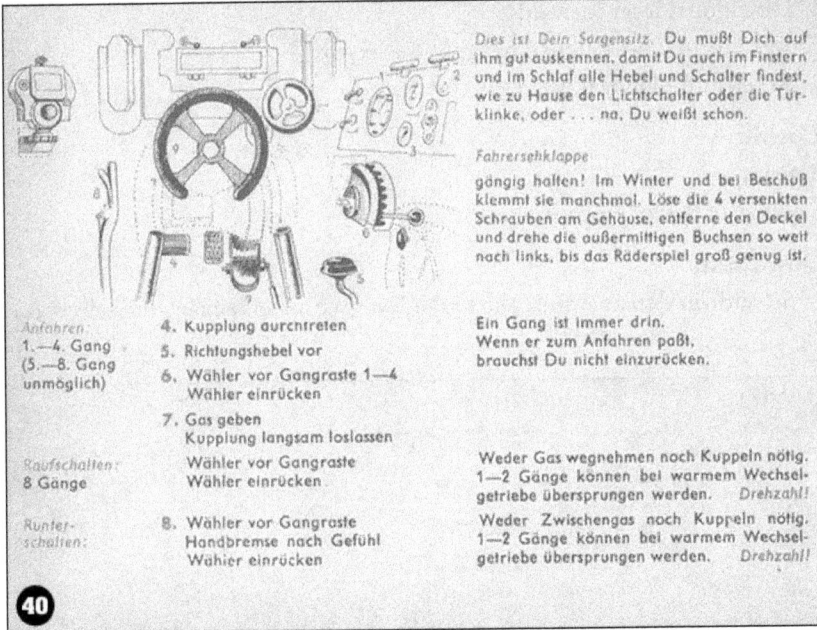

Original page 40 translation

This is your favorite chair. You need to know your way around here, so You'll find all the levers and switches even in the darkest of nights, like at home the light switch, the door handle or...well you know what.

Driver's lookout shield

Must be kept movable! In the wintertime and when under attack it can sometimes jam. Loosen the four countersunk screws in the frame. Remove the lid and turn the fixtures far enough to the left, until there is enough play in the adjustment knobs.

One gear is always engaged. If that one is suitable to start out. You will not need to change the selector.

No need to reduce engine speed or use the clutch. 1 or 2 gears can be skipped once the transmission is warmed up. Watch the tachometer!

No need to use the clutch, no need to double-clutch or speed up the engine. 1 to 2 gears can be skipped once the transmission is warmed up. Watch the tachometer!

To start out:
1st - 4th gear (5th - 8th gear impossible)
4. Depress clutch pedal

5. Directional lever forward

6. Selector to 1 - 4 detent Engage the selector

7. Accelerate, slowly engage the clutch.

Upshift:
8 gears
Selector in detent Engage selector lever

Downshift:
8. Selector in detent Adjust the brake lever with feel, engage the selector.

Original page 41 translation

In turns

9. Shift down before the turn. Pull in by the larger or smaller radius according to feel. Using any given gear, a wide or a narrow turn can be made. The smaller the turn, the lower the gear must be engaged. If it doesn't work out, brake lever, change gears.

Turning on the spot
Shift down to first through third gear, depress the clutch, pull left or right. Push the large button on the transmission housing.

Stopping

Shift down to first through fourth gear, brake lever, depress clutch, directional lever to "0", engage clutch.

Backing up, 4 gears

Depress clutch, reverse directional lever, selector lever to detent. Engage selector lever. Accelerate engine and slowly engage the clutch.

The directional lever cannot be moved to "0" or reverse as long as a gear above #4 is engaged. If you stopped while in 5th through 8th gear - depress the clutch - shift down.

Reverse is only possible in 1st through 4th gear.

Order to shoot

Depress clutch, apply hand brake lever. Try out position 10 1/2 and 1 1/2 o'clock and memorize. Commander and gunner give directions via intercom.

"In position"

Engage selector lever in second gear. The position of the three shafts and the respective gear can be noted on the plaque on the transmission housing.

"Breakfaaast"

Pull right, or...

"Lunch"

Pull left

(See "Daily meals")

(See "Spotting ")

Look out - estimate distance - report - look out.

Emergency shift

Directional lever to "0" Use a wrench to change gears Depress the clutch, Directional lever forward. Accelerate, engage the clutch.

> ***Moral: As with all things which are not compulsory,***
> ***driving is a pleasure.***

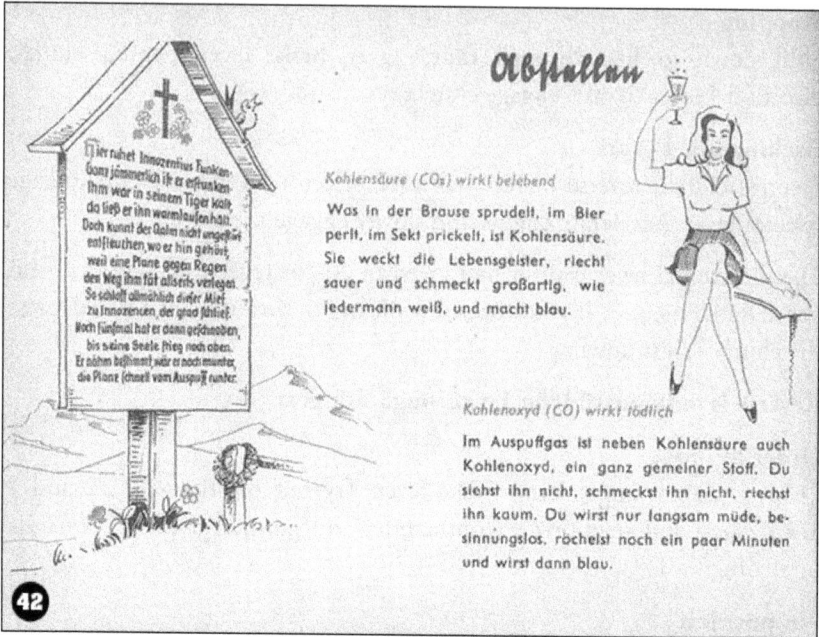

Original page 42 translation

Engine Shutoff

Carbonic Acid (CO2) is refreshing.

What sparkles in lemonade, foams in beer, tingles in champagne, is carbonic acid. It rejuvenates, smells sour and tastes great, as everyone knows it will get you drunk.

Carbon monoxide (CO) is deadly.

The exhaust gases contain carbon monoxide apart from carbon dioxide (CO 2), the former being a profoundly evil substance. You do not see it, you do not taste it, you do not smell it. You will slowly become tired, then fall unconscious, pant for a few minutes and then drop dead!

Sparky Innocent rests here, he died of tragic atmosphere
In his Tiger it was cold lo and behold....
So he let it run warm but the smoke was not forlorn since a tarp against the rain covered the pipe whence it came, so the fumes dlowly crept to Innocent who just slept.
Five more times he'd breathe, till upwards his soul did leave. Surely if still awake the tarpaulin off the exhaust he'd take.

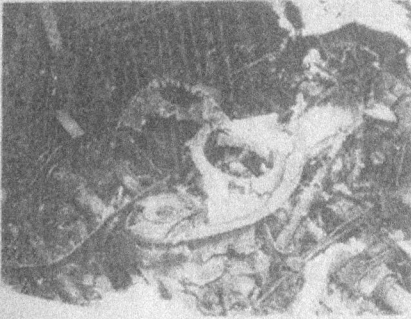

Manchmal geht's aber auch schnell.
Durch ein Leck in der Auspuffleitung sammelt sich Kohlenoxyd in der Wanne an. Du denkst an nichts Böses und drückst am Morgen auf den Anlasser, schon springt er an, der ganze Wagen nämlich und Du springst mit. Ein kleiner Funken eines schlecht isolierten Kabels jagt den ganzen Wagen hoch.

Lüften ist das einzige Mittel dagegen. CO ist schwerer als Luft und fließt langsam an die tiefste Stelle. Das mußt Du ausnützen.

Darum:

Beim Abstellen beide Hutzen auf, Bodenventil auf, Luken auf, Fenster auf, Türen auf, beide Sprithähne zu, Zündschlüssel abziehen. Bleibt er nicht stehen — Vollgas, Sammlerhauptschalter auf 0, Sonst platzt der Tiger.

Im Winter nicht auf den blanken Boden abstellen. Reisig, Bretter, dick Stroh, Bohlen, Holzwände oder Zäune unterlegen; Brocken, Eis, Matsch zwischen den Laufrädern hervorholen, alle 2 Stunden etwas bewegen, besonders gefährlich ist abwechselnd Wärme (tauen) und Frost (frieren). Sonst friert er an!

Öl verdünnen (siehe 6× Ölstand) und Sammler ausbauen, wenn Du für lange abstellst (siehe Strom). Lege den Gang ein, mit dem Du losfahren willst. Ein kaltes Wechselgetriebe läßt sich nicht schalten. Klemme den Kupplungsfußhebel so nach unten, daß die Kupplung gelöst bleibt und nicht zusammenfriert, Sonst kannst Du nicht losfahren.

Moral:

Den eignen Mief verträgt der Panzer genau so wenig wie der Landser.

(43)

Original page 43 translation

Sometimes it happens real fast:
A leak in the exhaust duct caused carbon monoxide to accumulate in the sump, you think no evil and push the starter button in the morning, and it starts right up, the whole tank that is! A tiny spark from a loosely insulated wire blows up the whole vehicle.

Ventilation is the only means of protection against it. Carbon monoxide is heavier than air and slowly settles in lower areas. You must use that condition to your advantage!

Therefore:
When turning off the engine, open both sides of the engine cover, open the sump vent, open the lookout, open windows, doors, close both fuel cocks. Remove ignition key. If the engine does not shut off – accelerate to wide open throttle position and turn the main battery switch to "0". - *Otherwise the Tiger bursts!*

In the wintertime do not stop on the barren ground. Lay twigs, brushwork, logs, straw or fences underneath. Remove dirt, mud and ice between the rollers. Move the tank a bit every two hours. A sudden change between warm weather (thawing) and cold weather (freezing) is especially dangerous. - *Otherwise it will freeze in place!*

Thin the oil, see "6 x Check Oil", and remove the batteries. If stopped for a longer period of time, see "Power". Engage the gear you intend to use when starting out later on. A cold transmission cannot be shifted through the gear range. Clamp down the clutch pedal so the clutch is disengaged and does not freeze onto the flywheel, - *Otherwise you cannot start out later!*

***Moral: The Tiger does not like its own odour,
much like the Landser doesn't care for his either!***

Motto: Mit Ruh', Umsicht und Bedacht —
dann: das Bergen bald vollbracht.

Das Bergen

Genau, wie Du Dei... m Kameraden in jeder Lage hilfst, mußt Du auch Dei... en stählernen Freund wieder heimholen, wenn er liegen blieb.

Notfalls kann Dir ein Tiger-Kamerad flottmachen; aber vermeide es.

Unternimm... ber er keine selbständigen Versuche weiterzukommen. D... quält Motor und Triebwerk, es nützt doch nichts —

Flußlauf

Sondern
Melde und laß Fachleute sprechen! Bereite inzwischen die Bergung vor, und zwar:

Gustav
macht Ketten frei oder öffnet sie — *damit Widerstände beim Schleppen beseitigt sind*
sieht das Laufwerk nach
baut die Vorgelegewellen aus, setzt — *damit das Wechselgetriebe ausgeschaltet ist, die Bremsen aber wirken.*
aber die Schrauben wieder ein.
Hilfsmann und Fugmann
beseitige die Hindernisse vor — *damit das Bergen erleichtert wird*
Ketten und Wanne
Schnellmerker
hat sich nach Verankerungspunkten für die Zugmaschine umgesehen und legt sich gleich das richtige Werkzeug zurecht:
Brech- und Abschleppstangen, S-Haken, Seile, Winden — *falls mit der Seilwinde geborgen wird*
Nicht koksen und Stullen streichen, sonst gibt's eins aufs Dach!
Unterrichte den Bergezugführer gleich über Schäden und Schleppfähigkeit des Panzers.
Und dann *fällt alles aus!*
Ist der Wagen frei, so wird er im Tandemzug abgeschleppt.
Paß auf wie ein Schießhund, besonders bei Brücken, Furten oder schmalen Wegstrecken.
Halte Verbindung mit den Zugmaschinen, hilf eifrig mit beim Einweisen.
Sonst rammst Du Kameraden, oder der Panzer sitzt wieder fest.

Moral: Die Bergung ist zwar sehr beschwerlich, indessen leider unentbehrlich.

44

Original page 44 translation

Field Recovery

Motto: With care, thought and logic - recovery is soon accomplished.

Just as you would help your comrade, no matter what, You must take care of your friend of steel too and take him home when he breaks down. If need be another Tiger can help you out, but it is better to avoid that avenue. It is better to skip any further attempts to get out on your own. You torment the engine and driveline, and it is no good anyway.

Instead:

Report and let the experts talk! In the meantime, prepare for recovery, paying attention to the following:

Gustav:

Frees up the tracks or opens them to check the running gear ...*so that resistance to towing is eliminated,*

Removes the steering gear box shaft and replaces the bolts ...*so that the transmission is disabled, but the brakes work.*

Hulsensacke and Piepmatz:

Remove obstacles in front of the tracks and hull ...*so that the recovery effort will be less difficult.*

Speedy Quickthinker:

has checked for anchor points for the tow tractor and prepares the appropriate tools: breaker bars, tow bars, hooks, ropes and winches ...*in case the recovery will be done using winches.*

Don't fiddle around and waste time, or you'll be reprimanded!

Inform the commander of the recovery team on damages to the tank and avenues for recovery right away. And then everyone lends a hand! Once the vehicle is free it will be towed in a tandem train. Be alert as a watchdog when crossing bridges, fording rivers, or passing narrow roadways. Keep in contact with the towing tractors, make an extra effort giving directions, otherwise your comrades will be broadsided or the tank ends up stuck once again.

Moral: Recovery is full of difficulty, yet is a necessity.

Motto: Selbst General Guderian
fährt manchmal auf der Eisenbahn.

Verladen

Das Verladen geht glatt und schnell, wenn Du alles gewissenhaft vorbereitest:

Den Waggon (SSyms) bremse fest und stütze die Wagenenden ab,

Sonst landet der Tiger auf den Schienen

Dem Tiger lege die Verladekette auf, verstaue die Zusatzlaufrollen und klappe aber die Kettenabdeckung hoch,

Sonst gefährdet er den Eisenbahnverkehr

Bevorzuge beim Verladen des Tigers Kopframpen, lege beide Geländeketten nebeneinander aus, fahre den Tiger darüber, mache die Ketten vorn fest und schleppe sie so auf den Wagen. Die überstehenden Enden werden umgeschlagen.

Steht der Panzer auf dem Waggon, vergiß nicht festzubremsen und zu verkeilen.

Prüfe öfters während der Fahrt, ob
die Bremsen fest sind.
die Holzkeile noch vernagelt sind
der Panzer in Wagenmitte steht.

Moral: Verladen ist für den, der viel Erfahrung hat, ein Kinderspiel.

45

Original page 45 translation

Loading for Transport

Motto: Even General Guderian sometimes takes the train!

Loading a tank onto the train is smooth and quick business if you have prepared everything properly:

Apply the railcar (SSyms) brake and support the overhang at each end of the railroad car - *Otherwise your Tiger ends up on the rails.*

Install the transport tracks and stow away the accessory rollers, but make sure the track cover is lifted up, so it will not endanger railroad traffic. When loading the Tiger prefer to use head ramps, lay out both all terrain tracks side by side, drive the Tiger over these, fasten the tracks on the front and pull them onto the railcar in this manner. The remaining ends are folded inward. Once the tank is on the rail car, do not forget to apply the brakes and chuck the tracks at each end.

While moving by train, frequently check: whether brake is firmly applied; whether the wooden chucks are still nailed down; whether the tank is still centered on the railcar.

Moral: Loading onto the train, for the old hands is child play!

THE RADIO OPERATOR

Original page 47 translation

Radio Operator

"Radio Operator the decrypter"

Your set reaches farther than the voice, the ear, the eye. It travels over distances faster than a tank or a projectile. The responsibility of whether it turns into a powerful and dangerous weapon or into a mean traitor is in your hands.

Motto: Oft gibt die rechte Rundfunksendung
dem Angriff erst die gute Wendung.

Das Gerät

Die richtige Stimmung und Lautstärke sind oft für Deine Zukunft
entscheidend. Indessen kann aber die lächerliche Ursache, falsche
Einstellung, fehlender Anschluß oder ein Wackelkontakt alles ver-
derben. Sei auf Draht!

Stets:
1. Kabel zum Umformer und zur Antenne in ihre Rasten stecken.
2. darauf achten, daß die Schalter auf „Aus" stehen,
   wenn die Geräte nicht benutzt werden.
3. Anschlüsse von der Batterie (+ an +, — an —) über den Anschlußkasten 23, die Sicherung in der Grundplatte und Umformer
   zum Gerät auf strammen Sitz prüfen. Achte auf Wackelkontakte und durchgescheuerte Stellen.

Vor dem Betrieb:
stecke alle Verbindungskabel so, wie Du es auf der Zeichnung rot eingezeichnet siehst.

Zum Betrieb des Empfängers:
Stelle 2 auf große Lautstärke.
Prüfe bei 6, ob die Skala leuchtet,
und bei 5, ob die Prüflampe brennt.
Stelle 6 auf „0".
Drehe 7 auf die befohlene Frequenz und raste ein.
Stelle 8 auf „Fern".
Drehe 6 auf größte Lautstärke.
Stelle 8 auf „Nah", wenn es zu laut wird.
Drehe 2 zurück, wenn es noch zu laut ist.

Zum Betrieb des Senders:
Stelle 2 auf „Tn".
Prüfe bei 6, ob die Skala leuchtet,
und bei 5, ob die Prüflampe brennt,
drehe 7 auf die Betriebsfrequenz
drücke 9.
drehe 10 so lange,
bis 11 am weitesten nach rechts ausschlägt.
Pendelt 11 wenn Du das Mikrofon besprichst?
Stelle 2 auf „Tg tönend", wenn Du morsen willst.

Nach dem Betrieb:
2 drehe die Schalter auf „0"
1 und stecke die Kabel in die Rasten.

Moral: Wer klug ist, rastet stets in sein
Gerät je 2 Frequenzen ein.

48

Original page 48 translation

The radio apparatus

Motto: Often the proper radio broadcast
will divert the attack to the better, at last!

The right wavelength and the proper volume are often decisive for your future. In turn, a ridiculous mishap, such as a wrong, adjustment, a missing connection or a loose contact can ruin everything. Be wired up.

Always:
1. Plug the wires to the transformer and to the antenna into their proper sockets.
2. Check that all switches are in the "off" position when the apparatus is not in use.
3. Check the connections from the battery, (+ on +, - on -) over connector box 23 in the base plate, and from the transformer to the apparatus for tight contact. Pay attention to loose wires and insulation.

Before using the apparatus:
Connect all wires as shown on the diagram.

To operate the receiver:

Adjust - 2 - for high volume

Check - 4 - whether the scale is lit.

And - 5 - for burning control light

Adjust - 6 - to "0"

Turn - 7 - on the ordered frequency and lock.

Adjust - 8 - for "far away"

Turn - 6 - to maximum volume

Adjust - 8 - to "near" if volume is too high.

Turn - 2 - back if it is still too loud.

To operate the transmitter:

Adjust - 2 - to position "Tn"

Check - 4 - if the scale is lit.

And - 5 - for burning light.

Turn - 7 - to operating frequency.

Push - 9

Turn - 10 - until 11 points to the far right of the scale.

Does - 11 - oscillate when you speak into the microphone?

Adjust - 2 - to "Tg sounding" if you want to use the Morse code

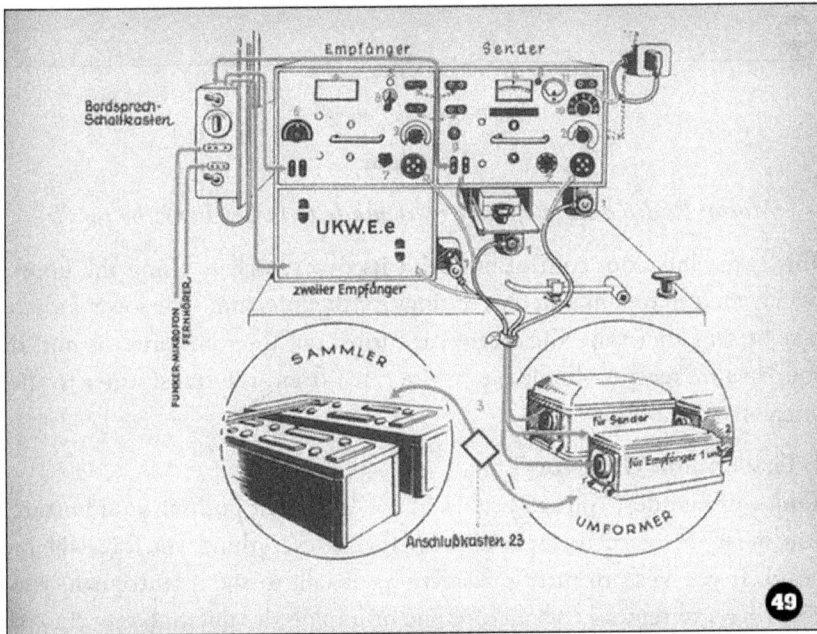

After operation:

2 Turn the switch to "0".

1 and stick the wires into their sockets.

Moral: He plugs his wiring for two frequencies.

Motto: Es dienen Telephon und Funk
der schnelleren Verständigung

Das Bordsprechen

Das ist der Bordsprechkasten mit seinen 2 Schaltern. Mit dem oberen kannst Du beim Bordsprechen 2 verschiedene Schaltungen erreichen Der untere kann stehen wie er will. Der Empfänger ist einge-schaltet, der Sender nicht. Wenn Du keinen Empfänger hast, schließt Du das 5fach-Kabel vom Umformer an den Bordsprech-kasten.

1. Fall: „Bord"

Panzerführer! Du kannst hören und sprechen ohne Deine Taste zu drücken. Du mußt deshalb besonders aufpassen, weil alles, was Du sagst, gehört wird. Willst Du einmal ordentlich fluchen oder Dich mit dem Grenadier unter-halten, dann mußt Du entweder das Mikrophon abnehmen, oder den Mikrophonstecker herausziehen, oder vom Funker die ganze Anlage abschalten lassen.

Willst Du dem Funker etwas sagen, dann mußt Du Deine Taste drücken.

Richtschütze und Fahrer! Ihr hört ständig mit. Wenn Ihr sprechen wollt, müßt Ihr Eure Tasten drücken.

Funker! Du kannst mit dem Pz. Führer erst sprechen, wenn Du Deine Taste drückst.

2. Fall: „Funk und Bord"

Funker! Wenn Du ständig ins Bordgespräch eingeschaltet sein willst, legst Du den oberen Hebel nach links auf „Funk und Bord". Wie der Pz. Führer hörst Du dann alles und kannst sprechen, ohne Deine Taste zu drücken.

Die 4 Bordsprecher sind als Kreise einge-zeichnet, Senden und Empfangen als Pfeile. Geht der Sendepfeil durch die Mikrophon-taste, dann muß sie beim Sprechen gedrückt werden.

Moral: Beim Bordfunk klappt's manchmal beinah so gut wie in der „Femina"!

50

Original page 50 translation

Intercom

Motto: Radio and telephone were made to better hear the tone!

This is the intercom control box with its two switches. Using the upper switch you can obtain different settings for the intercom. The lower switch may be set either way. The receiver is turned on, the transmitter is not. If you have no receiver, hook the 5-wire cable from, the transformer to the intercom control box.

1. First option: "Intercom"

Tank commander! You can listen and speak without pushing your button. You must therefore be especially careful, as everything you say will be heard. If you wish to utter maledictions or talk to the infantryman, you either have to remove the microphone or unplug the microphone wire, or have the radio operator turn off the whole apparatus. If you want to talk to the radioman you must push your button.

Gunner and Driver! You are constantly listening in. If you want to speak, you must push the button.

Radio operator! You can only talk to the commander after pushing your button.

2. Second option: "Broadcast and Intercom"

Radio operator! If you constantly want to be connected to the intercom, turn the upper switch to the left, position "Broadcast and Intercom". Like the commander you then hear everything and can speak without pushing your button.

The four speakers of the intercom are shown as circles, transmitting and receiving is denoted by arrows. If the arrow goes through a square then the button must be pushed on the microphone in order to talk.

Moral: Communication on the intercom works, as with a young woman!

Motto: Der Funkverkehr wär' unbeschreiblich mit einem Funker, welcher weiblich.

Senden und Empfangen

Hier sind 2 × 2 Fälle möglich, weil der untere Hebel jetzt mitspielt. Wir lassen ihn zunächst rechts liegen auf:

A. „Pz-Führer + Funker Empf. 1 und 2"

1. Fall „Bord"

Funker! Du kannst senden und empfangen, indem Du den Betriebsartenschalter auf „Tn" oder „Empfang" legst, während Pz. Führer Richtschütze, Fahrer ungestört bordsprechen.

Soll der Panzerführer mithören, was ankommt oder will er senden, dann mußt Du oder er die Taste drücken. Du hörst dann auch, was ankommt oder gesendet wird. Der Panzerführer ist solange vom Bordsprechen abgeschaltet.

Hier ist der Bordverkehr schwarz, der Funkverkehr rot eingezeichnet.

51

Original page 51 translation

Intercom

Motto: The broadcast would be beyond description with a female performing the encryption!

Here 2 x 2 options are possible as the lower switch is now part of the setting. For now, we will leave it set on the right, on:

A. "Commander and Radio operator, Receiver 1 and 2"

1. First option, "Intercom"

Radioman! You can send and receive by turning the operating mode switch to "Tn" or "reception" while the commander, gunner and driver talk on the intercom undisturbed.

Should the commander want to hear the incoming broadcast or if he wants to send out a message, then either you or him need to push the button. You will then hear what is coming in or being transmitted. In the meantime the commander is disconnected from the intercom.

The intercom is denoted together with broadcast mode in the above illustrations. On top intercom is to the left and above the dotted line, the radio operator being in broadcast mode.

Above, intercom is to the right and above the dotted line, only between gunner and driver.

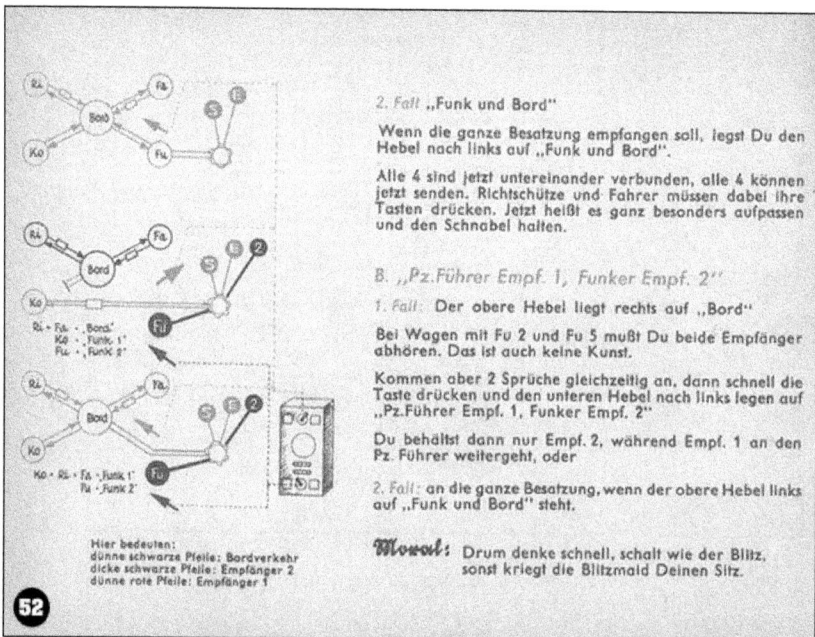

2. Fall „Funk und Bord"

Wenn die ganze Besatzung empfangen soll, legst Du den Hebel nach links auf „Funk und Bord".

Alle 4 sind jetzt untereinander verbunden, alle 4 können jetzt senden. Richtschütze und Fahrer müssen dabei ihre Tasten drücken. Jetzt heißt es ganz besonders aufpassen und den Schnabel halten.

B. „Pz.Führer Empf. 1, Funker Empf. 2"

1. Fall: Der obere Hebel liegt rechts auf „Bord"

Bei Wagen mit Fu 2 und Fu 5 mußt Du beide Empfänger abhören. Das ist auch keine Kunst.

Kommen aber 2 Sprüche gleichzeitig an, dann schnell die Taste drücken und den unteren Hebel nach links legen auf „Pz.Führer Empf. 1, Funker Empf. 2"

Du behältst dann nur Empf. 2, während Empf. 1 an den Pz. Führer weitergeht, oder

2. Fall: an die ganze Besatzung, wenn der obere Hebel links auf „Funk und Bord" steht.

Moral: Drum denke schnell, schalt wie der Blitz, sonst kriegt die Blitzmaid Deinen Sitz.

Hier bedeuten:
dünne schwarze Pfeile: Bordverkehr
dicke schwarze Pfeile: Empfänger 2
dünne rote Pfeile: Empfänger 1

52

In the illustrations, intercom is denoted as previously. On top only the radio op. is in broadcast mode. In the center one message is denoted by thick, another by thin lines, intercom is above to the right of the dotted line.

Above, thick lines denote message to radio op., the others message to the crew.

2. Second option: "Broadcast and Intercom"
If the whole crew is supposed to receive, switch to the left, position "Broadcast and Intercom".

All four crewmembers are now interconnected, all for can now send. Gunner and driver must push their buttons to do so.

Now special care is to be taken to shut up!

B. "Commander receive 1, Radio op. Receive 2"

1. First option:
The upper switch to the right, on "intercom" mode.

In vehicles with type Fu2 and Fu5 apparatus you must listen to both receivers, that does not require a Ph.D. either.

But if two messages arrive simultaneously, then push the button quickly and turn the lower switch to the left, on "Commander receive 1, Radio op. Receive 2".

In that case you only keep receiver No.2, while receiver No.1 goes to the commander, or...

2. Second option:
For the whole crew, if the upper switch is turned to the left on "Intercom and Broadcast".

Moral: Therefore, think fast and act quick,
or where you now a lightning bolt will sit.

191

THE LOADER

Original page 53 translation

Loader

"Loader Hulsensack the indefatigable"

60 tons of steel and 700 horsepower serve only one purpose, to set in motion and protect the weaponry you operate. If you fail, all of that will be in vain. If you prove yourself competent, a multitude of enemy tonnage and horsepower will be destroyed with your aid.

Original page 54 translation

Motto: *Often one cannot really fire as she will not as one desires.*

DO NOT unwrap too early!
DO NOT stand up but lovingly lay on a blanket.
DO NOT use the packaging material for heating, turn it back in,
DO NOT let moisture, dirt, sunlight or frost touch it!
DO NOT toss or dent like the bricklayers.

Shells with fractures or dents - **turn them out!**
Shells with marred rotating band - **turn them out!**
Shells with leaking explosive - **turn them out!**
Shells without base plate or crimping - **turn them out!**

Caution!!!
Inspect, clean, do not lubricate!
Hand tighten loose priming screws!
Priming screws must not protrude
Tighten nose fuse by hand!
Straighten out loose and rotating projectiles!
Ammunition with percussion primer will cause a short circuit!

Attention!

Insert shells tightly into their mounting brackets!

Rearrange storage on time!

When loading do not spoil the rotating band!

Anti-tank grenade #39 is black with white tip!

Anti-tank grenade A'40 is black!

HL - grenade is grey!

High explosive shell is yellow!

Only adjust delay using a wrench!

After unloading, set back on O.V., otherwise it will fail!

Turn in duds and used shells!

*Moral: Whether blond, black, turning grey, or white,
care for her like for your bride. Her temper you will come to
appreciate, at the touch of a finger she'll catch fire.*

Motto: Hemmung im Kanonenrohr
kommt, Gott sei Dank, nur selten vor.

Die vielseitige Kanone

Vorweg

Prüfe Deine Leitung, pflege die Munition, reinige den Verschluß,
mach alles Bewegliche gängig, reinige und entöle das Rohr vor
dem Schießen und öle es hinterher dick, wenn es wieder hand-
warm ist.

*Sonst schießt die
Kanone überhaupt
nicht.*

Achtung

Mündungskappe ab, bei Eis auch die durchschießbare.
Tarnmittel und Zweige weg von der Mündung.
In Feuerpausen durchs Rohr gucken.
Nachts mit der Taschenlampe reinleuchten.
Sprengstücke und Rückstände raus.
Heißgeschossene Rohre in Feuerpausen entladen.

*Sonst schießt die
Kanone zur Seite*

Nicht schießen

wenn die Mündungsbremse locker oder abgeschossen ist —
sie wirkt wie ein Segel und bremst 70% des Rückstoßes ab.

wenn die Rohrbremse Öl verliert,
sie wirkt wie ein Stoßdämpfer und bremst 25% des Rückstoßes ab

wenn der Luftvorholer Luft verliert oder nicht arbeitet,
er wirkt wie ein Türschließer und bremst 5% des Rückstoßes ab,

wenn der Rücklaufmesser auf „Feuerpause" steht.
Schiebe ihn nach jedem Schuß nach vorne

wenn der Splint am Öffnerhebel fehlt oder locker ist.

*Sonst schießt die
Kanone nach
hinten*

Indessen:

Bei geübten Schützen und auch.

*sonst schießt die
Kanone nach vorn.*

Moral: Nur ungern glaubt der Panzermann,
statt was zu treffen, selber dran!

55

194

The versatile cannon

Motto: A jam in the barrel - thank God, it doesn't happen often.

Beforehand...

Check your circuitry, care for the ammunition, clean the lock, rotate/ actuate all moving parts, clean and remove all the oil from the barrel before shooting. Apply oil liberally after use when the barrel is again warm to the touch. - *Otherwise the cannon will not shoot at all!*

Attention...

Remove the muzzle cover, also the disposable one, when covered with ice. Remove camouflage and brushwork away from the muzzle. Look through the barrel during a pause in firing. Shine inside with a flashlight at night. Remove fragments and residue. Unload a hot barrel during a pause in firing. - *Otherwise the cannon will shoot to the side.*

Do not shoot,

If the muzzle brake is loose or shot off - it works like a funnel and helps to absorb 70% of the recoil.

If the recoil brake loses oil - it works like a shock absorber and absorbs 25% of the recoil.

If the pneumatic recuperator leaks air or does not function. It works like a door closing link and absorbs 5% of the cannon's recoil.

If the recoil marker signals "pause in firing". It must be shifted forward after every shot.

If the cotter pin on the operating lever is lose or missing - *Otherwise the cannon will shoot backwards.*

Then again, with experienced marksmen and generally anyway - *the cannon will shoot forward!*

*Moral: Only with regret the tank man will admit,
instead of hitting he took a hit!*

Motto: Die 8.8 zündet wie ein Licht.
Bei manchem zündet's niemals nicht.

Die lange Leitung

Hemmung an:	Ursache:	Abhilfe:
Patronenlager	Grünspan oder Schmutz an der Patrone	Neu laden.
Zündschraube	Unbrauchbar (kann etwas versenkt sein)	Neue Schraube.
Schlagbolzen	Zu kurz, stumpf oder abgebrochen	Neuer Schlagbolzen.
Brücke	Feder gebrochen	Neue Brücke.
Blöckchen	Wird von Brücke nicht erreicht	Kanone vordrücken, Luft auf 55 at nachfüllen (4,4 Liter Öl).
Druckknopfstecker	Kabelschuh lose	Stecker instandsetzen.
Signallampen	Du kannst feuern, auch wenn die Lampe ausgebrannt oder aus den Klemmfedern gefallen ist	Neue Lampe. Feder zurechtbiegen.
Ölsicherung	Rohrbremse verliert Öl (Inhalt 5,1 Liter)	Dichtung nachsehen, Schrauben nachziehen, Öl nachfüllen.
Boschstecker	Kabel klemmt, Stecker nicht ganz eingesteckt	Dose und Stecker prüfen, neues Kabel, Feder zurechtbiegen.
15-Amp.-Sicherung	Erst Kurzschluß suchen, Kabel eingeklemmt	Neue Sicherung vom Fahrer.
40-Amp.-Sicherung	Flakmunition, durchgescheuerte Leitung	Schlagzündschraube durch Glühzündschraube ersetzen.
Sammler	Klemme lose oder verschmutzt	Säubern, anziehen, fetten.
Hilfe bei Störungen bis 15-Amp.-Sicherung	Lampe am Abzug brennt nicht, Signallampe brennt	Notbatterie mit Notschalter einschalten.
bis Boschstecker	Lampe am Abzug brennt, Signallampe brennt nicht	Kabel in den Stecker der Turmbeleuchtung stecken, mit Ladeschützensicherung abziehen.

Prüfen: Kanone entladen, Abzug gezogen halten, Prüflampe mit einem Pol an blanke Masse legen, mit dem anderen Ende an die blanke Leitung.
Vorsicht! Keinen Kurzschluß machen! Leitung gegen die Kanone zu so lange prüfen, bis die Lampe erlischt. Kurz davor liegt der Fehler!
Achtung! Wenn die Ölsicherung ausgeschaltet hat, darf nicht geschossen werden.

Moral: Gar mancher biß ins grüne Gras, weil er den Leitungsweg vergaß.

56

Original page 56 translation

Slow Response

Motto: The 8.8 is rapidly fired but some of them never light.

Jamming at Chamber
Cause: Corrosion or dirt on shell
Remedy: Reload.

Jamming at Priming screw
Cause: Useless (can be recessed)
Remedy: New priming screw.

Jamming at Striker
Cause: Too short, dull or broken
Remedy: New striker.

Jamming at Bridge
Cause: Broken spring
Remedy: New bridge.

Jamming at Block
Cause: Not reached by the bridge
Remedy: Push cannon forward, refill air to 55 at, (44L oil)

Jamming at Socket on pushbutton
Cause: Loose wire connection
Remedy: Repair socket and plug.

Jamming at Signal lamps
Cause: You can fire, even with lamp is burnt or has fallen out
Remedy: Install a new lamp, bend the spring as needed.

Jamming at Oil fuse
Cause: Recoil brake is leaking oil (contains 5.1 Litres of oil)
Remedy: Check seal, tighten screws, fill up oil.

Jamming at Bosch type plug
Cause: Wire pinched, plug is not fully inserted.
Remedy: Check socket and plug, new wire, bend spring.

Jamming at 15 Amp. fuse
Cause: First find the short or pinched wire.
Remedy: Obtain new fuse from driver.

Jamming at 40 Amp. Fuse
Cause: Anti-aircraft ammunition, chafed wire
Remedy: Replace percussion primer with electric igniter.

Jamming at Batteries
Cause: Loose clamps or dirty batteries
Remedy: Clean, tighten clamps, apply grease.

Solution for malfunctions up to 15 Amp fuse
Symptom - Lamp on the trigger does not burn, signal lamp does burn!
Remedy: Switch to emergency battery on emergency switch.

Solution for malfunctions up to Bosch type plug
Symptom - Lamp on the trigger signal lamp does not light.
Remedy: Insert wire into socket for turret lights, pull through with the loader fuse.

Check: Unload cannon, hold trigger pulled, lay test light with one end to ground, (bare metal), with the other end on the wire, (insulation removed). **Be careful!**Do not cause a short circuit! Check the wiring towards the cannon until the test light no longer lights up. The malfunction is located shortly before that point!

Attention! If the oil fuse has turned power off, shooting must not occur.

Abfeuerstromkreis

Original page 58 translation

5 Cures for Jamming

Motto: When it comes to fire the poorly machine gun will jam!

Bullets:

With dents or fractures, rust or deformation ...throw out! Install only German made ammunition straight out of the package, do not use suspicious Russian ammunition dropped by air (explosive ammunition). Check every bullet, clean, do not lubricate.

Belts:

- With pockets that were stepped on, are bent or corroded...throw them out!
- With broken or bent claws...throw them out!
- With links torn off or stepped on...throw them out!
- With worn off link connectors...throw them out!
- Do it like the skiers!
- Dip the belts into boiling kerosene, shake off well!

That will last for an average campaign. Install the belts properly, the claw must sit in its groove snugly. Assemble with care, the stud must be centered in the opening.

Machine gun:

Assemble properly. Check the length of the recoil spring (forward to center insert). Check the length of the firing pin string, three turns over end of bolt. The firing pin nut must snap audibly. Do not insert the belt feed the wrong way.

Oil:

Apply oil only on moving parts and locking cams. Use high sulfur oil or even better, some engine oil. Remove the oil from the barrel and locking cams, - otherwise you'll have inhibitions.

Installation:

Proceed so that the machine gun is not distorted. The mounting fork must fit over the pins on the housing without binding. Adjust the trigger linkage with locknut. The machine gun must be set for continuous fire. Move the cocking slide forward, so that the tang does not break. Empty the deflector bag.

...But before installation:

Lege die Hand aufs Herz und frage 5 Fragen:

Frage 1: Sind Mantel und Lauf verbogen, arbeitet die Vorholstange?

Probe 1: MG spannen, Mündungsfeuerdämpfer ab. Der Lauf muß sich mit dem Finger leicht bis zum Anschlag zurückdrücken lassen und muß sofort wieder nach vorne kommen.

Frage 2: Schießt das MG Dauerfeuer?

Probe 2: Abzug treten, Schloß anziehen und vorschnellen lassen. Es darf erst beim Loslassen des Abzuges gefangen werden, dann aber sofort.

Frage 3: Ist das Schloß gängig?

Probe 3: Bodenstück mit Schließfeder ab. Schloß muß sich mit Spannschieber federleicht bewegen lassen.

Frage 4: Verriegelt das Schloß vollständig?

Probe 4: Schloß vorschnellen lassen. Deckel auf. Stirnfläche des Schloßgehäuses muß mit der Kante des Zuführerunterteiles abschneiden.

Frage 5: Klappt das Zuführen, Ausstoßen, Ausziehen und Auswerfen?

Probe 5: Ein paar Hülsen mit aufgesetztem Geschoß gurten. Schloß vorschnellen lassen und zurückziehen. Hülse muß scharf ausgeworfen werden.

Neu! Schnelle Feuerbereitschaft:

Beim Laden bleibt das Schloß vorne!
Du kannst in aller Gemütsruhe laden.
Wenn die Sicherung versagt, kann kein Schuß fallen.
Gurt so einlegen, daß nur eine Patrone zugeführt wird.
Deckel nicht zuwürgen.
Willst Du schießen, dann brauchst Du nur durchzuladen.

Falsch!
Dieser Abstand zeigt, daß das Schloß nicht verriegelt.

Richtig!
Diese beiden Kanten müssen zusammen fallen.

Merke: Drum prüfe nebst Patronengurt, ob auch die Spritze sauber spurt.

59

Original page 59 translation

...Lay your hand over your heart and ask five questions:

200

Question #1:
Is the barrel bent? Does the counter recoil mechanism operate?

Check #1:
Cock the machine gun, remove the flash damper. The barrel must be easily pushed to the stud using just one finger, but rebound immediately.

Question #2:
Does the machine gun operate in continuous fire mode?

Check #2:
Kick the trigger, pull the lock and let it snap forward. It must catch only when releasing the trigger, and immediately.

Question #3:
Does the lock operate freely?

Check #3:
Remove the base plate with locking spring. The lock must be movable together with the locking slide without effort.

Question #4:
Does the lock engage completely?

Check #4:
Let the lock snap forward, open the lid. The mating surface of the lower lock housing must be even with the edge of the lower half of the feed mechanism.

Question #5:
Does the process of delivery, deflection, extraction and ejection work properly?

Check #5:
Insert a few cases with projectiles on top, let the lock snap forward and pull back. The case must be ejected sharply.

New! Swift readiness to fire:
When loading the lock is left in forward position! You can take your time loading. If the safety stop fails, no shot can be fired!

Do not close the lid with the use of force. If you want to shoot you only need to load through.

> *Moral: Check besides the belt,*
> *does the sprayer work as well?*

Original page 60 translation

A Mules's Barometer

Motto: A mule's tail will tell, whether it's wet out, windy, or hot and thick. Watching the machine gun's behaviour, the gunner finds the jam!

If the tail is dry and does not wiggle - nice weather
If the tail is dry but wiggles - windy
If the tail is wet but does not wiggle - rain
If the tail is wet and wiggles - storm
If the tail is nowhere to be seen - fog

Just as easily, you can determine what the problem is with your machine gun when it jams:

Pay attention!
Remove the foot from the trigger, on the right side, move the cocking slide back, while at the same time checking:

1. Position of the lock?
2. What is being ejected?
3. What is in the way of the lock?

Secure on the left, on the right, remove the lid and check.
And now look at....

Das MG-Barometer

Wo steht das Schloß?	Was wird ausgeworfen?	Was hemmt?	Was hilft sofort?	Was war schuld?
vorne	Patrone angeschlagen	Versager	weiter schießen	**Schmutz** reinigen, entölen, ölen, Graphit
	Patrone blank	Schlagbolzen	Schloßwechsel	
	nichts	klemmender Gurt	Gurt nachziehen	
		Ausstoßer	Schloßwechsel	
		Zubringer	Gurt ziehen	
fast vorne	Patrone blank	verspanntes MG	Kralle lösen	**Schlamperei** nachgurten, geraderichtet nachstellen
	nichts	Verriegelungsstück	Laufwechsel	
		verbeulte Patrone	Laufwechsel	
	Was macht die Patrone?			
mitte	Patrone klemmt, Lauf frei	schlechtes Gurten	weiter schießen	
		Ausstoßer	Schloßwechsel	
	Patrone klemmt, Hülse im Lauf	Hülsensack	Hülsensack leeren	
		Auszieher	Schloßwechsel	
		Patronenlager	Laufwechsel	
	Patrone klemmt, Bodenreißer im Lauf	lose Bolzenmutter	Schloß- u. Laufwechsel	**Ermüdung** lahme Federn längen
	Hülse klemmt, Patrone im Lauf	Verschlußsperre	Laufwechsel	
		Auswerfer	Schloßwechsel	
fast hinten	Patrone nicht ausgestoßen	verbogene Tasche	weiter schießen	
		Verbindungstasche	weiter schießen	
		Schloßbahn	reinigen	
		krummer Auswerfer	Schloßwechsel	
	Patrone eckt	eckender Gurt	weiter schießen	**Bruch und Verschleiß** neues Teil aus dem Ersatzteilkasten od. Waffenmeister
		Zuführeroberteil	weiter schießen	
hinten (gefangen nach dem 1. Schuß)		kurzes Gestänge	von Hand abziehen	
Schloß steht nicht still	(wenn es stehen bleiben soll, Gurt festhalten)	klemmend. Gestänge	von Hand abziehen	
		verschmutz. Abzug	oft durchladen	
		Abzugsstollen	das andere MG	

Deine Schuld / Nicht Deine Schuld

Moral: Du siehst, o Freund, wenn es nicht schießt, daß Du meist selber schuldig bist.

61

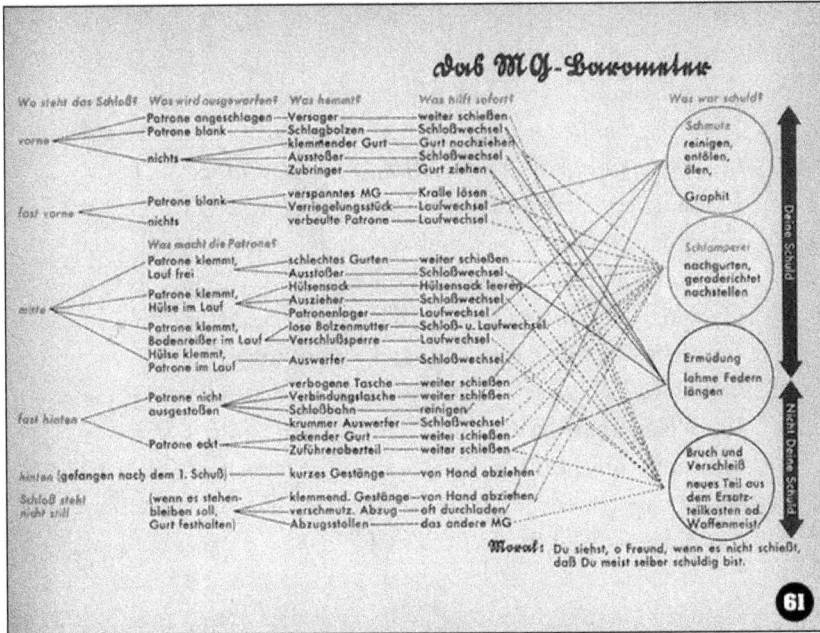

Original page 61 translation

The Machine Gun Barometer

LOCK POSITION FORWARD:

- What is ejected: cartridge, dud. What jams: failure.
  Immediate remedy: continue fire. Root cause: 4 Wear
- What is ejected: cartridge, intact. What jams: striker.
  Immediate remedy: exchange lock   Root cause: Fatigue/4 Wear
- What is ejected: nothing. What jams: belt binds.
  Immediate remedy: pull belt through   Root cause: 2 Sloppiness
- What is ejected: nothing. What jams: Ejector rod.
  Immediate remedy: exchange locks   Root cause: 3 Fatigue/4 Wear
- What is ejected: nothing. What jams: carrier.
  Immediate remedy: pull on belt   Root cause: 3 Fatigue/4 Wear

ALMOST FORWARD

- What is ejected: cartridge, intact What jams: distorted gun.
  Immediate remedy: loosen claw   Root cause: 2 Sloppiness
- What is ejected: cartridge, intact What jams: locking catch
  Immediate remedy: exchange barrel   Root cause: 1 Dirt
- What is ejected: nothing. What jams: cartridge dented
  Immediate remedy: exchange barrel   Root cause: 2 Sloppiness

CENTER

What is the cartridge doing?

- Cartridge jams, barrel free What jams: improper load
Immediate remedy: continue fire   Root cause: 2 Sloppiness
- Cartridge jams, barrel free What jams: ejector rod
Immediate remedy: exchange lock   Root cause: 3 Fatigue/4 Wear
- Cartridge jams, case in barrel What jams: deflector bag
Immediate remedy: empty bag   Root cause: 2 Sloppiness
- Cartridge jams, case in barrel What jams: extractor
Immediate remedy: exchange lock   Root cause: 4 Wear
- Cartridge jams, case in barrel What jams: Chamber
Immediate remedy: exchange barrel   Root cause: 1 Dirt
- Cartridge jams, split case in barrel What jams: loose striker nut
Immediate remedy: exchange lock/barrel   Root cause: 2 Sloppiness
- Cartridge jams, split case in barrel What jams: bolt stop
Immediate remedy: exchange barrel   Root cause: 4 Wear
- Case jams cartridge in barrel What jams: ejector
Immediate remedy: exchange lock   Root cause: 4 Wear

ALMOST BACK

What is the cartridge doing?

- Cartridge not ejected What jams: bent pocket
Immediate remedy: continue fire   Root cause: 2 Sloppiness
- Cartridge not ejected What jams: connector
Immediate remedy: continue fire   Root cause: 2 Sloppiness
- Cartridge not ejected What jams: lock travel
Immediate remedy: clean   Root cause: 1 Dirt
- Cartridge not ejected What jams: bent ejector
Immediate remedy: exchange lock   Root cause: 2 Sloppiness
- Cartridge travel What jams: belt travel
Immediate remedy: continue fire   Root cause: 2 Sloppiness
- Cartridge travel What jams: feed, upper part-continue fire
Root cause: 3 Fatigue/4 Wear

ALL THE WAY BACK

- Caught after 1st. shot: What jams: Linkage short
Immediate remedy: pull off by hand   Root cause: 2 Sloppiness
- Lock does not stay in place (if it is to stop, hold the belt) What jams: linkage binds Immediate remedy: pull off by hand   Root cause: 2 Sloppiness

- Lock does not stay in place (if it is to stop, hold the belt) What jams:trigger dirty Immediate remedy: reload often   Root cause: 1 Dirt
- Lock does not stay in place (if it is to stop, hold the belt) What jams:wear on trigger Immediate remedy: get another machine gun Root cause: 4 Wear

Root cause:

YOUR FAULT

1. Dirt! Clean, remove oil. Apply oil and graphite.
2. Sloppiness! Reload the belt, Straighten out, readjust

NOT YOUR FAULT

3. Fatigue! Sagging springs the springs.
4. Fracture and wear! New part from spare parts bin or ordinance shop

Moral: You see, if the shots don't go as they came,
usually it's you who is to blame.

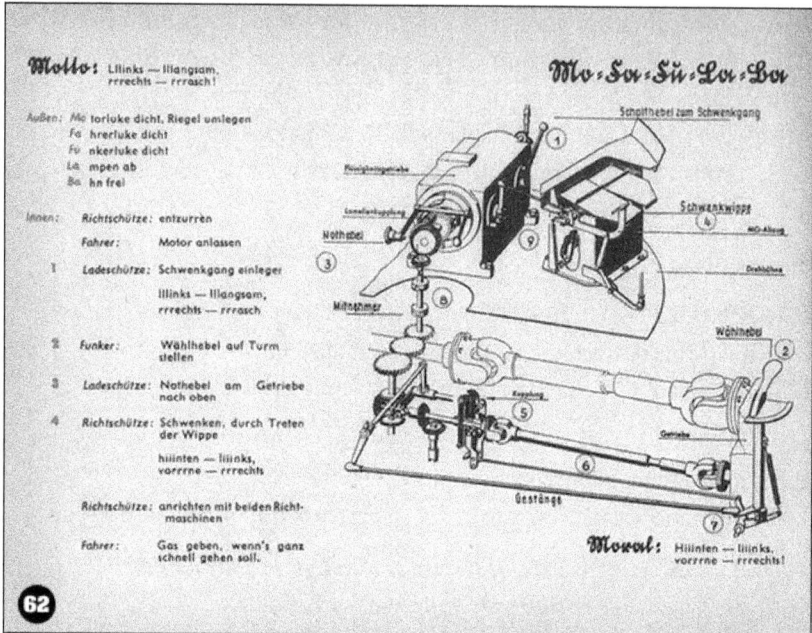

Original page 62 translation

MO-FÜ-FA-LA-BA (mnemonic)

Motto: Lllleft – slllow, rrright – rraapid!

Exterior:

MO-tor (engine) cover closed, engage lock

FÜ-nker (radio operator's) hatch closed

FA-hrer (driver's) hatch closed

LA-ampen (lights) removed

BA-hn (clear) tracks

Interior:

Gunner, disengage lock

Driver, start engine

1. Loader, engage rotating gear lllleft – slllow, rrright – swwwift!

2. Radio op. Selector lever on "turret"

3. Loader, Emergency lever on transmission upwards

4. Gunner, Rotate, by stepping on pedal.

Reeear – leeeft, frooont – riiight!

Gunner, aim using elevating and traversing mechanism.

Driver, accelerate, when it has to happen quickly.

Moral: Reeear – Leeeft, frooont – riiight!

Motto: Bei manchem rastet schon zu Haus
der Turm mit dem Verstande aus.

Der Durchforben

Hemmung:	Ursache:	Abhilfe:
Turm läßt sich vom Fuß nicht schwenken	Kupplung sitzt fest	5 Motor laufen lassen, Kupplung abklopfen!
	Kupplungsgestänge zu kurz oder zu lang	6 Mutter am Kupplungsgestänge lösen und Gabel verstellen!
	Gestänge an Kugelpfanne ausgesprungen	7 Kugelpfanne einklinken und umrandeln!
	Mitnehmer über Schleifring-übertrager ausgehoben	8 Glocke abnehmen und Mitnehmerklauen einrasten!
	Kein Öldruck	Öl nachfüllen!
	Wippengestänge gelöst	9 Gestänge einhängen, neuer Sicherungssplint!
Turm bleibt auf 4 Uhr oder 8 Uhr stehen	Turm klemmt an Motorluke	Turm von Hand auf 12 Uhr drehen, dabei mit Seil an Kanone ziehen! Luke dicht!
Turm schwenkt vom Fuß nur rechts	Feder unter Wippe zu lang	4 Feder verstellen oder Wippe waagrecht richten!
Turm schwenkt vom Fuß nach einer Seite schneller als nach der anderen	Wippengestänge zu kurz oder zu lang	9 Wippengestänge kürzen oder längen!
Turm schwenkt ununterbrochen	Kupplung und Gestänge sitzen fest	6 Motor abstellen und Gestänge lösen!
	Widerlager der Druckfeder sitzt schräg	8 Antriebswelle anflanschen, Druckmutter des Widerlagers abschrauben, Kupplung abziehen, dabei Nadellager nicht beschädigen. Federwiderlager gerade einsetzen, Kupplung einbauen!
Nothebel arbeitet nicht	Nothebel dreht sich auf Welle, Sicherungsstift abgedreht	3 Neuer Sicherungsstift!

Moral: Wer Köpfchen hat, schwenkt elegant —
Wer keines hat, würgt mit der Hand.

Original page 63 translation

Turret trouble

*Motto: Still at home, for some there went
the turret and their head out of detent.*

TURRET CANNOT BE ROTATED BY FOOT

Cause: Clutch stuck
Remedy: 5 Leave engine running, knock clutch loose!

Cause: Clutch linkage too short or too long
Remedy: 6 Loosen nut on clutch linkage and adjust fork!

Cause: Linkage jumped out of ball pivot
Remedy: 7 Connect ball pivot and secure!

Cause: Center shaft dislodged on top of slip ring connector
Remedy: 8 Remove bell housing and engage center shaft dogs!

Cause: No oil pressure
Remedy: Refill to proper level!

Cause: Pedal off hinges
Remedy: 9 Install linkage, new cotterpin

TURRET HANGS UP AT 4 OR 8 O'CLOCK POSITION

Cause: Turret hanging up on open engine cover
Remedy: Using a rope attached to the cannon, pull to 12 o'clock position, close engine cover!

TURRET SWINGS ONLY TO THE RIGHT WHEN OPERATED BY FOOT

Cause: Spring under pedal is too long
Remedy: 4 Adjust spring or set pedal in horizontal position!

TURRET SWINGS AT DIFFERENT SPEEDS LEFT OR RIGHT, WHEN OPERATED BY FOOT

Cause: Pedal linkage too short or too long
Remedy: 9 Shorten or lengthen pedal linkage!

TURRET SWINGS WITHOUT INTERRUPTION

Cause: Clutch and linkage binding
Remedy: 6 Turn off engine and free up linkage!

Cause: Compression spring stop not seated right
Remedy: 5 Remove drive shaft at flange, unscrew the locknut, pull off the clutch, do not damage the needle bearing, insert spring stop straight, install clutch.

EMERGENCY LEVER DOES NOT FUNCTION

Cause: Emergency lever is turning with shaft, pin sheared off
Remedy: 3 Install new pin to secure emergency lever!

Moral: With sense we swivel elegant – who has none labours by hand.

THE GUNNER

Das Schießen ins Schwarze ist eine
Kunst, aber keine Schwarzkunst. Damit
Du besser schießt als Dein Gegner, hast
Du die schärfere Waffe und den
schärferen Verstand.
Mit der 8.8 kannst Du einer Mücke den
rechten Eckzahn wegschießen, hier
lernst Du, wie:

Original page 65 translation

Gunner
"Holzauge the infallible"

Aiming a shot into dead center is a matter of art, but not black magic. In order to shoot better than your opponent. You have been given the sharper weapon and the sharper mind. Using the 8.8 You can shoot off a mosquito's right canine tooth.

Here you learn how:

Original page 66 translation

Motto: You won't learn to aim or shoot, if you haven't eaten your way up this book!

Hülsensack had received a gigantic cake from his bride Elvira on the occasion of his birthday. The cake had a diameter of 2 kilometers.

This cake was to be shared with every man in the division so Hülsensack cut it into 6400 pieces.

Those were very strange pieces of cake. If you started eating at the tip, there was hardly anything because it was so thin. At the back it became much wider, going up to 1 meter in width at the outer fringe. Each piece of cake was 1000m long.

Elvira would have liked to bake a cake where each piece would have been 2000 m long, but the field post declined submission to the unit. Those would have been 2 m wide at the end.

You can easily figure out the width for such a piece of cake, if you only know the distance from your mouth:
- For 1000 m, it is 1m wide
- For 2000 m, it is 2 m wide
- For 800 m, it is 0.8 m wide, and so on...

The brightest will say the width is always 1/1000 or one thousandth of the distance from your mouth.

Such a piece of cake is called a notch!

4 notch for instance is as wide as 4 pieces of cake side by side. Look out! That is where the reticules in your scope are located!

Die Spitzen von 2 Stacheln sind genau 4 Strich auseinander.
Wenn Du über sie hinwegpeilst, dann ist das genau so, als würdest Du an den Kanten Deines Tortenstückes entlanggucken.

Wenn also dahinten auf 2000 m ein Haus genau zwischen 2 Spitzen paßt, dann weißt Du: „Aha!"
1 Stachelzwischenraum ist   4 Strich
1 Strich (auf 2000 m) ist 2 m   4 Strich × 2 = 8 m,
das Haus ist 8 m breit   Ist das nicht eine Mordssache!

Frage: 1 Panzer steht 500 m weit, er reicht, wie auf dem Bild z. B., über 3 Stachelzwischenräume hinweg. Wie breit ist er?

Du rechnest: 3 Stachelzwischenräume zu je 4 Strich = 12 Strich
1 Strich (auf 300 m) = 0,5 m   12 Strich × 0,5 = 6 m.

Antwort: Der Panzer ist 6 m breit.

Genau so kannst Du auch die Zielhöhe ausrechnen, weil Du weißt,
der Hauptstachel ist 4 Strich hoch und jeder Nebenstachel 2 Strich.
Das mußt Du dir genau merken, Du brauchst es stets beim Nabelvisier.

Frage: Wie hoch ist der Panzer?

Du rechnest: angenommen, er ist 3mal so hoch wie ein Nebenstachel,
3mal Nebenstachelhöhe zu je 2 Strich ...
Na jetzt kannst Du schon allein weiter.

Die ganz Schlauen wissen, daß auch im Fernglas eine Stricheinteilung ist, mit der man genau so arbeiten kann! Aber auch in Deinem Daumen! Strecke ihn ordentlich weg, dann ist er haargenau 40 Strich breit! Ein Daumensprung mißt 100 Strich (Einmal das eine und dann das andere Auge zukneifen, und immer über die gleiche Daumenkante anvisieren.)
Dann kannst Du mit bloßem Auge die Zielgrößen und Zwischenräume auf 5 Strich genau angeben, daß jeder staunt. Probier's mal!

Also:
Wenn Du die Entfernung kennst, kannst Du ausrechnen, wie groß Dein Ziel ist.

STRICH
Auf 2000 m sind 4 Strich
auf 1000 m sind es
Entfernung: 2000 m.
Entfernung: 500 m.

Moral:
Bist Du um einen Strich gescheitert?
Wenn nicht, lies lieber gar nicht weiter!

67

Original page 67 translation

The Notch

Motto: Are you wiser by one notch? Don't read further if not!

The tips of each set of reticules are exactly four notch apart. If you bear over ahead of them, it is the same as if you looked along the edges of your piece of cake. So if there is a house 2000 m distant, which fits right between the tips of two reticules. You know:

"Look at here"!

The gap between two tips is 4 notch
One notch at 2000 m is 2m wide
4 notch x 2 = 8 m
The house is 8 m wide
Isn't that a killer?

Question:
1 tank is 500 m distant, it reaches across 3 gaps between reticule tips. How wide is the tank?

You calculate:
  3 gaps at 4 notch each = 12 notch
  1 notch at 500 m is 0.5 m
  12 notch x 0.5 = 6 m.

Answer: The tank is 6 m wide.
You can calculate the height of the target in the same manner, if you know: The center reticule is 4 notch high, the side reticules are each 2 notch high. You must remember this well. You need it constantly when using the scope.

Question:
How tall is the tank?

You figure:
Assume it is 3 times as tall as a minor reticule,
3 times 2 notch, that is ... You take it from here.

The real smart ones know that such a scale is also found in the sights of binoculars and may be used in the same manner! But it is also in your thumb! Hold it far away and it is exactly 40 notch wide. One jump of the thumb measures 100 notch. (Close one eye, then the other, while looking along the same edge of your thumb). That way you determine the target size and distance in between to an accuracy of 5 notch, stunning everyone! Try it! So if you know the distance. You can calculate the size of the target!

Motto: Beim Schatz hat man die Nähe gerne.
Beim Schätzen teilt man nah und ferne.

Das Schätzen

Die Entfernung genau schätzen — kann niemand.
Das „Messen" — lernen viele.
Das Visier richtig stellen — lernt aber jeder!

Du mußt lernen, Dich bis 1200 m höchstens um 200 m rauf und 200 m runter zu verschätzen. Wenn 500 die richtige Entfernung ist, muß Deine Schätzung zwischen 300 m und 700 m liegen. Das ist nun wirklich keine Kunst. Über 1200 m wird aus dem Schätzen schon mehr ein Raten.

Schätze kürzer!
Bei dunklen Zielen,
wenn's trüb und unklar ist,
bei unruhiger, dunstiger Luft,
bei dunklem Untergrund,
wenn Dir die Sonne und Reflexe
in die Augen funkeln.

Schätze weiter!
Bei hellen Zielen,
wenn's frisch und heiter ist,
bei stiller, reiner Luft,
bei hellem Hintergrund,
mit der Sonne, über Ebenen.
Durch das Zielfernrohr,
wenn Du nicht sehen kannst,
was zwischen Dir und dem Ziel liegt.

Schätze 2mal: 1. Das Ziel ist bestimmt näher als X m (z. B. 900 m)
2. Das Ziel ist bestimmt weiter als Y m (z. B. 500 m)
und nimm dann das Mittel zwischen beiden Schätzungen (z. B. 700 m).

Die Entfernung können nur der Fahrer und der Pz. Führer richtig schätze, weil sie unmittelbar mit dem blanken Auge sehen können. Durch das Zielfernrohr geht es nämlich schlecht.
1. weil das Zielfernrohr alles 2½ mal vergrößert und
2. weil Du mit einem Auge gar nicht schätzen kannst.

Halte Dir ein Auge zu und laß Dir von einem Kameraden einen Finger ½ m vor die Nase halten. Jetzt versuche, ihn mit Deinem Zeigefinger von der Seite schnell auszustoßen.

Achtung: Nicht selbst den Finger hochhalten und nicht vorher mit beiden Augen hinsehen.

Der Richtschütze und der Pz. Führer können aber „Messen", mit dem Zielfernrohr und der Optik nämlich. Du wirst das auch gleich lernen!

zu viel

zu wenig

die Mittelste ist goldrichtig!

68

Original page 68 translation

Spotting

Motto: Your sweetheart sees into your eyes,
when spotting we separate close and distant, very wise.

Estimating a distance exactly - cannot be done.
"Measuring" is learned by many -
Adjusting the range correctly - must be learned by all!

When estimating a distance of 1200 m or less you must learn to be off by no more than 200 m up or down. If 500 m is the correct distance, then your estimate must be between 300 m and 700 m. That really is not much of a challenge. Above 1200 m estimating turns into guesswork.

Estimate closer by!
- For dark targets
- If it's dreary and cloudy
- In windy and foggy air
- Against a dark background
- If the sun or reflections hit your eye.

213

Estimate Farther away!

- For lighter targets
- In fresh and sunny weather
- In clear air without wind
- Against a light background
- With the sunlight across the plain
- Through the scope if you cannot see what is between you and your target.

Estimate twice:

1. The target is surely closer than X m (e.g. 900 m)
2. The target is surely farther away than Y m (500 m)

Take the average of the two estimates, in this case 700 m.

Distance can only be estimated by the driver or the commander, since they have a clear line of sight. It cannot be done well through the scope because

1. the scope magnifies 2 1/2 fold, and
2. You cannot possibly estimate with one eye.

Close one eye and let a comrade hold his finger 1/2 m in front of You. Then try to quickly grab it with your index finger.

Attention: do not use your finger and do not look with both eyes beforehand. However, the gunner and the commander can "measure" using the scope and the optics. You will now learn to do that.

Wenn ihr Zeit habt, macht es so.

Der Panzerführer
mißt oder schätzt seine Entfernung — siehe „Messen"

Der Fahrer
(er braucht etwas länger) meldet seine Entfernung — siehe „Schätzen"

Der Panzerführer
rechnet das „Mittel" aus — siehe 1. Klasse Volksschule

Der Richtschütze
(hat inzwischen gemessen oder geschätzt) meldet seine Entfernung — siehe „Messen"

Der Panzerführer
rechnet wieder das „Mittel" aus und befiehlt die richtige Entfernung — siehe „Schießbefehl"

Der Richtschütze
(die Entfernung ist nicht das richtige Visier) — stellt das Visier ein — siehe „Nabelvisier"

Ihr habt aber immer Zeit!
denn wenn ihr ins Blaue schießt, kostet das viel mehr Zeit, kostet das viel mehr Granaten, verratet ihr euch, bevor ihr wirken könnt.

3 mal 2 Augen sehen mehr als zwei — ihr schätzt auf 100 m genau
3 mal muß der Panzerführer rechnen — dafür bekommt er mehr Geld
3 mal wird gemeldet oder befohlen — dazu ist der Bordfunk da.

Übung ist alles.

Achtung! Die richtige Entfernung ist nicht das richtige Visier!

900 1300 1000 1600 800 1000
Panzerführer 1100   Fahrer 1300   Richtschütze 900
Meldung
Mittel 1200
Meldung
Richtige Entfernung 1050
Befehl
Richtiges Visier eingestellt 1200

Moral: Kürzer, unklar, trüb, im Dunkeln, Dunst, unruhig, Sonne funkeln! Hell, mit Sonne, rein und heiter, eben, zwischen, Optik — weiter!

69

Original page 69 translation

If you have the time, do it like this:

THE TANK COMMANDER
Measures or estimates his distance,   see "measuring"

THE DRIVER
(He needs a little longer) reports his distance - see "spotting"

THE TANK COMMANDER
Calculates the average - see grade 1 in preschool

THE GUNNER
In the meantime having measured or estimated for himself reports his distance. See "Order to shoot"

THE GUNNER
(Distance is not the correct range) adjusts the correct range - see "Belly Button Rule"

You always have the time!
If you miss it will take far longer, cost more ammunition, you give away your position before your action takes any effect.

3 times 2 eyes see more than two - You estimate +/- 100,

3 times, the commander must calculate - he gets more money
3 times, reports and orders are exchanged - that is the purpose of the intercom.

Practice does it all!

Attention! The correct distance is not the correct range.

> *Moral: Closer - foggy, dreary dark, mist, moving, against the sun*
> *Further - bright, with the sun, clear, plain*

Original page 70 translation

Measuring

Motto: Even artists measure as estimating by eye is not reliable.

If the painter wants to accurately measure a line he will compare the size of the pencil with his model. You compare the size of the reticule with the target! Because if you know the size of your target. You can use the notch to figure out how far away it is.

Look out:
The Russian tanks are all 3 m wide. Assume that it is at a distance that lets it cover 1 1/2 gaps between the tips of reticules. Then you say:

Look at here! 1 1/5 gaps at 4 notch each = 6 notch
6 notch = 3 m
1 notch = 3 : 6 = 0.5 m
0.5 m x 1000 = 500 m

If the tank is positioned at an angle, you cannot calculate using length or width. You use height. Let us assume that the optics display a picture as shown in the illustration. Then you figure:

3 minor reticules 2 notch high = 6 notch
6 notch = 3 m, etc

Through the scope graduation looks like this:

Problem: Calculate the distance of this truck

A few measurements:

Attention! The correct distance is not the correct range!

> *Moral: Instead of measuring how far off measure by meters and divide the meters by the notch you divide times 1000.*

Original page 71 translation

Seven Goodies

Motto: Save ammunition, avoid waste - a wagon full is enough for the "Ritterkreuz"!

Pistol: through the hatch at guests on the rear.

Sub.-M.G.: through the hatch into ditches and nests in obstructed areas.

Pineapples: through the hatch into holes and at hidden targets.

Smokeshells: in case of fire, jamming, needed for tactical retreat, if things get difficult.

M.G., front: as far as 200 m at man, horse and wagon.

M.G., turret: as far as 400 m at man, horse and wagon,(farther if several present), set fire to buildings, help the infantry by nailing the enemy on the ground.

Cannon: High Explosive shell:

(No delay) Generates shrapnel 20 m to each side and 10m forward. Therefore, better to miss to the side than to the rear of the target. Tried and tested against anti-tank guns, howitzers, massed infantry targets, nests. Destroys armor, wheels, tracks, lookouts.

(Delay) A mine, if delivered vertically: Intrudes and detonates wooden bunkers, buildings, shelters, forest and juvenile tanks. Incinerates everything and overturns vehicles.

(Ricochet) Upon impact after shallow trajectory it will bounce back up off firm ground and detonate 50 m further away at a height of 4 - 8 m in midair. Use against invisible positions which cannot be fired on otherwise.

Armor-piercing shell, #39: Cracks tanks and trenches as far as 2000 m.

Armor-piercing shell, #40: Cracks heaviest tanks as far as 1500m (deviation). Use only when #39 does not penetrate. Attention! There is more thrust behind it! For 600 to 1000m you must decrease the range by 100m, for 1100 m to 1500m always by 200m.

HL-shell: Against heaviest tanks as far as 1000 m (substantial deviation). Blasts enormous holes, but travels slowly. Therefore the range must always be increased by 1/4 compared to the rule. (For instance not 600 m but 750 m). Do not use if camouflage, brushwork, nets are in front of the target. Otherwise it will detonate too early!

Attention: The correct distance is not the correct range

> ### *Moral: Shoot less, hit more, stay tight,*
> ### *and delight "Reichsminister Speer"!*

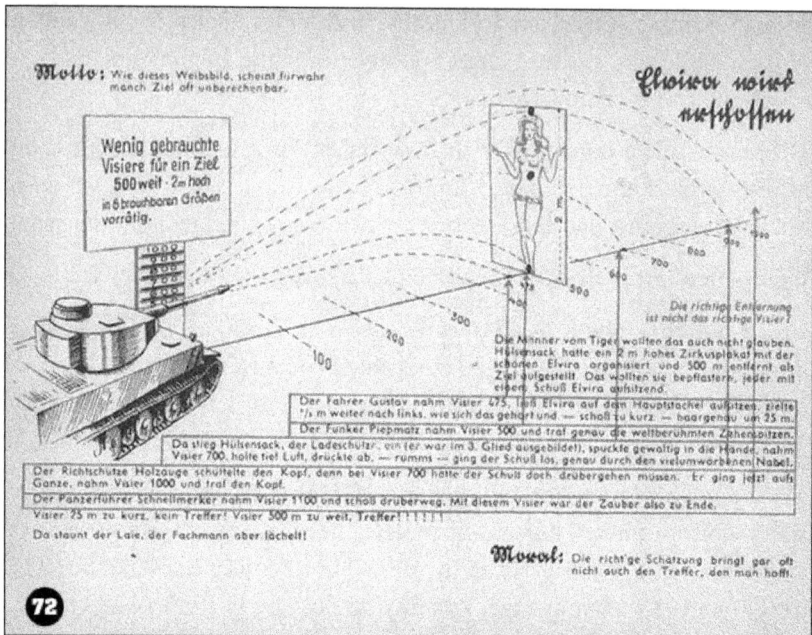

Original page 72 translation

Elvira gets shot

Motto: Many targets appear incalculable as the girl is unpredictable!

The correct distance is not the correct range.

The men of the TIGER didn't want to believe it either. Hülsensacke the Indefatigable had obtained a circus banner 2 m high with the pretty Elvira on it and posted it 500 m away as a target. That they wanted to plaster, everyone taking a shot at Elvira.

Driver Gustav took range at 475, let Elvira sit on the main reticule, took 1/2 m to the left, like you're supposed to, and fell short - by exactly 25 m.

Piepmatz the radio operator used range 500 and hit the world-famous toes, - precisely.

Then Hülsensacke the Indefatigable went in, the loader, (having been trained in the third rank), mightily spat into his hands, took range 700, took a deep breath and hit the trigger - boom - the shot went off, right through the much adorned belly button.

Gunner Richtschutze Holzauge the Infallible shook his head and said that with ranged 700 the shot should have gone over the top of it. Now he went for it all, took range 1000 and hit the head.

Commander Speedy Quickthinker took 1100 and went over it. With that range the magic had ended!

Range 25 m short, no hit! Range 50mm too far, direct hit!!!!!

The layman marvels, the expert just looks on!

Moral: The right estimate sometimes doesn't give the hit you need!

Original page 73 translation

The loader always hits

Motto: The old Panzermann will always strive for a hit.

The cannon shoots point blank. The shot therefore goes up to the range adjusted but no further.

If you know the exact distance and fire with range the same as distance, then you will hit the point of aim. But you never know the exact distance. If your guess is short by 25 m, then you will hit the dirt 25 m before the target, just like driver Oscar did.

The 8.8's trajectory is amazingly flat. So you need to elevate the barrel only a little to shoot much farther. You will then still hit your target close by with a distant range, if the target is only tall enough. For instance, using range 1000 you will hit all targets within 0 and 1000 m, if they are 2 m high. Isn't that wonderful?

However, shooting at Elvira using range 1000 is still not on the safe side, because if she were only a bit shorter, the shot would go overhead, as it did with Commander Speedy.

There are several usable ranges for one target! The smallest of them is the distance, all others lie above that. You can hit Elvira with 6 different ranges.

500 - 600 - 700 - 800 - 900 - 1000.

Do not adjust range equal to distance! Because if you are short by 25 m in your estimate. You will miss by 25 m. Do it like the loader, be moderate, then you'll hit the center of the target, the belly button.

In estimating the distance he can afford a glitch of 200 m either way, and he will still hit. The Loader always hits, because he can't be off by more in estimating a distance.

Moral: The old foxes will adjust the optics further they estimate!

Motto: $V_{Nabel} = E + \dfrac{\frac{H}{2}}{1000} \cdot 100$

Das ist das einzige, was Du Dir nicht zu merken brauchst.

A Wäre Elvira doppelt so groß, dann wären doppelt so viele Visiere brauchbar. Nabelvisier ist dann 1000. Du kannst Dich rauf wie runter um 500 m verschätzen!

B Ist das Ziel ganz klein, z. B. die Zehenspitzen, dann taugt nur ein Visier (500), die genaue Entfernung: Paknester, Panzer in Hinterhangstellung, Scharten, schwache Stellen an Panzern z. B. Turm (damit der Schuß senkrecht auftrifft) mußt Du so bekämpfen. Du darfst Dich nicht verschätzen.

C Entfernt sich Elvira, dann taugen immer weniger Visiere.

D Schließlich bleibt nur noch eines übrig: Visier gleich Entfernung.

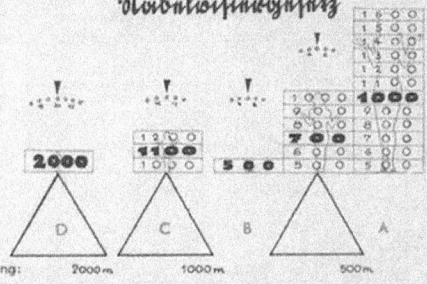

Das Sültanfout'fhe Nabelvisierungsatz

Entfernung: 2000 m 1000 m 500 m

Ist das Ziel ganz klein, oder erscheint es nur klein weil es weit weg ist, dann ist die Zahl der brauchbaren Visiere auch klein, weil das Ziel nur wenige oder gar kein Strich hoch ist.
Nur *kleine* Schätzfehler sind erlaubt.

Ist das Ziel *groß* oder sieht es *groß* aus, weil es nahe ist, dann ist die Zahl der brauchbaren Visiere auch *groß.* Große Schätzfehler sind erlaubt.

74

Original page 74 translation

The Loader's Belly Button Rule

That is the only thing you do not need to remember.

A. If Elvira were twice as tall, then twice as many ranges could be used. Bellybutton range would then be 1000. You can be off either way by 500 m!

B. If the target is very small, as for instance the toes, then only one range (500) will do, the exact distance: Anti-tank positions, tanks behind a hill, trenches, weak spots on tanks, as for instance the turret (so that the shot will hit vertically), must be fought in this manner. Your estimate must not be off.

C. If Elvira moves further away, then ever fewer ranges will suffice.

D. In the end there is only one course left to take: Range equals distance, If the target is very small, or if it only appears small because it is far away, then the number of useable ranges is also small since the target is only a few or not even one notch tall. Only small errors in estimating are permitted.

If the target is large or if it looks large because it is close by, the number of useable ranges is also large. Large errors are permitted.

Wie finde ich das richtige Visier?

1. Schätze die Entfernung
2. Schätze die Höhe des halben Zieles (Nabel) in Strich durch Vergleich mit dem Stachel (oder die Höhe des ganzen Zieles und nimm die Hälfte).
3. Das halbe Ziel in Strich mal Hundert Meter zähle zur Entfernung dazu, dann hast Du das Nabelvisier und triffst den Nabel.

Um wieviel darf ich mich verschätzen?

Strich mal Hundert Meter darfst Du zu weit und auch zu kurz schätzen und triffst trotzdem.

Beispiel:

1. weniger als 600 m
   mehr als   400 m . . . . Mittel =   500 m
2. Zielhöhe ist   4 Strich
   Nabelhöhe somit 2 Strich
3. 2 mal 100 m . . . . = + 200 m
   Nabelvisier . . . . =   700 m

Erlaubter Schätzfehler

2 mal 100 m . . . . =   200 m
es taugen somit alle Schätzungen
zwischen 500 m + 200 m . . . . =   700 m
und   500 m — 200 m . . . . =   300 m

Visiere
in allen brauch-
baren Größen

600
1000   700
Visier   Visier
500   200

Moral:

Mit der Stachelhöhe vergleicht sich die Nabelhöhe leicht.
Zur Entfernung rechnest Du Strich mal Hundert noch hinzu.
100 Meter für den Strich höchstens nur verschätze Dich.

75

Original page 75 translation

How do I find the correct range?

1. Estimate the distance.
2. Estimate the height of half the target, (bellybutton), in terms of notch by comparison with the reticule (or take the height of the entire target and divide it by two).
3. Half the target in notch times 100 meters, add that to the distance, that gives you the belly button range and you will hit the belly button.

By how much can I be off in the estimate?

Notch by 100 meters, is how far you may be over or under in estimating the correct distance and still hit.

Example:

1. Less than 600m more than 400m, average = 500m.
2. Target height is 4 notch belly button thus at 2 notch
3. Permissible error in estimate 2 times 100 m = 200 m, therefore all estimates between 500 m + 200 m = 700 m, 500 m - 200 m. = 300 m are applicable.

Moral: The reticule compare to the belly button where you stare,
to the distance you add notch by 100, not so bad,
100 m times the notch is how far you can deviate.

Original page 76 translation

Sensible Use of Ordnance

Motto: Just as Max Schmeling saves his right,
you must save the shells for the fight.

Always hold below the target, take aim from low down.

Attention!
The cannon always fires 1/2 m, the machine gun 1 m to the side. Because the cannon is positioned 1/2 m, the machine gun 1 m to the right of the optics.

Therefore always aim the cannon 1/2 m, the machine gun 1 m to the left!

Under 1200 m
You can't possibly miss, when correctly using the belly button rule.

Over 1200 m
Most of the time you have to adjust range equal to distance. Since you

estimated very accurately you will fire too close or too far. Then you adjust the range, because it was off, even if only by 50 or 25 m. Do not alter the point of aim, as that makes less of a difference over 1200 m.

Only if the shot misses to the left or to the right, are you permitted to change the point of aim sideways. If that is over 2 notch, then use the minor reticule to hold the target.

If the first shot is not a hit, you either made a mistake in estimating or you did not properly adjust the weapon.

You are at fault, not the cannon.
Up to 2000 m the 8.8 will fire point blank. Only if firing as far as 3000 m, one of three shots will miss. At a distance of 4000 m only every forth shot will produce a hit. (deviation.)

Therefore, always consider, whether shooting over great distances is worth it.

After every substantial firing sequence -
Elevate the barrel, Open the lock, let it cool and air out. In the wintertime remove the muzzle cover.

Wet the ground in front of the muzzle, otherwise firing the weapon will generate dust.

In the winter time, camouflage that spot, as it will turn black.

> *Moral: Use the sun from the back and the wind from the side,*
> *fire from stationary.*

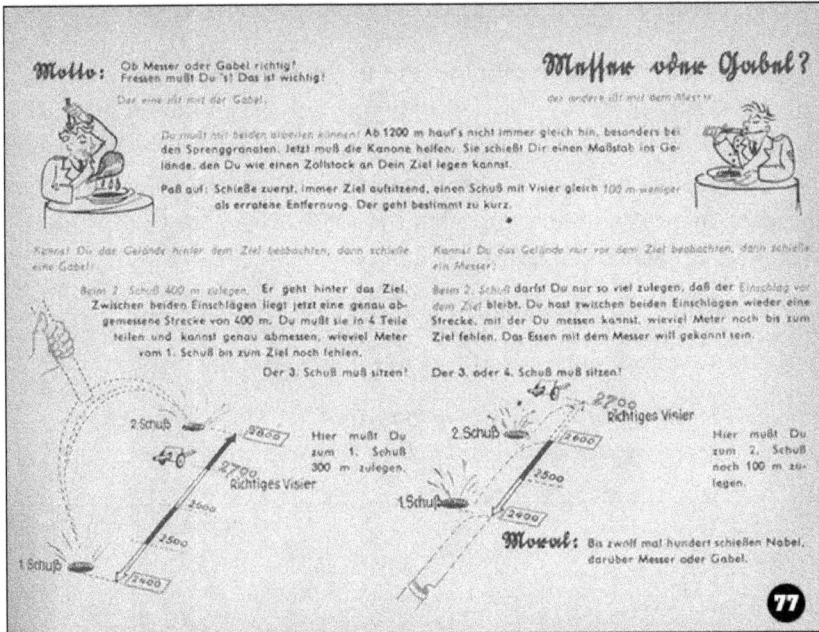

Original page 77 translation

Knife or fork?

Motto: Whether knife or fork is used on the platter, you have to eat it, that's what matters!

Some eat with a fork, others use a knife. You must be able to use both!

Over 1200 m it doesn't always work out right away, especially when using explosive shells. Now the cannon must come to your aid. It will shoot a scale for you in the field, which you can lay onto your target just like a yardstick.

Pay attention:
Firstly always fire one shot with the range 100 m less than the distance you guessed. Surely that one will fall short.

If you can see the terrain behind the target, then use a fork:
For the second shot, add 400 m.

It will go behind the target. Between both locations of impact there now lies an accurately measured distance of 400 m. You must divide it into four equal parts. And now the distance in meters from the first shot to the target can be measured accurately.

The third shot must be right on target!

If you can only see the terrain in front of the target, then use a knife:
For the second shot, you can add only so much. The location of impact must still be in front of the target. Again you have a distance between both locations of impact which can be used to measure how far you are short of the target in meters. Eating with a knife is not that easy. The third or fourth shot must be right on target!

In this instance you must add 300 m to the first shot.

In this instance you must add 100 m to the second shot.

Moral: Up to twelve by one hundred fire by button rule,
over greater distances knife or fork apply with cool.

Original page 78 translation

The Lead

Motto: Easy to kill your enemy, if you get the lead right.

The five men of the Tiger had requisitioned some cherries while the leave-train had stopped. They began to spit the stones at the telegraph poles adjacent to the track. That worked ok. The train slowly started to roll. At first they still managed to hit the poles, but all of the sudden they all missed.

Everyone was shocked. Then, the loader curled his tongue into the barrel of a howitzer, closed one eye, and with the other he aimed a good distance in front of a telegraph pole, pressed real hard, and - boom - the shot went off. Right on the telegraph pole. The faster the train went, the further ahead he aimed in front of a pole.

If your target is closer than 200 m - aim at it!
If an enemy wants to cross your line of sight at a distance between 200 m and 1200 m - **lead ahead of him!**

Because if you aim exactly at him, the enemy will have gone a few meters further in the time your shell takes to get there. It will not hit the place where he is, but where he was!

First, you must estimate how fast he is going:
Slow 10 km - Average 20 km - Fast 30 km

and then take a lead with the main reticule:
- **for armor-piercing shells 39/40:** Slow 3 - Average 6 - Fast 9 notch
- **for high-explosive shells:** Slow 4 - Average 8 - Fast 12 notch

Example: Truck is passing straight across at average speed.

"Machine gun 20 shots - 10 o'clock – 600 - truck - take lead 8 notch"!

Always use the minor reticule that fixes the target. That is what they are there for. And always let it run into the main reticule. If he is not going straight across but coming at you at an angle, then you take half the lead.

Example: Tank is approaching at an angle traveling at average speed.

"Anti-tank 39 - 1 o'clock - 600 - tank - take lead 3 notch!"

If your target is farther away than 1200 m - stop!

You will waste too much ammunition on moving targets.

The lead measurements are easily remembered by...

Moral: 9 and 6 and 3 - for tanks use we, 12 and 8 and 4 - only for explosive, no chore.

Motto: Benutzt am Okular Du zwecks
Justieren einen Fliegenklecks
und zielst dann sauber und verbissen,
wirst Du trotzdem danebenschießen.

Das Justieren

Beim Marsch immer Waffen zurren. Trotzdem wandern sie durch die Erschütterung aus.
Selber justieren, dann kennst Du Deine Waffe!

erst Kanone: Hierzu brauchst Du Bindfaden und Isolierband oder Fett.
1. Klebe ein Fadenkreuz über die Mündung.
2. Nimm den Schlagbolzen heraus.
3. Visiere ein Fernziel durch das Rohr an.

dann Rechtes Fernrohr: Hierzu brauchst Du einen Vierkant für die Optik.
1. Stelle die richtige Sehschärfe ein.
2. Stelle das Kanonenvisier auf 0.
3. Nimm die Schutzkappen am Optikkopf ab.
4. Justiere den Hauptstachel nach der Seite auf das Ziel.
5. Justiere den Hauptstachel nach der Höhe auf das Ziel.

dann Linkes Fernrohr: Hierzu brauchst Du einen Vierkant für die Optik.
1. Stelle das Kanonenvisier auf 1000 m.
2. Richte mit dem rechten Fernrohr das Ziel an.
3. Schwenke den Stachel nach links.
4. Stelle links die richtige Sehschärfe ein.
5. Verstelle den Augenabstand, bis die Sichtkreise zusammenfallen.
6. Justiere den Hilfsstachel nach der Seite auf das Ziel.
7. Justiere den Hilfsstachel nach der Höhe auf das Ziel.

Das Notvisier ist jetzt auf 1000 m starr justiert. Du kannst damit aufsitzend alle 2 m hohen
Ziele zwischen 0 und 1000 m treffen. Über 1000 m mußt Du ins Ziel gehen, oder Ziel ver-
schwinden lassen.

zuletzt Turm-MG: Hierzu brauchst Du eine gelochte Hülse. Hülsensack trägt sie stets bei sich.
1. Bodenstück ab, Schloß heraus, Hülse in den Lauf.
2. Stelle das MG-Visier auf die Justiermarke zwischen 200 und 300 m.
3. Richte mit dem rechten Fernrohr über Hauptstachel das Ziel an.
4. Justiere das MG über den gelochten Hülsenboden und Mündung auf das Ziel.
5. Überprüfe durch Anschießen.

Bug-MG: Überprüfe durch Anschießen.

Moral: Justiere öfters die Kanone,
dann schießt Du mit Erfolg, sonst ohne.

79

Original page 79 translation

Centering

Motto: If it's by a hair's breadth,
without the optics means you'll still miss!

When on the move always fasten down your gun. Still, they will deviate
due to vibration. Adjust them yourself, then you know your weapon!

First the cannon: To do this you need a piece of thread and electrical tape
or grease.
1. Attach a cross hairs across the muzzle.
2. Remove the firing pin.
3. Hold on to a distant target through the barrel.

Then the right scope: you will need a square head wrench for the optics.
1. Adjust to obtain a correct focus.
2. Adjust the range for the cannon to 0.
3. Remove the protector caps on the head-piece of the optics.
4. Centre the main reticule sideways on the target,
5. Centre the main reticule up or down on the target.

230

Then the left scope: You will need a square head wrench for the optics.

1. Adjust the range for the cannon to 1000 m.
2. Aim on to the target with the right scope.
3. Turn the reticule to the left.
4. Adjust to correct focus on the left.
5. Adjust the eye gap until both sights fall into one.
6. Adjust the auxiliary reticule sideways on the target.
7. Adjust the auxiliary reticule up or down on the target.

The emergency range is now fixed at 1000 m. Holding onto a target You can use it to hit any object that is 2 m high at a distance between 0 and 1000 m. Over 1000 m you must go into the target, or let the target vanish.

In the end, the turret - machine gun: You will need a perforated case. The loader always carries one with him.

1. Remove the base plate, take the lock out, insert the case into the barrel.
2. Adjust the machine gun range to the mark between 200 and 300 m.
3. Using the right scope take aim at the target over the main reticule.
4. Center the machine gun through the perforated base plate and the muzzle onto the target.
5. Check by shooting at the target.

Machine gun - front: Check by shooting at the target.

Moral: Regularly centre your cannon and you'll fire with success!

THE TANK COMMANDER

Original page 81 translation

Tank Commander

"TANK COMMANDER SPEEDY QUICKTHINKER"

Only your clarity of thought, your assured order will give life to the Panzer, direction to speed, decisive impact to the projectile. You hold a hand full of trump cards, now learn to play the game.

Motto: Seit Anno Tobak bis onnitzt, befiehlt dem Schuß man, daß er sitzt.

Der Schießbefehl

1. Stellt das Gewehr schräg vor den Leib
2. Kolben zu dem linken Fuß
3. Patrone aus der Tasch'
4. Patrone auf den Lauf
5. Ladstock heraus
6. Verkürzt den Ladstock vor der Brust
7. Stößt zu 1 — 2 — 3
8. Pfropfenstange aus der Tasch'
9. Pfropfenstange in das Maul
10. Beißt den Pfropfen ab
11. Pfropfen auf den Lauf
12. Ladstock drauf
13. Stößt zu 1 — 2 — 3
14. Feder von dem Hut
15. Das Gewehr in die Schwebe
16. Putzt das Zündloch aus
17. Feder auf den Hut
18. Pulverhorn heraus
19. "Pulver auf die Pfann'"
20. Pulverhorn an Ort
21. Macht ein grimmiges Gesicht'
22. Spannt den Hahn
23. Legt an
24. Zielt gut
25. Gebt Feuer
26. Herr hilf
27. Feuer

27 Kommandos wären im Dreißigjährigen Krieg nötig, um einen Schuß zu schießen. Deshalb hat er auch so lang gedauert. Indessen wurde der Schießbefehl in den Regimentern noch verschieden gehandhabt. Manche taten es nicht unter 90 Kommandos!

Fasse Dich kurz! Presse Deinen Willen in einen Befehl von 8 Kommandos!

82

Original page 82 translation

Order to Shoot

Motto: From past times until today, the order to shoot is sequenced.

1. Angle te musket in front.
2. Brace with left foot
3. Take out cartridge
4. Powder into barrel
5. Pull out ramrod
6. Brace ramrod against chest
7. Ram home 1-2-3
8. Take wadding out of pocket
9. Hold wadding in mouth
10. Bite off wadding
11. Insert into barrel
12. Ram home
13. Push in 1 - 2 - 3
14. Cock weapon
15. Suspend the weapon
16. Clean out the vent hole
17. Close pan

18. Take out powder horn
19. Powder in the pan
20. Return powder horn in place
21. Grimace
22. Cock the weapon
23. Point
24. Aim well
25. Give fire
26. Short prayer
27. Fire

In the war of 1618 - 1648, 27 commands were necessary to fire one shot. That is why it took so long. On top of that, the order to shoot was handled differently in various regiments. Some of them used no fewer than 90 commands!

Make it short! Compress your order into one short sequence consisting of 8 commands!

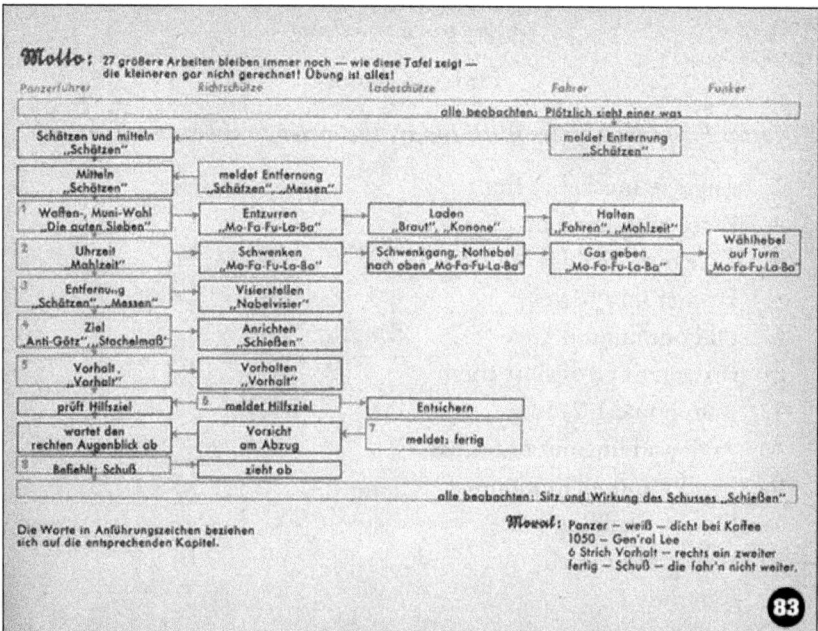

Motto: 27 main tasks still remain - as shown in this chart not counting the minor ones! Practice does it all!

Tank commander, Gunner, Loader, Driver, Radio operator: All are on the lookout, suddenly one of them spots something...

Driver: Reports distance "Contact"

Commander: Estimate, average "Contact"

Commander: Average "Contact"

Gunner: Reports distance "Contact", "measuring"

Commander: 1. Select Weapon/ammo "7 goodies"

Gunner: 1. Remove tiedown "MO-FÜ-FA-LA-BA"

Loader:1. load "Bride", "cannon"

Driver: 1. Stop "Driving", "Daily meals"

Commander: 2. Turret position "Daily meals"

Gunner: 2. Rotate Turret "MO-FÜ-FA-LA-BA"

Loader: 2. Select gear emergency lever up

Driver: 2. Accelerate "MO-FÜ-FA-LA-BA"

Radio: 2. Selector lever to turret pos. "MO-FÜ-FA-LA-BA"

Commander: 3. Distance "Contact", "Measuring"

Gunner: 3. Adjust range, "Belly Button rule"

Commander: 4. Target "Goetz Outreach" "Reticule"

Gunner: 4. Aim "Fire"

Commander: 5. Lead, "Lead"

Gunner: 5. Take lead, "Lead"

Commander: Checks auxiliary target

Gunner: 6. Reports auxiliary target

Loader: 6. Release

Commander: Wait for right moment

Gunner: Care with trigger

Loader: 7. reports ready

Commander: 8. Orders: Fire

Gunner: 8. lets off

All watch effect of the shot, "Fire"

Words in quotation marks refer to the respective chapters.

Original page 84 translation

Daily Meals

Motto: Not just the soldier is kept alive meals, but also the Panzer.

Your tank is

12 cm thick at the turret plate
10 cm thick at the front plate
8 cm thick at the side and rear plates
No-one else is!

But you yourself can make it even thicker!

When mother cuts the sausage straight, then that will yield one slice just as wide as the sausage is thick. But if she cuts at an angle, then the slice gets twice as wide!

We want more sausage now!

If you let someone fire at your tank straight on, then it is 10 cm thick and will sustain all calibers up to and including 75mm. But if you stand at an angle, then it is 13 cm thick.

A shot that hits at an angle penetrates much less, than one that hits head on. Therefore 13 cm thick plates hit at an angle gives the equivalent protection of armor that is 18 cm thick against a shot fired head on. (If you want to cut the sausage at an angle you need a sharper knife) Your armor placed at an angle is therefore in reality as strong as 18 cm and withstands all calibers up to and including 152 mm

Then you cannot be penetrated at all!

You see, just turning your tank from 12 to 1 o'clock makes it thicker by 2 cm. In order to penetrate these 2 cm your adversary has to come 1000 m closer.

1 cm of armor weighs the same as a firing range of 500 m!

If you stand at an angle this has the effect of placing your adversary 4 km farther distant, in one fell swoop. From there he can fire all he wants.

Here you can read all the positions and corresponding armor strength... and this shows your effective armor protection.

Die günstigsten Stellungen zum Feind liegen bei
10¹/₂   1¹/₂   4¹/₂   und   7¹/₂ Uhr.

Sie heißen nach den passenden Stunden Mahlzeiten.

Die 2. Silbe wird zwecks guter Verständigung immer l a n g gezogen — (Mittaaag) —.

Sie sind leicht zu merken nach dem Malzeichen.

Fahrer!   Bei Stellung immer links oder rechts anziehen, bis Feind auf Frühstück oder Mittag steht. (Richtung ausprobieren und merken.)

Richtschütze!   Gefährliche Ziele immer in Richtung Mahlzeiten bekämpfen. (Stellung des Turmes am Zifferblatt ablesen, Fahrer verbessern.)

Pz-Führer!   Gefährlichen Feind schräg anfahren. Stellung über Eck befehlen, so daß Feind in Richtung der Mahlzeiten steht. (Stellung des Zieles am Zifferblatt ablesen, Fahrer verbessern.)

Moral: Auf „Mahlzeit" — selbst mit 15,2 — bringt man Dir höchstens Schrammen bei. Der Gegner findet das abscheulich, für Dich, mein Freund, ist es erfreulich.

Original page 85 translation

The best positions towards the enemy are at
10 1/2, 1 1/2, 4 1/2 and 7 1/2 o'clock

According to the respective hours they are called meals.

To make communication easier, the second syllable is always stretched out - (breakfaaast) -

They are easy to learn when compared to the X-mark.

Driver!

When taking position always veer to the left or right, until the enemy stands at breakfast or lunch. (Try out the direction and memorize).

Gunner!

Fight dangerous targets from the direction of meals at all times. (Read position of turret on the clock and correct the driver).

Tank - Commander!

Approach dangerous enemy at an angle. Order 45 ° angle position, so that the enemy faces in direction of the meals. (Read position of target on the clock, correct the driver).

Moral: At mealtime - even with a 15.2 - you might get a scratch or two. Your adversary has nothing but frustration, it's a cakewalk for you.

Motto: Tritt Feind in dieses Kleeblatt rein,
so kann's für Dich gefährlich sein.

Das Kleeblatt

Wir sehen uns den Tiger
von oben an.

Auf welche Entfernung durchschlägt mich der T-34 mit der 7.62 cm lang?
Aus Richtung 12   Uhr unter 500 m
Aus Richtung 12¹/₂ Uhr unter 300 m
Aus Richtung 1   Uhr bin ich sicher
Aus Richtung „Mittag" bin ich am sichersten
Aus Richtung 2   Uhr unter 500 m
Aus Richtung 2¹/₄ Uhr unter 1300 m
Aus Richtung 3   Uhr unter 1500 m
Aus Richtung 3¹/₂ Uhr unter 1300 m
Aus Richtung 4   Uhr unter 500 m
Aus Richtung „Kaffee" bin ich sicher usw.

legen unsere Uhr drum

und tragen diese
Entfernungen ein.

Steht der Gegner im Kleeblatt, dann werde ich durchschlagen.
Steht er draußen, dann bin ich sicher.

An den „Mahlzeiten" kann der Tiger nicht geknackt werden.

Manöver vom Tiger!

Ihr selbst habt es in der Hand, ob der Tiger sicher ist, oder nicht. Prost Mahlzeit!

Wenn wir das für alle
Stunden machen und
die Endpunkte dieser
Sicherheitsabstände
verbinden, dann
gibt das ein Klee-
blatt.

Steht der Feind wirklich im Kleeblatt, dann mach Dir nicht gleich in die Hosen, sondern dreh den Tiger auf „Mahlzeit". Dann ist der Kerl gleich wieder draußen. Beschießen Dich zwei gleichzeitig, dann dreh den einen auf „Mahlzeit", und klotze auf den anderen.

Der Betreten des
Kleeblattes ist
verboten

86

The Cloverleaf

Motto: If enemy moves inside in this cloverleaf, you may be in danger.

At what distance does a T-34 7,62 en long-barrel penetrate my armor?

- From direction 12 o'clock under 500 m.
- From direction 12 1/2 o'clock under 300 m.
- From direction 1 o'clock I am safe.
- From direction "Lunch" I am in the safest position.
- From direction 2 o'clock under 500 m.
- From direction 2 1/2 o'clock under 1300 m.
- From direction 3 o'clock under 1500 m.
- From direction 3 1/2 o'clock under 1300 m.
- From direction 4 o'clock under 500 m.
- From direction "Coffee", I am safe, and so on.

If the enemy is located inside the cloverleaf, I will be penetrated. If he stays outside, I will be safe.

At "mealtime" the Tiger cannot be penetrated.

Men of the Tiger! It is in your own hands, whether the Tiger is safe or not. Enjoy your meals!

Should the enemy actually encroach inside the cloverleaf, don't wet your pants right a way. Instead, turn the TIGER towards "mealtime". Immediately the other guy is outside of it again. If two are firing at you simultaneously, turn one onto "mealtime" and blast the other one.

We look at the Tiger from up above

Lay our watch around it

And chart these distances.

If done for all hours, the lines connecting the charted dots yield a cloverleaf.

Das Kleeblatt ist für einen Gegner mit längerer Kanone größer.

Bei Feindwaffen, die weniger durchschlagen, hat es nur drei Blätter,
weil Deine Front dann auf jede Entfernung sicher ist.

Eine einzige Zahl
    mußt Du Dir für jeden Feindpanzer merken, dann weißt
    Du genau, wie groß Dein Kleeblatt ist!
    Für den T-34 mit der 7.62 cm lang ist sie 15.
1500 m sind die drei großen Blätter lang!
    (weil der Tiger seitlich und hinten gleich dick ist).
    Immer 1000 m kürzer als die großen Blätter, hier also
500 m. ist das kleine Blatt lang
    (weil vorn der Tiger 2 cm dicker ist).

Die ganz Schlauen
    können außerdem noch für 2, 4, 5, 7, 8 und 10 Uhr aus-
    rechnen, wie weit sie den Gegner heranlassen dürfen, ohne
    durchschlagen zu werden.
    Diese Entfernung ist ebenfalls
1000 m kürzer als die großen Blätter
    (weil dort der Panzer 2 cm dicker ist).

Die Überschlauen
    machen das auch noch für 11 und 1 Uhr.
    Die Entfernung ist
1000 m kürzer als das kleine Blatt
    (weil der Tiger dort 2 cm dicker ist als vorn).

Moral: Steht so ein Kerl in Deinem Klee,
Dann schmeiß ihn raus durch einen Dreh.

87

Original page 87 translation

For an opponent with a longer cannon, the cloverleaf is larger.

For enemy weaponry which can only penetrate less, it only has three leaves, because the front is then safe at any distance.

Only one number is what you need to memorize for each enemy tank, Then you will know the exact size of your cloverleaf!

For the T-34 with a 7.62 long-barrel it is...

1500m is the length of the three long leaves! (because the Tiger is equally thick on the side and arrears). Always 1000 m shorter than the longer leaves is the short one.

500 m (because the TIGER is 2 cm thicker in front).

The really smart ones can also calculate how far they may let the enemy approach them for positions 2, 4, 5, 1, 8 and 10 o'clock, and not be penetrated.

1000m This distance is also shorter than the large leaves, (because in that location the tank is 2 cm thicker)

240

The really extra smart ones will do the same for 11 and 1 o'clock The distance is 1000 m shorter than the smaller leaf, (because the Tiger is 2 cm thicker in that location than it is in front).

**Moral: *Should one of them be in your cloverleaf,*
*then throw him out with a dance.***

Motto: Der Mäßige verschießt gar viel,
der Meister schießt mit Maß und Ziel.

Das Stachelmaß

Der Bildhauer vergleicht sein Modell mit seiner Arbeit! Wenn die Plastik genau zwischen die zwei Spitzen der Rachenlehre paßt, weiß er, daß sie das richtige Maß hat.
Der Panzermann vergleicht den Feind mit dem Stachelmaß! Wenn der T-34 (Front) genau zwischen die zwei Spitzen der Stacheln paßt, dann hat er zum Abschuß das richtige Maß. Du weißt dann
1. daß Du ihn jetzt durchschlagen kannst und
2. welche Entfernung das ist.

Durch Seite und Heck kannst Du alle Feindpanzer unter 2000 m knacken. Das ist leicht zu merken. Die Front ist bei allen dicker. Du mußt dann näher heran, oder sie näher herankommen lassen, den T-34 z. B. auf 800 m. Diese Entfernung ist bei allen Panzern verschieden. Studiere die Panzerbeschußtafel in der Deckeltasche!

Das Stachelmaß sagt Dir, wann Du auf Abschußentfernung heran bist. Es ist für den T-34 z. B. 43.

4 = Stachelmaß-Front: 4 Strich muß der T-34 breit sein, damit Du ihn durch die Front abschießen kannst (oder er muß zwischen zwei Stachelspitzen passen). Er ist dann 800 m weit.

3 = Stachelmaß-Seite: 3 Strich muß der T-34 breit sein, damit Du an der Seite durchkommst. Er ist dann 2000 m weit.

Stachelmaß-Heck: ist immer die Hälfte von Stachelmaß-Seite, hier also 1½ Strich. Er ist dann 2000 m weit.

Für ganz Schlaue:
Dreht sich ein Feindpanzer von „Seite" seinerseits auf „Mahlzeit", dann wird er als Ziel höchstens 10% breiter. Diese 10% Fehler sind eingerechnet. Du mußt dann Turm-Mitte schießen, damit Dein Schuß senkrecht auftrifft.

Moral:
Das Maß der Stacheln zeigt Dir an, daß Du ihn knacken kannst, und wann.

88

Original page 88 translation

The Reticule Gap

**Motto: *The average one will shoot a lot,*
*the master shoots by chart and plot.***

The artist compares his model with his work! If the sculpture fits right in between the two tips of the gauge, then he knows that he has the correct measurement.

The tanker compares the enemy to the reticule! If the T-34, seen from the front, fits exactly in between two reticules, then he has the correct measurement to fire at. You will then know:
1. **That you will penetrate him, and**
2. **Which distance that is.**

Through side and rear you can crack all enemy tanks under 2000 m. That is easy to remember.

All of them have a thicker front. In that case you must go closer, or let them get closer, for the T-34 that is 800 m. This distance is different for all tanks. Study the chart on armor location supplied with the manual. The reticule-gap will tell you when you are close enough to shoot. For the T-34 it is 43, for instance.

4 = reticule-gap, front:

The T-34 must be 4 notch wide, so that you may kill him head on. (He has to fit between two reticules). He is then 800 m distant.

3 = reticule-gap, side:

The T-34 must be 3 notch wide, so that you can penetrate the side. He is then 2000 m distant.

Reticule-gap, rear: is always half of reticule-gap, side, in this case 1 1/2 notch. He is then 2000 m distant.

For really smart ones:

If an enemy tank turns "side" to his own "mealtime", then his target size will be enlarged by 10% at the most. This error of 10% is included. You must then shoot at the turret center, so that your shot will hit vertically.

Moral: The reticule-gap will show you that you can crack him and when.

"Wanted"

Motto: This reference you must remember your bride's picture and number.

Every kid knows the Spitfire and the HE 111.

Every youngster can tell a Ford V-8 from an Opel Kapitaen at 500 m distance. The old foxes recognize a DKW-250 by its sound.

Surely then you must be able to learn the differences between each enemy tank and learn to recognise them! Immediately sit down and study the tank identification chart supplied with this manual.

Memorise the appearance and the following 5 typical features:

T34: 15 - 8 - 43
KW1: 9 - 4 - 84
Churchill III: 7 - 15 - 24
Lee: 8 - 20 - 13
Sherman: 8 - 8 - 43

You will then master the tank-duel with each of the enemies in your sleep.

T - 34 Type

15: Clover-leaf I will be penetrated side and rear closer than 1500 m. Front always 1000 m less, in this case on from 500 m, never at "mealtime"

8: Distance I penetrate front at 800m side and rear at 2000 m for all tanks.

4: Reticule-gap, front 4 notch is width of T-34 at 800m.

3: Reticule-gap, side 3 notch is width of T-34 at 2000 m rear is always half of reticule-gap, side in this case 1 1/2 notch

Moral: Often the same number is fatal or fabulous.
Do you stand to lose or gain? One will rise and one will fall.

Original page 90 translation

Goetz Outreaches Ivan

Motto: He who reaches farther easily can knock the other one in the face!

You hold the enemy at a distance with your iron fist and knock him out without him being able to even nibble on you.

You are further away from the opponent than he is from you!

The Goetz Outreach is the space between your cloverleaf and your maximum range.

Pay attention!

You can kill the T-34 head on at 800 m. The T-34 can kill you only starting at 500 m.

Goetz Outreach: Between 500 m and 800 m you can kill him but he cannot kill you. You must try to be in that range for battle!

If you stand at "mealtime", you cannot possibly lose this round!

You take more weight and more range into the ring. You always beat him!

Isn't that a killer thing?

The 5 charts supplied with the manual lay out your potential opponents in a tank-duel. They contain cloverleaf, reticule-gap, character reference and Goetz Outreach for your most dangerous enemies. Look at them for however long it takes to memorize them, so that you will know the entire chapter as soon as their description is on your lips. Just the same, as you do with the picture in your shirt-pocket, when thinking of "her".

***Moral: It's the moral of the story I can hit you,
but you can't hit me***

Panzerklau

Für jede Granate, die Du verschießt,
　　　hat Dein Vater 100 RM Steuern bezahlt,
　　　hat Deine Mutter eine Woche in der Fabrik
　　　gearbeitet,
　　　ist die Eisenbahn 10 000 km weit gefahren!

Das bedenke vor jedem Schuß!

Sprenggranaten auf nicht erkannte Ziele „auf Ver-
dacht" verschossen, auf Ziele, die mit MG erledigt
werden können, sind ein Verbrechen.

Panzergranaten auf unbrauchbare Entfernung, auf
erledigte Panzer, oder schlecht gezielt verschossen,
geben nur Kerbschnitzarbeiten im Stahl!

Männer vom Tiger! Sparen!
　　　Nützt den dicken Panzer aus! Ran!
　　　Walzen ist billiger als MG!
　　　MG ist billiger als Kanone!
　　　Hülsen und Packgefäße abliefern!

Der Tiger säuft den Sprit kanisterweise.
Jeder Liter muß 3000 km weit gekarrt werden:

Männer vom Tiger! Sparen!
　　　Geizt mit jedem Liter!
　　　Laßt den Motor nicht unnütz laufen!
　　　Weißt Du, wann der nächste Sprit kommt?

Der Tiger kostet mit allem Drum und Dran 800 000 RM
und 300 000 Arbeitsstunden. 30 000 Menschen müssen
einen ganzen Wochenlohn geben, 6000 Menschen
eine Woche schuften, damit Du einen Tiger be-
kommst. Sie arbeiten alle für Dich.

Männer vom Tiger!
　　　Bedenkt, was Ihr in den Händen habt!
　　　Haltet Ihn in Schuß!
　　　Panzerklau geht um!
　　　Schlagt ihn, wo Ihr ihn trefft!

91

Original page 91 translation

For every shell, that you fire off

Your father has paid 100 RM in taxes, your mother worked one week in the factory. The trains had to travel 10,000 km.

Think of that each time you want to fire!

Explosive shells onto targets not positively identified or onto targets that can be destroyed with the machine gun are a criminal waste.

Anti-tank grenades fired at useless range, at tanks already damaged, or poorly aimed only chisel off some steel!

Men of the Tiger!

Save! Make good use of the thick armor! Be resolute ! It's cheaper to overrun than to fire the machine gun! The Machine gun is cheaper than cannon! Return the cases and packaging material.

The Tiger guzzles down the fuel by the can.

Every litre has to be hauled from 3000 km away:

Men of the Tiger!

Save! Be stingy with every Litre! Don't let the engine run needlessly! Are you sure when the next fuel ration will arrive?

All included the Tiger costs 800,000 RM and 300,000 man-hours to produce. 30,000 people have to give a whole weeks pay and 6000 men have to work a whole week, so that you will get one Tiger. They all work for you.

Men of the Tiger!
Consider what you hold in your grasp! Keep it in good shape! They are stealing the tanks! Grab them where the thieves are found!

92

Original page 92 translation

Supplied with this manual are:

1. Tank identification chart Russia
2. Armor location chart 8.8 KwK 36
3. Anti-Goetz T - 34

   K V 1

   Churchill III

   Lee

   Sherman

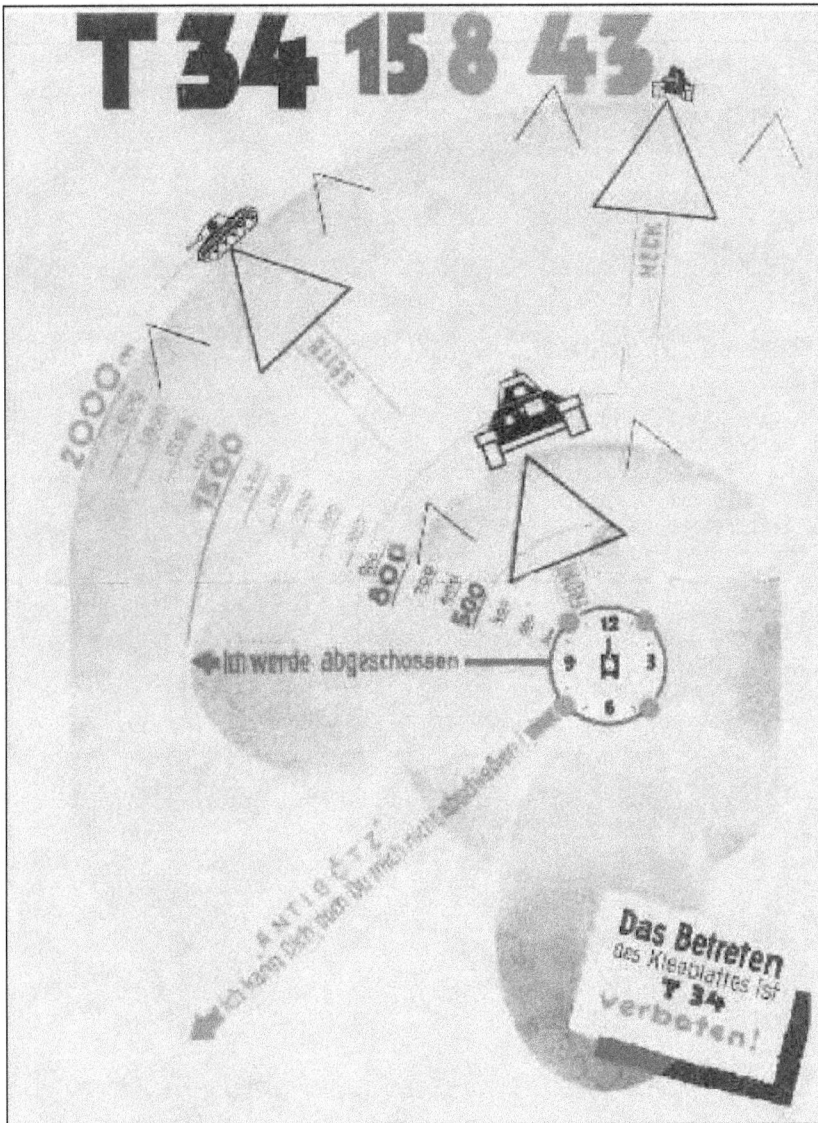

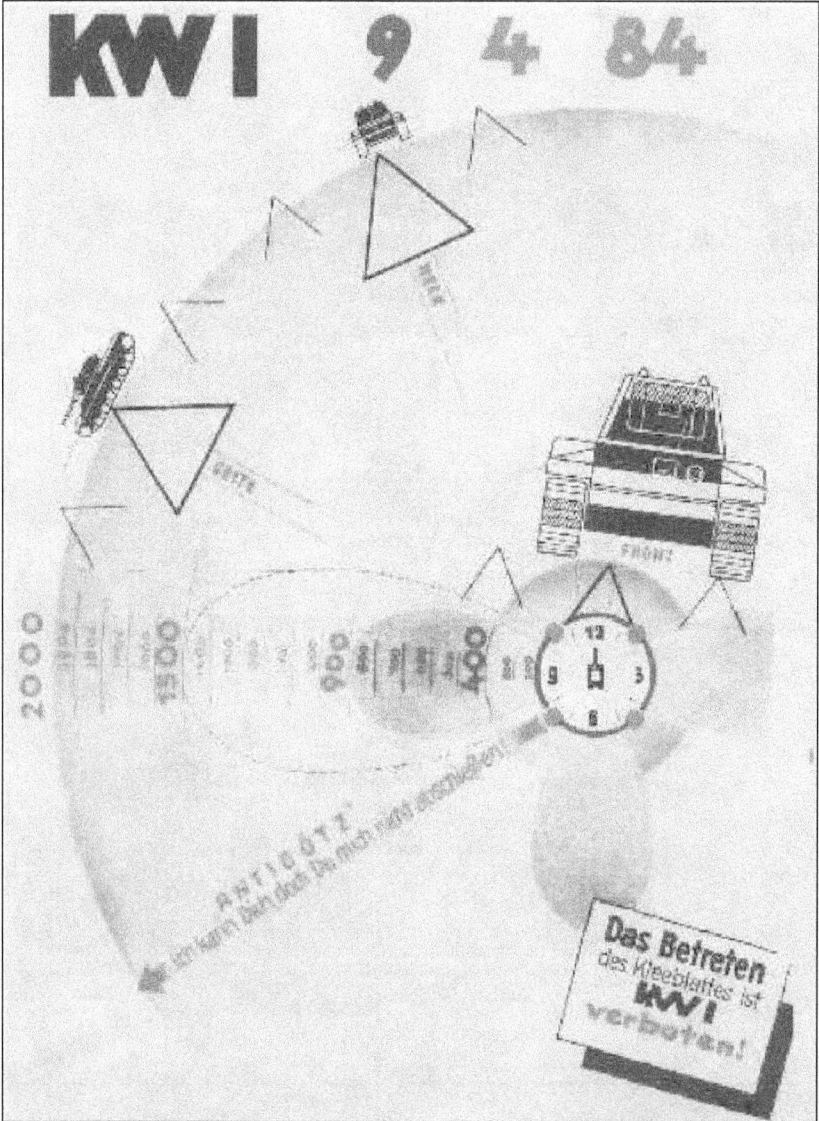

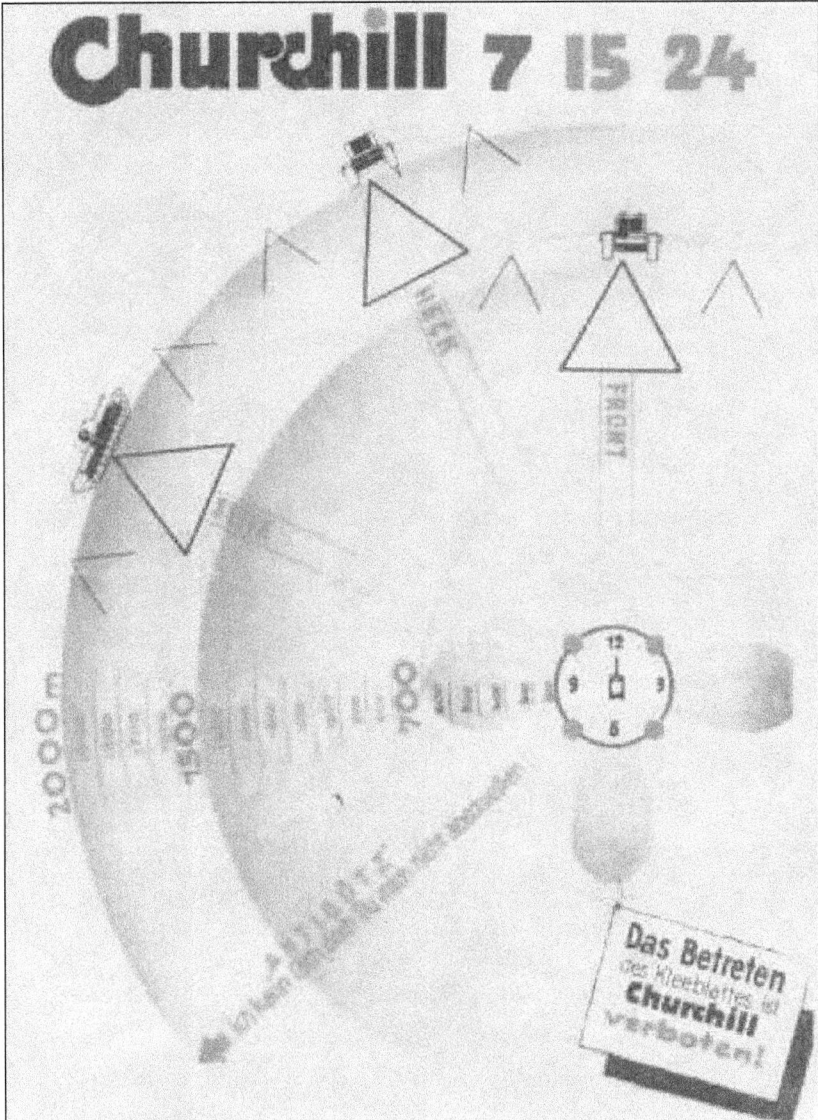

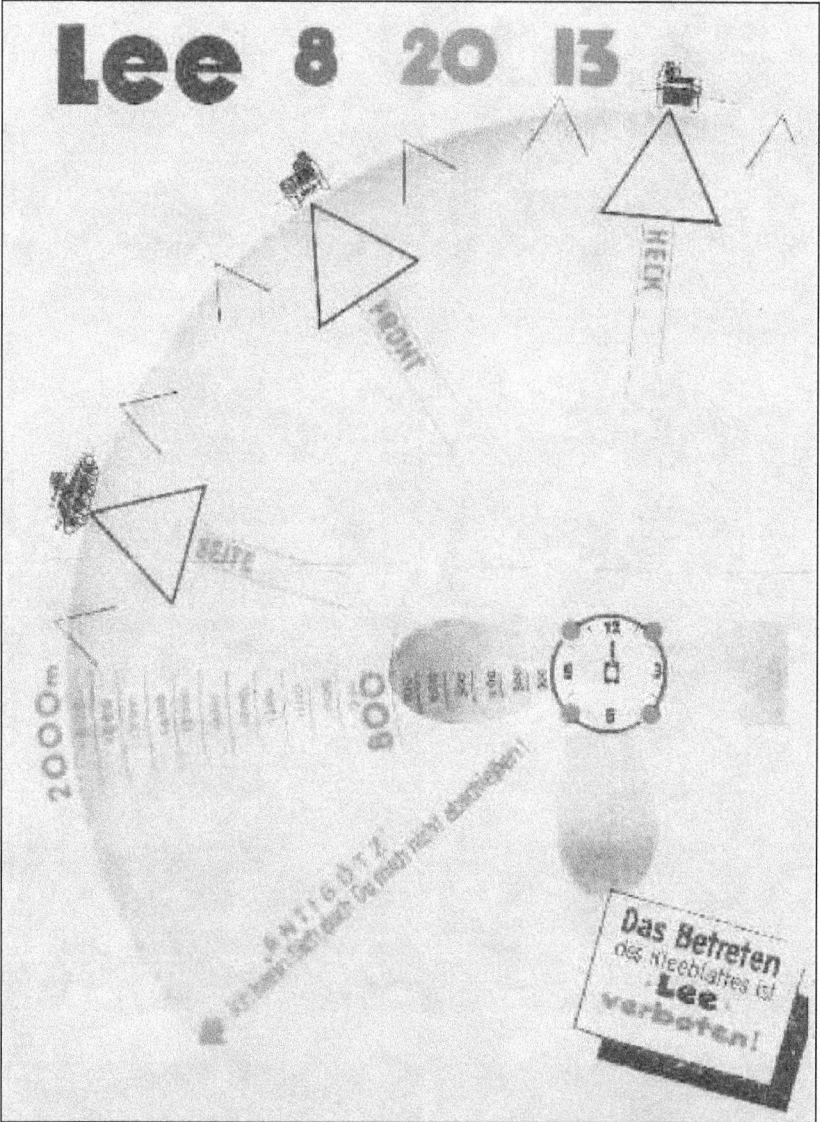

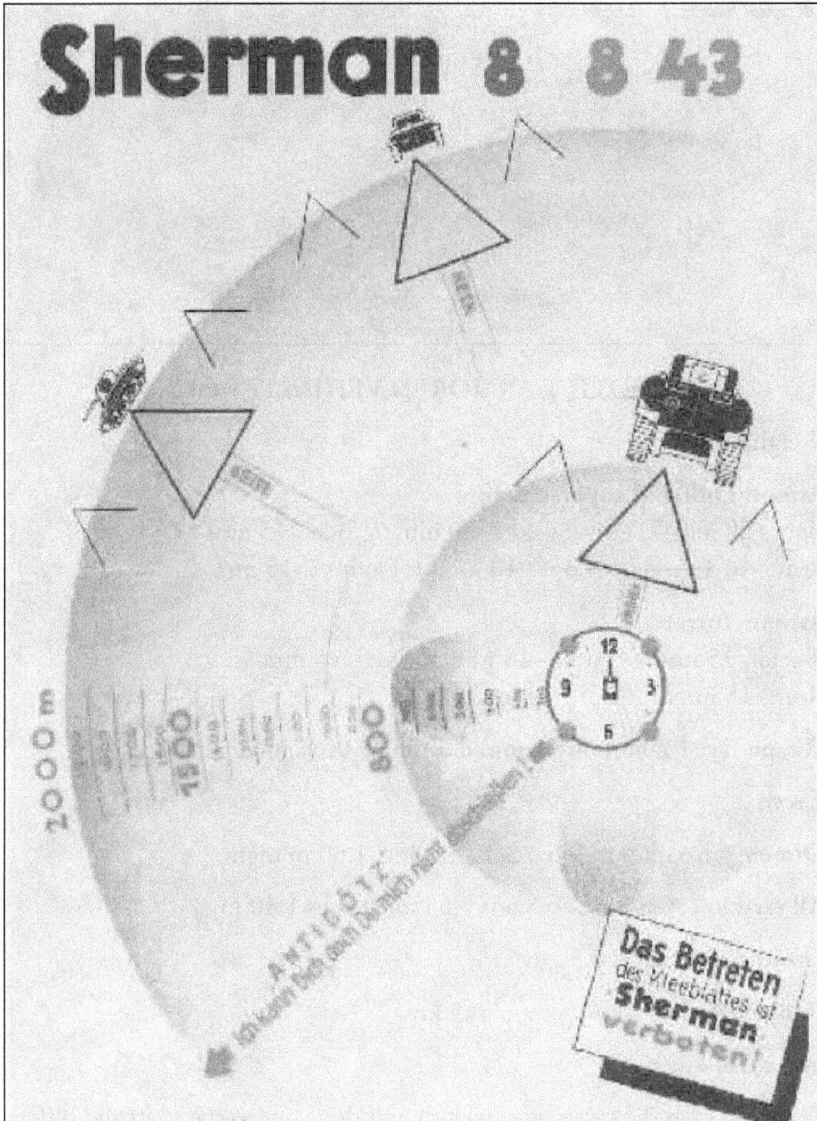

LIGHT ARMOURED VEHICLES

T 60

SOVIET ARMORED VEHICLE: T 60

Weight: 5.5 t

Armor: Hull and superstructure
Bow - 20 mm / Driver's side - 20 mm / Side - 15 mm
Rear - 10-13 mm / Roof - 10 mm / Floor - 7-10 mm

Armor: Turret
Shield - 15 mm / Front - 15 mm / Side - 15 mm
Rear - 15 mm / Roof - 7 mm

Weaponry: 1 20mm mechanized cannon, 1 machine gun.

Crew: 2

Dimensions: 4.00 m long, 2.35 m wide, 1.80 m high

All terrain capability: Ascends 0.55 m, crosses 1.40 m,

Ground clearance: 0.30 m

Range: Road 615 km, terrain 315 km

Speed: 44 km/h

Features: Uses the same running gear and drive line as the T 40 and differs from it in appearance only in the shape of the upper armor case and the missing propeller drive in the rear.

Use: Light armored vehicle for battle reconnaissance, usually comprise the (3.) light company of an armored detachment

Evaluation: Very small and light armored vehicle of most recent production, (used since Nov. 1941), weak armor, minimal combat use. Has mechanical limitations.

SOVIET ARMORED VEHICLE T 70

Weight: 9.2 t

Armor: Hull and superstructure
Bow - 45 mm / Driver's front - 35 mm / Side - 16 mm
Rear - 25 mm / Roof - 10 mm / Floor - 10 mm

Armor: Turret
Shield - 60 mm / Front - 35 mm / Side - 35 mm
Rear - 35 mm / Roof - 10 mm

Weaponry: 1 45mm mechanized cannon, L/46, 1 machine gun, 1 machine pistol.

Crew: 2

Dimensions: 4.29 m long, 2.33 m wide, 2 m high

All terrain capability: Ascends 0.65 m, crosses 1.80 m, fords 0.90 m

Range: Road 450 km, terrain 300 km

Speed: 45 km/h

Indentifying features: Outer appearance similar to the T 60, but longer and more imposing stance. Has 5 rollers and a sharply protruding mantlet for cylindrical mount.

Use: Light armored vehicle for battle reconnaissance, usually comprise the (3.) light company of an armored, detachment.

Evaluation: Light armored vehicle of most recent production.(In use since summer of 1942)

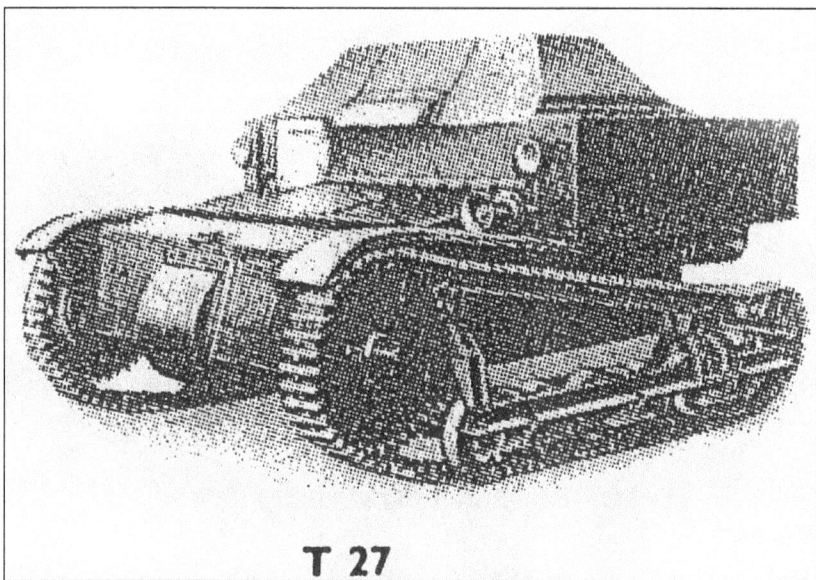

T 27

SOVIET ARMORED VEHICLE: T 27
(Series denomination T 27 A, small armored vehicle, "tankette", armored tractor)

Weight: 1.7 up to 2.7 t

Armor: 4 up to 10 mm

Weaponry: 1 machine gun

Crew: 2

Dimensions: 2.60 m long, 1.80 m wide, 1.45 m high

All terrain capability: ascends 0.50 m, crosses 1.30 m, fords 0.70 m

Ground clearance: 0.34 m

Range: Road 110 km, terrain 60 km

Speed: 40 km/h

Indentifying features: Low, boxlike armored vehicle, appears almost as wide as long.

Use: Originally intended as armored reconnaissance vehicle it was soon proven to be useless and is now - usually unarmed - used only as an armored artillery tractor.

Evaluation: Useless as an armored vehicle. Only limited use as a tractor (weak motor).

T 37

SOVIET 3 AND 5 TON AMPHIBIOUS ARMORED VEHICLES: T37, T38 AND T40

Indentifying features: Low, flat, boxlike construction. Propeller drive in the rear.

Use: Light armored vehicle for combat reconnaissance and attack with infantry. Also used commonly when the crossing of rivers is not expected.

In terms of overall battle formation amphibious armored vehicles were deployed in large numbers within the Soviet-Russian armored force.

Evaluation: Weak armor and weaponry, only limited combat use, easy to defeat. In light of the few existing bridges in the East, this vehicle's amphibious capability can prove an advantage. T 37 and T 38 are obsolete pre-war designs.

T 37 and T 38

Weight: 3.2 t

Armor: turret. Bow, Armor case 10 mm, otherwise 4 to 6 mm

Weaponry: 1 machine gun (T 38 occasionally has heavier weapons)

T 38

T 40

Crew: 2

Dimensions: 3.75 m long, 2.00 m wide, 1.80 m high

Ground clearance: 0.30 m

Range: Road 185 km, terrain 115 km

<u>T 40</u>

Weight: 5.5 t

Armor: 10-14 mm, turret, bow, armor case otherwise 6 mm

Weaponry: 1 extra heavy machine gun, 1 machine gun

Crew: 2

Dimensions: 4.10 m long, 2.35 m wide, 1.95 m high

Ground clearance: 0.34 m

Range: Road 360 km, terrain 185 km

All terrain capability: ascends 0.60 m, crosses 1.70 m, floats

Speed: on land 45 km/h, in the water 5-10 km/h

SOVIET ARMORED VEHICLE: T 26
Series denomination: T 26 A, T 26 B, T 26 C

Weight: 9.5 t

Armor: Bow and driver's front - 16 mm, Turret - 16 mm, Side - 16 mm, Rear - 16 mm

Weaponry: 1 45mm mechanized cannon, 2-3 machine guns

Crew: 3

Dimensions: 4.60 m long, 2.45 m wide, 2.65 m high

All terrain capability: ascends 0.80 m, crosses 2.20 m, fords 0.80 m

Ground clearance: 0.37 m

Range: Road 350 km, terrain 175 km

Speed: 30 km/h

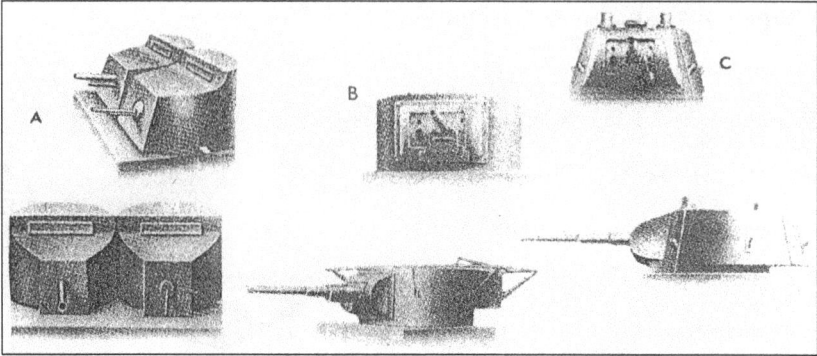

Various turret shapes: Left Series A (2 turrets), centre Series B, right Series C

Indentifying features: Rear of turret on versions B and C cantilevers far out. Low type of construction, descending towards the rear.

Use: Formerly a common light Soviet-Russian armored vehicle used in attack (in conjunction with infantry). After heavy losses in the summer of 1941 it is only rarely seen.

Evaluation: Weak armor. Good weaponry. Weak engine, slow speed. Obsolete pre-war design that is easy to defeat. Further production likely ceased.

SOVIET FLAMETHROWER ARMORED VEHICLE:
T 26 B with flamethrowing device

Weaponry: Flamethrowing device (400 liters of flame oil), 1 machine gun.

Crew: 3

Indentifying features: Wide box-shaped container on the front of the turret with two openings, one for the machine gun, one for the flame bucket.

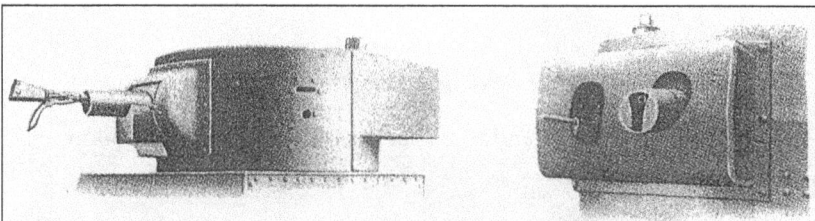

T 26 B with flamethrowing device. On the left is Version 1 which is more common than Version 2 on the right.

Use: Light armored vehicle for attack with infantry support, especially onto fortified positions. In terms of battle formations intended for use in larger numbers, yet use is comparatively rare.

Evaluation: Characteristics same as light armored vehicle. T 26, limited tactical value.

BT 7

SOVIET ARMORED VEHICLE:
Christie armored vehicle BT 1-7 (various series)

"BT" - Bystrochodni tank: a fast armored vehicle

Weight: 12.2 up to 13.7t (varies by series)

Armor: Bow and driver's front - 13-22 mm , Turret - 15 mm, Side - 13 mm, Rear - 13 mm

Weaponry: 1 45 mm mechanized cannon on wheels 70 km/h, 1 machine gun. (Some have additional machine gun in rear of turret - BT 7 sometimes has short 76.2mm motorized cannon)

Crew: 3

Dimensions: 5.80 m long, 2.30 m wide, 2.40 m high

All terrain capability: ascends 0.75 m, crosses 2.10 m, fords 1 m

Ground clearance: 0.36 m

Range: on tracks 430 km, on wheels 570 km

Speed: on tracks 50 km/h

Indentifying features: Large roadwheels (Christie system), flat construction, pointed towards the front (shape of turret changed frequently). The BT 7 armored vehicle equipped with the 7.62 cm motorized cannon is very similar in appearance to the somewhat wider and heavily armored T 34. It is often confused with the T 34. Differences to the T 34 see there.

Use: Light armored vehicle on wheels (rare) for tactical and operational reconnaissance. On tracks (almost always), used for attack with infantry support. Was used in the Soviet-Russian tank corps in large numbers, together with the T 26 originally about 3/4 of all armored vehicles. Only rarely seen now.

Evaluation: Fast, light armored vehicle with good pickup, however armor is insufficient. Production likely ceased.

M 3 General Stuart

US ARMORED VEHICLE: M 3 GENERAL STUART

Light armored Vvehicle of American origin, the use of which can be counted on in the Soviet-Russian theatre of war

Armor: Hull and superstructure
Bow (cast) - 50 mm / Driver's front - 38 mm / Side - 25 mm
Rear - 25 mm / Roof - 10 mm / Floor - 10 mm

Armor: Turret
Shield (cast) - 43 mm / Front - 55 mm / Side - 32 mm

Rear - 32 mm / Roof - 12 mm

Weight: 13 t

Weaponry: 1 37mm mechanized cannon

Crew: 4

Dimensions: 4.46 m long, 2.46 m wide, 2.65 m high

All terrain capability: ascends 0.65 m, crosses 1.80 m, fords 1.10m

Ground clearance: 0.42 m

Range: 160 km

Speed: 56 km/h

Indentifying features: Short, high construction. The front drive wheel is star shaped. Three different turret shapes:
  a) round, without commander's cupola elevated
  b) round with commander's cupola elevated
  c) angular, with commander's cupola elevated

Guard for tracks on the side only on version for the tropics.

Use: Light armored vehicle for tactical and operational reconnaissance.

Evaluation: Fast, light and agile armored vehicle with good pickup. A lot of wear on the tracks.

MEDIUM ARMOURED VEHICLES

T 34

Soviet armored vehicle: T 34
Series denomination: T 34 A, T 34 B, T 34 B with cast turret

For the newest version, the driver's front is to be reinforced to a strength of 100 mm.

Weight: 26.3 t

Armor: T 34 A

Hull and superstructure
Bow - 45 mm / Driver's front - 45 mm / Side - 40-45 mm
Rear - 40 mm / Roof - 18-22 mm / Floor - 14 mm

Turret
Shield - 45+25 mm / Front - 45 mm / Side - 45 mm
Rear - 40-45 mm / Roof - 16 mm

Armor: T 34 B

Hull and superstructure
Bow - 45 mm / Driver's front - 45+15 mm / Side - 45 mm
Rear - 45 mm / Roof - 18-22 mm / Floor - 14 mm

Turret
Shield - 45+25 mm / Front - 45+17 mm / Side - 45+17 mm
Rear - 45 mm / Roof - 16 mm

Armor: T 34 B with cast turret

Hull and superstructure
Bow - 45 mm / Driver's front - 45+15 mm / Side - 45 mm
Rear - 45 mm / Roof - 18-22 mm / Floor - 14 mm

Turret
Shield - 45+25 mm / Front - 60-70 mm / Side - 60-70 mm
Rear - 60-70 mm / Floor - 20 mm

Weaponry: 1 motorized cannon 7.62 cm, 2 machine guns

Dimensions: 5.90 m long, 3.00 m wide, 2.45 m high

Crew: 4

All terrain capability: ascends 0.90 m, crosses 3.00 m, fords 1.10 m

Ground clearance: 0.38 m

Range: Road 450 km, Terrain 260 km

Speed: 50 km/h

Indentifying features: Flat construction, angled bow, Christie-running gear (road wheels). Lead vehicles with longer 76.2mm mechanized cannon L/41.5, all other vehicles equipped with shorter mechanized cannon L/30.5.

Features that are different on T 34 as opposed to BT 7, which has a similar appearance:

T 34

Bow plate: Round edges, upper bow plate including driver's front at shallow angle (30° incline from horizontal)

Armor case: Angled surfaces

Turret shape: Round edges, angled shape

Running gear: 5 road wheels

BT 7

Bow-plate: Sharp edges, steep, separate from driver's front.

Armor case: Steep surfaces

Turret shape: Steep side, sharp edges

Running gear: 4 road wheels

In general, the T 34 has a more imposing and streamlined appearance.

Use: Most important armored vehicle for armored attack.

Evaluation: By far the best and most practical Soviet-Russian armored vehicle. Fast, agile, very powerful weaponry and strong armor. Most difficult to combat of all Soviet-Russian designs, due to its very beneficial construction (incline from horizontal is 30° at bow-plate, 40°-45° at rear plate, 50° at armor case sides).

M 4 General Sherman

US ARMORED VEHICLE:
M4 General Sherman

Weight: circa 31 t

Armor: Hull and superstructure
Bow - 55 mm / Driver's front - 65 mm / Side - 26-39 mm
Rear - 26-60 mm / Roof - 13-26 mm / Floor - 14-18 mm

Armor: Turret
Shield - 244 mm / Front - 85 mm / Side - 85 mm
Rear - 85 mm / Roof - 30 mm

Weaponry: 1 75mm mechanized cannon, 1 machine gun in rotating turret, 1 anti-aircraft machine gun, 1 machine gun in bow

Crew: 5

Dimensions: 5.65 m long, 2.75 m wide, 2.75 m high

All terrain capability: ascends 0.70 m, crosses 2.20 m, fords 1.28 m

Ground clearance: 0.38 m

Range: Road surface 300 km, terrain 160 km

Speed: 36 km/h

Identifying features: Stocky appearance, rounded off design on all sides.

Use: Most important USA armored vehicle for armored attack and infantry support.

Evaluation: Most practical USA armored vehicle. Fast, agile, heavy armor and powerful weaponry.

M 3 General Lee I

US ARMORED VEHICLE:
M3 General Lee I, General Lee

Weight: 28 t

Armor: Hull and superstructure
Bow - 65 mm / Driver's front - 50 mm / Side - 38 mm
Rear - 26-38 mm / Roof - 14 mm / Floor - 14-18 mm

M 3 General Grant I

Armor: Turret
Shield - 55 mm / Front - 88 mm / Side - 50-60 mm
Rear - 50 mm / Roof - 30 mm

Weaponry: 1 75mm mechanized cannon L/31 mounted in bay on one side, 1 37mm mechanized cannon L/56.6 + 1 machine gun in rotating turret, 1 anti-aircraft machine gun mounted in rotating turret-top, 2 machine guns fixed in bow.

Crew: 7

Dimensions: 5.65 m long, 2.75 m wide, 3.05 m high

All terrain capability: ascends 0.70 m, crosses 2.20 m, fords 1.28 m

Ground clearance: 0.38m

Range: Road surface 300 km, Terrain 160 km

Speed: 0.38 m

"General Lee II" has cast upper part of armor case. Specifications same as "Lee I". Chassis and superstructure the same as armored vehicle M 3 "General lee I". Turret without rotating top and cantilevered rear. "General Grant II" has a cast upper armor case. Specifications same as "Lee I", but lower, 2.75 m high.

Identifying features: Elevated construction with bay-like bumpout on the side. Strong weaponry. The front drive wheel has a star-like shape.

30-ton Armored vehicle M 3 (Canadian)
Another version of the M 3 manufactured in Canada is the armored vehicle "Ram". It is manufactured of cast armor and features no side bump-out.

Weaponry: "Ram I" 1 40mm mechanized cannon L/52, 2 machine guns, "Ram II" 1 57mm mechanized cannon L/45, 2 machine guns

US ARMORED VEHICLE:
M3 "General Grant I"

Use: Armored vehicle for armored attack and infantry support.

Evaluation: Comparatively fast and maneuverable armored vehicle with high firepower

The armored vehicle M 3's chassis is also used as a self-propelled assault gun with 105mm caliber cannon.

Mk II Matilda

ENGLISH ARMORED PURSUIT VEHICLE:
Mk II "Matilda"

Weight: 26 t

Armor: Hull and superstructure
Bow - 75-80 mm / Driver's front - 80 mm / Side - 65-70 mm
Rear - 55 mm / Roof - 16-23 mm / Floor - 14 mm

Armor: Turret
Shield - 80mm / Front - 75-80mm / Side - 77mm
Rear - 70mm / Floor - 20mm

Weaponry: Matilda III C.S. (close support) 1 76.2 mechanized cannon. L/26.5, 1 machine gun, 2 smoke pistols. Matilda I, II, III - 1 40iinm mechanized cannon L/52, 1 machine gun, 2 smoke pistols

Crew: 4

Dimensions: 6.00 m long, 2.55 m wide, 2.50 m high

All terrain capability: ascends 0.60 m, crosses 1.80 m, fords 0.80 m

Ground clearance: 0.33 m

Range: Road surface 100 km. Terrain 60 km

Speed: 23 km/h

Identifying features: Angled sides on turret, round edges (cast steel), strong armor on running gear with large; cavities (service openings).

Use: Armored vehicle for infantry support in an attack.

Evaluation: Heavily armored and especially difficult to combat from the side. Tactically slow and cumbersome. Not suitable for operational use.

ENGLISH ARMORED PURSUIT VEHICLE:
Mk III "Valentine"

Weight: 16 t

Armor: Hull and superstructure
Bow - 60 mm / Driver's front - 60 mm / Side - 60 mm
Rear - 16-60 mm / Roof - 10-30 mm / Floor - 8-20 mm

Armor: Turret
Shield - 26 mm / Front - 65 mm / Side - 60 mm
Rear - 45-60 mm / Floor - 16-20 mm

Weaponry: 1 40mm mechanized cannon L/52, 1 machine gun, 1 smoke pistol

Crew: 3

Dimensions: 5.45 m long, 2.75m wide, 2.25 m high

All terrain capability: ascends 0.70 m, crosses 2.40 m, fords 1.20 m

Mk II Valentine

Ground clearance: 0.42 m

Range: Road surface 150 km, terrain 103 km

Speed: circa 30 km/h

Identifying features: Round turret with vertical sides, running-gear armor (as opposed to Mk II) is missing.

Use: Same as Mark II

Evaluation: Lighter than Mk II, but faster and more maneuverable.

SOVIET ARMORED VEHICLE: 30-TON T28

Weight: 28 to 32 t

Armor T 28:
Bow and driver's front - 30 mm / Turrets - 23 mm
Side - 20+7 mm / Rear - 20 mm

Weaponry: 1 76.2mm mechanized cannon (L/16.5 or L/24), 3 machine guns,(some have additional rear machine gun and anti- aircraft machine gun).

Armor T 28 (reinforced):
Bow and driver's front - 38-52 mm / Turrets - 53 mm
Side - 48+7 mm / Rear - 52 mm

Crew: 6

Dimensions: 7.25 m long, 2.80 m wide, 2.75 m high

T 38

All terrain capability: ascends 0.90 m, crosses 3 m, fords 0.80 m

Ground clearance: 0.43 m

Range: 180 km

Speed: 35 km/h

Identifying features: Noticeably large (longer than KV II 52 t), 3 turrets = 1 main turret with mechanized cannon, 2 side turrets with machine guns, armored running gear.

Use: The T 28 was the main medium pre-war-tank for support of light armored vehicles in an attack.

Evaluation: Obsolete design with numerous mechanical defects, (down time). Slow and difficult to maneuver. Comparatively weak armor for its size, easy to combat. No longer in production. Already mainly used only as an armored artillery tractor.

HEAVY ARMOURED VEHICLES

KV 1

SOVIET 44-TON ARMORED VEHICLE KV I
Series denomination: KW I A, KW I B, KW I C, KW I S, KW 8
("KV" = Klim Voroschilov)
Misleading classification: "52t KV"

Weight: 43.5 t

Armor KV I A

Hull and superstructure
Bow - 5 mm / Driver's front - 75 mm / Side - 75 mm
Rear - 75 mm / Roof - 35 mm / Floor - 35 mm

Turret
Shield - 60+25 mm / Front - 75+25 mm / Side - 75mm
Rear - 75mm / Roof - 35mm

Armor KV II B (reinforced)

Hull and superstructure
Bow - 75+25-35 mm / Driver's front 75+25-35 mm
Side - 75, sometimes 75+35 mm / Rear - 75 mm
Roof - 35 mm / Floor - 35 mm

Turret
Shield - 100 mm / Front - 75+35 mm / Side - 75+30 mm
Rear - 75mm / Roof - 35mm

Armor: KV I C

Hull and superstructure
Bow - 75+25-35 mm / Driver's front - 75+25-35 mm
Side - 90 mm, sometimes 90 + 40 mm / Rear - 75 mm
Roof - 40 mm

Turret (cast)
Shield - 105 mm (rolled steel) / Front - 120 mm
Side - 120 mm / Rear - 120 mm
Roof - 40 mm

Weaponry: 1 76.2mm mechanized cannon L/30.2, 2 to 3 machine guns

Crew: 5

Dimensions: 6.80 m long, 3.35 m wide, 2.75 m high

All terrain capability: Ascends 0.90 m, Crosses 2.80 m, Cords 1.45 m

Ground clearance: 0.52 m

Range: Road 335 km, Terrain 200 km

Speed: 35 km/h

The KV I S is a new version of this armored vehicle, featuring reinforced armor, and a motorized cannon 7.62 cm L/41.5.

The KV 8 armored vehicle is equipped with a flamethrower and a motorized cannon 4.5 cm as well as 4 machine guns.

Identifying features: Comparatively small for its size, sleek shape, rear of turret cantilevers far out, (as opposed to KV II 52 t). Additional armor bolted onto turret and chassis as identified by large hex bolts. Armor welded on in places of weaponry impact, only visible from up close.

Use: Armored vehicle used for fire support in an armored attack. Deployment similar to that of a self-propelled assault gun.

Evaluation: Armored vehicle with heavy armor and weaponry little operational use. May force results in the course of trench-warfare. Especially version B and C is difficult to combat.

M 1 Dreadnought

US ARMORED VEHICLE:
60-Ton M1 "Dreadnought"

Weight: circa 57 t

Crew: 6 – 7

Dimensions: circa 7.00 m long, circa 3.10m wide, circa 3.35m high.

All terrain capability: ascends circa 1.50 m, crosses 3.30 m, fords 1.20 m

Ground clearance: circa 0.50 m

Range: 220 km

Speed: ca. 30 km/h

Armor: 75-200 mm

Weaponry: 1 105mm long mechanized cannon in turret, 2 37mm mechanized cannons, L/56.5 in driver's front, 2 side machine guns and 2 machine guns

Identifying features: Stretched out vehicle with armored running gear.

Use: Heavy armored vehicle for breakthrough and infantry support during an attack.

Evaluation: Heavy armor and difficult to combat.

KV II

SOVIET ARMORED VEHICLE:
KV II ("KV" with 15.2 cm motorized howitzer)
Erroneously named "58t", "64t", "58t", "64t", "70t", etc.

Weight: 52 t

Crew: 6 – 7

Dimensions: 6.80m long, (incl. weapon 7.20m), 3.35m wide, 3.30m high.

All terrain capability: ascends 0.90 m, crosses 2.80 m, fords 1.45 m. (Can only pass over bridges of high weight rating)

Ground clearance: 0.52 m

Range: Road 280 km, terrain 170 km

Speed: 30 km/h

Armor:
Bow and driver's front - 75 mm / Turret, rolled steel - 75 mm
Side - 75 mm / Rear - 75 mm

Weaponry: 1 152Mm mechanized howitzer, 1-2 machine guns. Sometimes additional machine gun in rear.

Identifying features: Steep, cube-shaped turret case, high overall height, heavy weaponry (howitzer!) Tank chassis, hull and running gear are the same as KV 1 44 t.

Use: Heavy armored vehicle used for fire support in an armored attack. Deployment similar to that of a self-propelled assault gun. Now only rarely seen.

Evaluation: Heavy armor. Very substantial firepower, however limited maneuverability. Useful in trench warfare. Even according to Soviet-Russian evaluation the over-burdened chassis was not satisfactory.

T 35 A

SOVIET HEAVY ARMORED VEHICLE:
45 ton armored vehicle T 35
T35 A (TP, BS, S II, M II, T 32 older model, AV T 35 A-B-C different versions)

Weight: 45 t

Armor:
Bow and driver's front - 30 mm / Turrets - 20-25 mm
Side - 23+11 mm / Rear - 22-27 mm

Weaponry: 1 76.2mm mechanized cannon L/16.5 or L/24, 2 45mm mechanized cannon, 6-7 machine guns.

Crew: 5

Dimensions: 9.60m long, 3.20m wide, 3.50 high

All terrain capability: ascends 1.30 m, crosses 4.75 m, fords 1.25 m

Ground clearance: 0.58 m

Range: Road 150 km

T 35 C

Speed: 30 km/h

Soviet heavy armored vehicle: T35 C

Weight: 45 t

Armor: up to 60 mm

Weaponry: 1 76.2mm mechanized cannon, 1 45mm mechanized cannon, 2-3 machine guns

Crew: 6

Dimensions: 9.60 m long, 3.20m wide, 3.50 m high

All terrain capability: ascends 1.30 m, crosses 4.75 m, fords 1.25m

Ground clearance: 0.58 m

Range: Road 150 km

Speed: 30 km/h

Identifying features: Production varies widely. Number of turret varies by series.

T 35 A: 5 turrets, (1 main, 4 side turrets).

T 35 C: 2 turrets, some have armored running gear.

Use: Heavy armored vehicle for armored attack with infantry support.

Evaluation: Obsolete design, big, cumbersome, limited maneuverability. Especially the T 35 A has little combat use in spite of its number of turrets. Both versions are no longer made and will only rarely be seen.

Mark IV Churchill I/II

ENGLISH HEAVY INFANTRY-ARMORED VEHICLE
Armored Pursuit Vehicle 40-Ton MkIV "Churchill I/II"

Weight: approximately 38 t

Armor: Hull and superstructure
Bow - 38-75mmm / Driver's front - 88+14 - some 88+88mm
Side - 14+38 up to 14+64mm / Rear - 28-50mm
Floor - 16mm / Top - 16-20mm

Armor: Turret
Shield - 100m / Front - 100mm / Side - 100mm
Rear - 100mm / Roof - 40-50mm

Weaponry: Churchill I - In turret: 1 40mm mechanized cannon L752, 1 machine gun, 1 anti-aircraft machine gun, 1 smoke pistol. In driver's front: 1 76.2mm mechanized cannon L/26.5, 2 machine pistols

Weaponry: Churchill II - In turret: same as Churchill I. In driver's front: 1 machine gun, 1 flamethrower, fixed, 2 machine pistols

Crew: 5

Dimensions: Churchill I 7.10m long. Churchill II, 7.60m long, 3.25 m wide, 2.65 m high.

All terrain capability: ascends 1.13m, crosses 2.80m, fords up to 2.40m

Ground clearance: 0.51m

Driving Range: Road 260 km. Terrain 80 km

Speed: 26 km/h

Identifying features: Flat, stretched construction. Unprotected running gear. Rounded off shape of turret

Use: Heavy armored vehicle used for infantry support during an attack.

Evaluation: Heavy armor and difficult to combat. Slow tactical effect and cumbersome. Not suitable for operational use.

Mark IV Churchill III

ENGLISH HEAVY INFANTRY-ARMORED VEHICLE
Armored Pursuit Vehicle 40t MkIV "Churchill III"

Weight: approximately 38t

Armor: Hull and superstructure
Bow - 38-75mm / Driver's front 88+14 - some 88+88mm
Side - 14+38 up to 14+64mm / Rear - 28-50mm
Roof - 16-20mm / Floor - 16mm

Turret
Shield - 55 mm / Front - 88 mm / Side - 75-88 mm
Rear - 75 mm / Roof - 20 mm

Weaponry: Churchill III - In turret: 1 57mm mechanized cannon L/45, 1 machine gun, 1 anti-aircraft-machine gun, 1 smoke pistol. In driver's front: 1 machine gun, 2 machine pistols

Crew: 5

Dimensions: 7.10mlong, 3.25m wide, 2.65m high

All terrain capability: ascends 1.13m, crosses 2.80m, fords 2.40m.

Ground clearance: 0.51 m

Range: Road 260 km, Terrain 80 km

Speed: 26 km/h

Identifying features: Flat, stretched out design. Unprotected running gear. Angular shape of turret.

Use: Heavy armored vehicle used for infantry support during an attack.

Evaluation: Heavy armor and difficult to combat. Slow tactical effect and cumbersome. Not suitable for operational use.

OLDER DESIGNS
ONLY RARELY EXPECTED TO BE SEEN

ARMORED RECONNAISSANCE VEHICLES
Arm. Rec. veh. "BA" (Bronieford)
Arm. Rec. Veh. "BA" (Ford)

"BA" Bronieford

Vehicle weight: 1.7 to 2.1t

Armor: 5 to 6 mm

Weaponry: 1 machine gun

Crew: 3

Dimensions: 4.20 m long, 1.70 m wide, 2.10 m high

Ground clearance: 0.26 m

All terrain capability: limited

Driving range: 320 km (road surface)

Vehicle speed: 50 km/h

Identifying features: Two - axle running gear, short edged shape.

"BA" (Bronieford)

Evaluation: Obsolete version, inferior armor and weaponry.

"BA" Ford

Vehicle weight: 5t

Armor: 7 to 13 mm

Weaponry: 1 motorized cannon 4,5 cm, 2 machine guns

Crew: 4

Dimensions: 4.70 m long, 2.10 m wide, 2.40 m high

Ground clearance: 0.22 m

All terrain capability: limited

Driving range: 320 km (road surface)

Vehicle speed: 50 km/h

Identifying features: Three - axle running gear, edged shape. (Turret on new edition of conical shape and rounded off.)

Use: Light or medium armored reconnaissance vehicle, respectively. Used for tactical and operational reconnaissance by mechanized units.

Evaluation: Improved version. Reconnaissance vehicle with combat capability, does however exhibit numerous mechanical shortcomings.

"BA" (Ford)

FOR OFFICIAL USE ONLY!
DO NOT LET FALL IN ENEMY HANDS!

(Defence against armored vehicles difficult to combat)
ARMOR PENETRATION CHART
8.8 cm "KwK" 36

<u>Issued: 2/15/43</u>

Fundamentals on procedure of shooting against armored vehicles difficult to combat

1. Maintain coldbloodedness: Strive to obtain suitable distance to detect "weak spots" and facilitate effective destruction!

2. Combat enemy tanks from hidden position and unexpected direction! In open terrain, attack enemy tanks "over the corner" of own tank (highest possible protection by the given armor).

3. In spite of careful aim for each individual shot, maintain high firing frequency!

4. Alert inspection of projectile impact! Not every hit is always immediately destructive.

5. Strive to obtain favorable angle of impact! Highest impact is obtained when front or side are fully visible, the least when traveling at an angle (45°). For round or curved turrets, always hold at center of turret.

6. Select the correct grade of ammunition! Consider the data in this chart. Solid core shells, use only up to a distance of 2000m and then only if regular piercing-piercing shells or HD shells turn out to have no effect.

Explosive shells - ignitor position "without delay" – can cause disabling circumstances, (setting on fire), destructive effect for hitting the front of the turret just above the turret ring or under the cantilevered rear of the turret by means of lifting or diverting installed position of turret on armored vehicles T 34 A and B, also for hitting the front of the turret on the MK II underneath the cannon. These hits on the turret however are rare.

7. In this armor penetration chart the following symbols mean:

Ammunition:
AT= 88mm piercing-piercing shell Kwk 36
HD = 88mm Heavy Duty shell KwK 36
SC = 88mm #40 solid core sell KwK36
EG = 88mmm inserted explosive cartridge

Effect:
Black = Destructive effect
Hatched = Disabling or destructive effect
White = No effect

The weak spots of armored vehicles which can be fired at successfully are marked with Indicating lines connected to the abbreviations of the proper grade of ammunition.

Figures in meters next to the abbreviations for grade of ammunition indicate the upper limit of the distance at which a successful penetration of the armor can be counted on. For HD-grenades no distances were given, as these projectiles can penetrate all outlined black areas up to a distance of 2000 m. The combat distance however, will in most cases be far shorter, when taking into account the size of the target and the surrounding circumstances, (enemy impact, vision, etc.).

For details on the effect of different grades of ammunition, study the text part of this manual, (H.Dv. 469/3b).

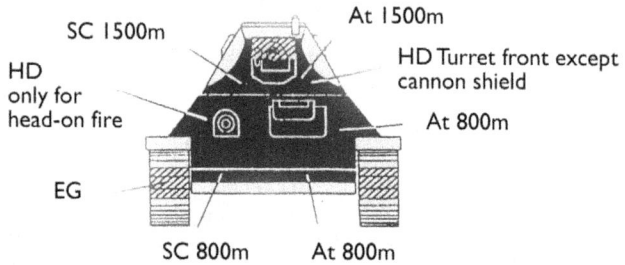

SC 1500m

At 1500m

HD Turret front except cannon shield

HD only for head-on fire

At 800m

EG

SC 800m   At 800m

For all black areas
At 2000m
SC 2000m
HD Every viable
combat distance

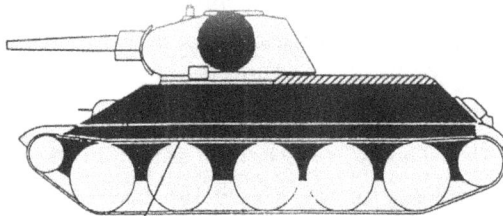

EG For firing at track and running gear

For all black areas
At 2000m
HD Every viable
combat distance

SC 2000m

SC 1800m

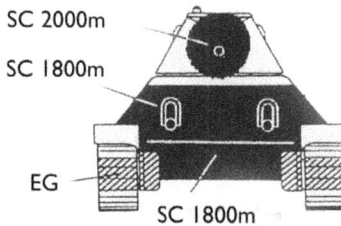

EG

SC 1800m

Medium armored vehicle T 34 A

The data for this armored vehicle has been determined through calculation. It is to serve as a preliminary guideline.

SC 1500m

At 1500m

HD
only for
head-on fire

HD Turret front except
cannon shield

At 300m Only for almost
head-on fire

EG

SC 800m   At 800m

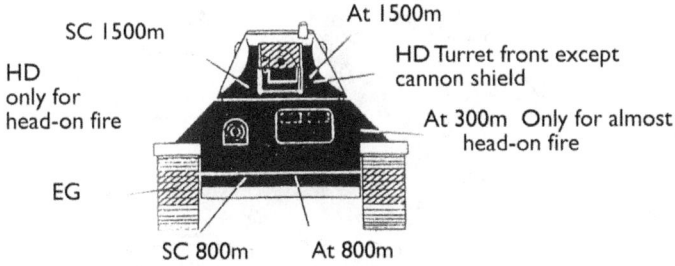

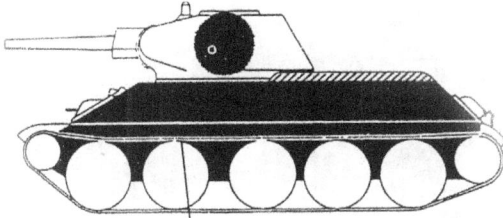

For all black areas
At 2000m
SC 2000m
HD Every viable
combat distance

EG For firing at track and running gear

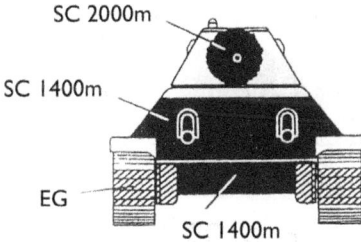

SC 2000m

SC 1400m

For all black areas
At 2000m
HD Every viable
combat distance

EG

SC 1400m

Medium armored vehicle T34 B (reinforced)

The data for this armored vehicle has been determined through calculation.
It is to serve as a preliminary guideline.

SC 1500m

At 800m

SC 1500m

At 1500m

HD

HD

SC 1500m   At 1500m

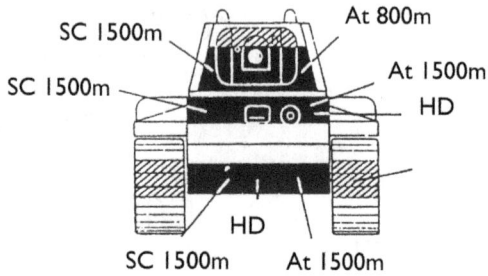

For all black areas
At 2000m
SC 2000m
HD Every viable
combat distance

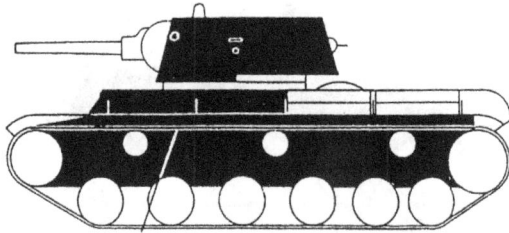

EG For firing at track and running gear

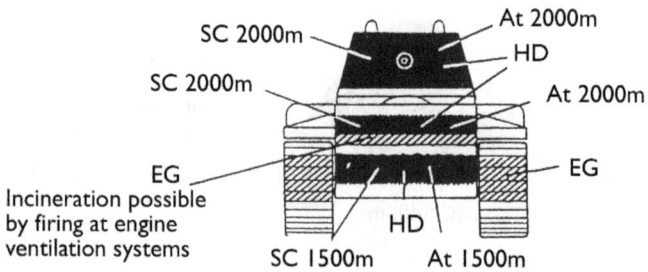

SC 2000m

At 2000m

HD

SC 2000m

At 2000m

EG

EG

Incineration possible
by firing at engine
ventilation systems

HD

SC 1500m   At 1500m

Heavy armored vehicle KV IA

The data for this armored vehicle has been determined through calculation. It is to serve as a preliminary guideline.

SC 1500m

At 800m
HD Turret front except
cannon shield

SC 1500m

At 1500m
HD
EG

HD

SC 1500m   HD Turret front except
cannon shield

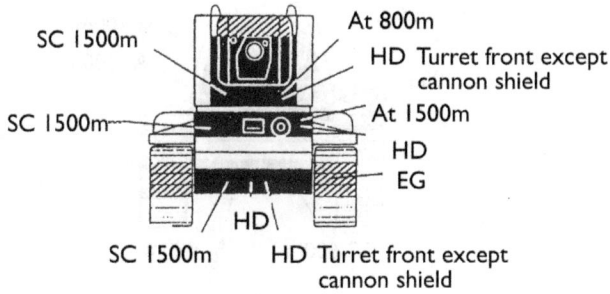

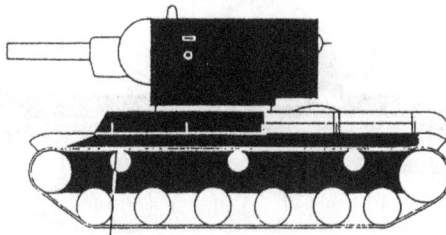

For all black areas
At 2000m
SC 2000m
HD Every viable
combat distance

EG For firing at track and running gear

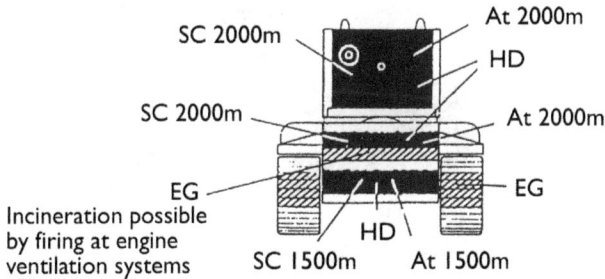

SC 2000m

At 2000m
HD

SC 2000m

At 2000m

EG

EG

Incineration possible
by firing at engine
ventilation systems

HD

SC 1500m   At 1500m

Heavy armored vehicle KV II

The data for this armored vehicle has been determined through calculation.
It is to serve as a preliminary guideline.

SC 1200m
At 700m
SC 400m
At 300m
EG
SC 600m
At 400m

SC 1200m
At 700m
At 1500m
SC 2000m
HD

EG For firing at track and running gear

SC 1200m
At 700m
At 1500m
SC 1500m
HD
EG
EG
HD
Incineration possible
by firing at engine
ventilation systems
SC 1500m
At 1500m

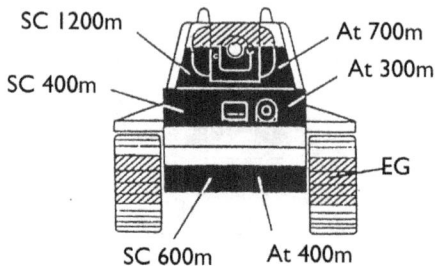

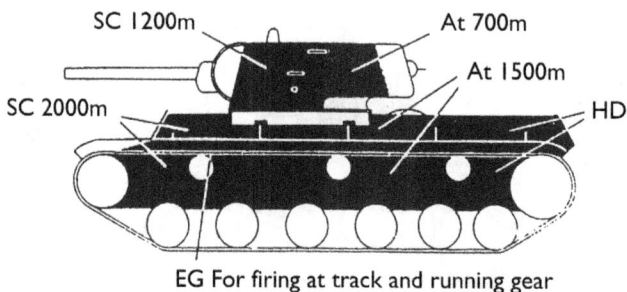

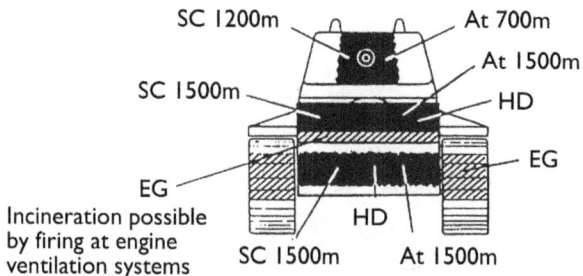

Heavy armored vehicle KV 1C (reinforced)

The data for this armored vehicle has been determined through calculation. It is to serve as a preliminary guideline.

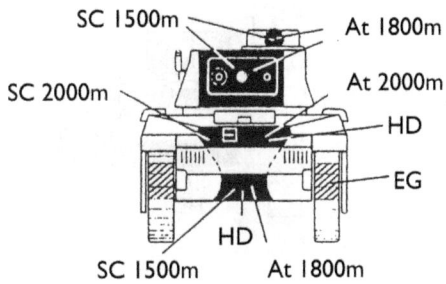

SC 1500m · At 1800m · SC 2000m · At 2000m · HD · EG · HD · SC 1500m · At 1800m

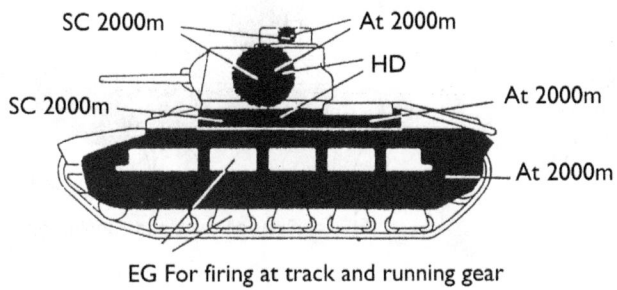

SC 2000m · At 2000m · HD · SC 2000m · At 2000m · At 2000m

EG For firing at track and running gear

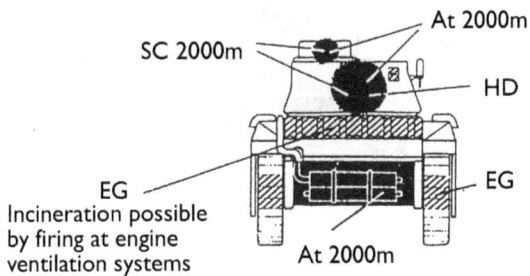

At 2000m · SC 2000m · HD · EG · Incineration possible by firing at engine ventilation systems · EG · At 2000m

Medium armored vehicle Mk II

The data for this armored vehicle has been determined through calculation. It is to serve as a preliminary guideline.

For all black areas
At 2000m
SC 2000m

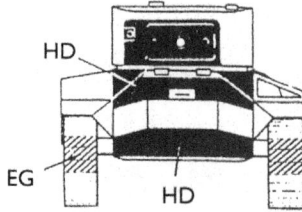

HD

EG

HD

For all black areas
At 2000m
SC 2000m
HD Every viable
combat distance

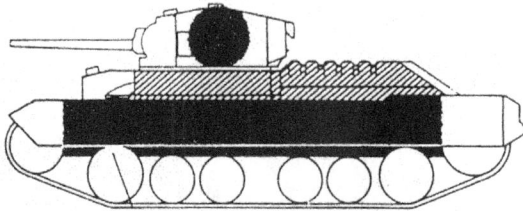

EG For firing at track and running gear

EG
Incineration possible
by firing at engine
ventilation systems

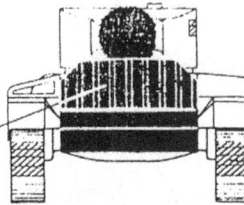

For all black areas
At 2000m
SC 2000m
HD Every viable
combat distance

EG

Medium armored vehicle Mk III (Valentine)

The data for this armored vehicle has been determined through calculation. It is to serve as a preliminary guideline.

SC 2000m

At 1500m

SC 2000m

HD

At 900m

EG

HD

SC 2000m

At 1800m

At 1500m

For all black areas
SC 2000m
HD Every viable
combat distance

At 2000m

EG For firing at track and running gear

For all black areas
At 2000m
SC 2000m

EG

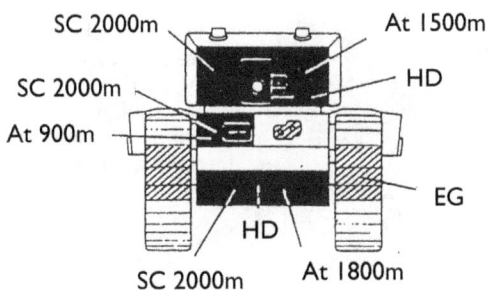

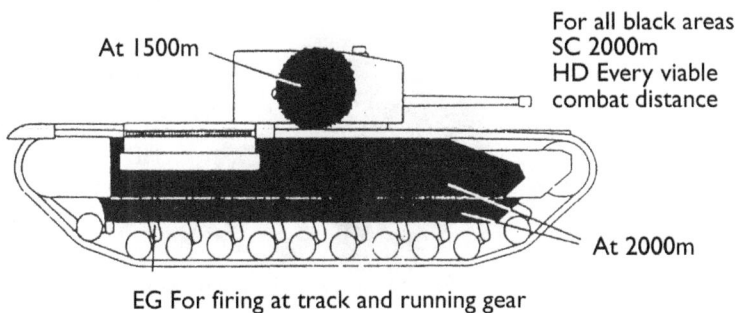

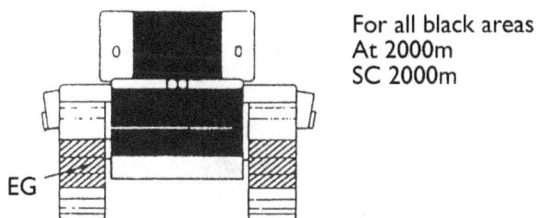

Heavy armored vehicle Mk IV (Churchill III)

The data for this armored vehicle has been determined through calculation. It is to serve as a preliminary guideline. The figures are also valid for the type I and II Churchill equipped with cast turrets.

At 400m

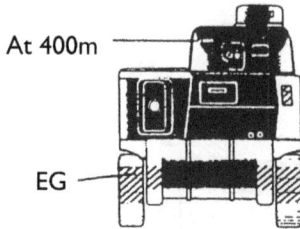

For all black areas
(except turret front)
At 2000m
SC 2000m
HD Every viable
combat distance

EG

For all black areas
At 2000m
SC 2000m
HD Every viable
combat distance

EG For firing at track and running gear

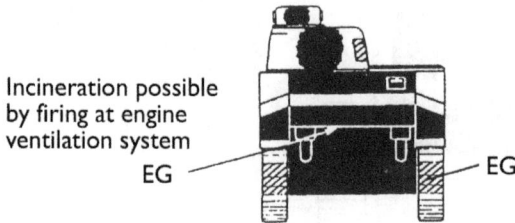

Incineration possible
by firing at engine
ventilation system
EG

For all black areas
At 2000m
SC 2000m

EG

Medium armored vehicle M3 (General Lee)

The data for this armored vehicle has been determined through calculation. It is to serve as a preliminary guideline.

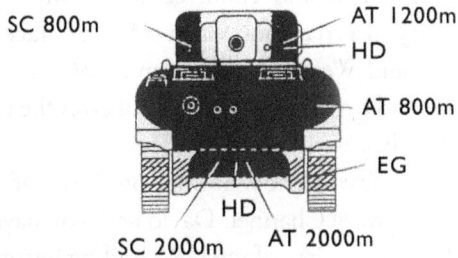

SC 800m

AT 1200m

HD

AT 800m

EG

HD

SC 2000m   AT 2000m

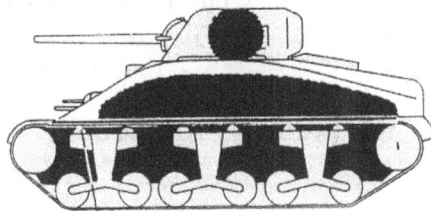

For all black areas
At 2000m
SC 2000m
HD Every viable
combat distance

EG For firing at track and running gear

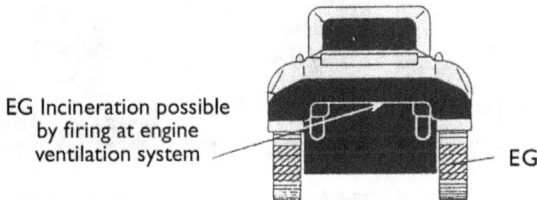

EG Incineration possible
by firing at engine
ventilation system

For all black areas
At 2000m
SC 2000m
HD Every viable
combat distance

EG

Medium armored vehicle M4 (General Sherman)

The data for this armored vehicle has been determined through calculation. It is to serve as a preliminary guideline.

ABOUT CODA BOOKS

Most Coda books are edited and endorsed by Emmy Award winning film maker and military historian Bob Carruthers, producer of Discovery Channel's Line of Fire and Weapons of War and BBC's Both Sides of the Line. Long experience and strong editorial control gives the military history enthusiast the ability to buy with confidence.

The series advisor is David McWhinnie, producer of the acclaimed Battlefield series for Discovery Channel. David and Bob have co-produced books and films with a wide variety of the UK's leading historians including Professor John Erickson and Dr David Chandler.

Where possible the books draw on rare primary sources to give the military enthusiast new insights into a fascinating subject.

www.codabooks.com

The English Civil Wars

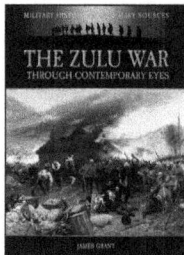

The Zulu Wars

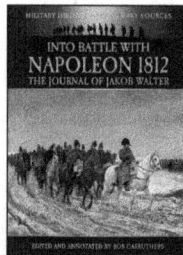

Into Battle with Napoleon 1812

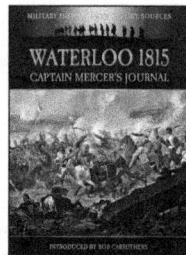

Waterloo 1815

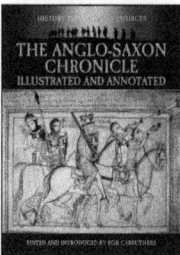

The Anglo-Saxon Chronicle

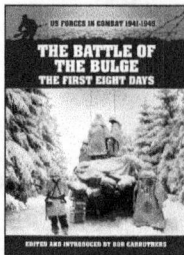

The Battle of the Bulge

The Normandy Campaign 1944

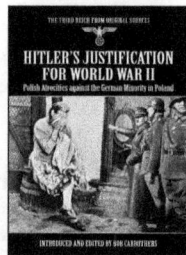

Hitler's Justification for WWII

Hitler's Mein Kampf - The Roots of Evil	I Knew Hitler	Mein Kampf - The 1939 Illustrated Edition	The Nuremberg Trials Volume 1
Tiger I in Combat	Tiger I Crew Manual	Panzers at War 1939-1942	Panzers at War 1943-1945
Wolf Pack - the U boats	Poland 1939	Luftwaffe Combat Reports	Eastern Front Night Combat
Eastern Front Encirclement	Panzer Combat Reports	The Panther V in Combat	The Red Army in Combat
Barbarossa - Hitler Turns East	The Russian Front	The Wehrmacht in Russia	Servants of Evil

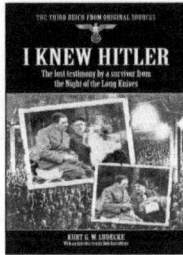

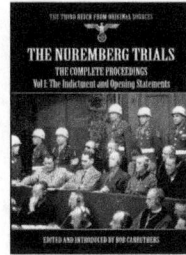

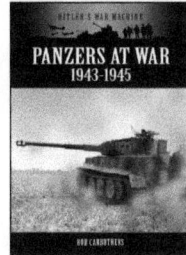

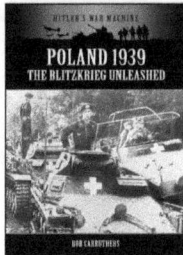

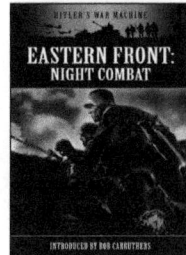

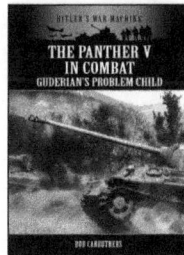

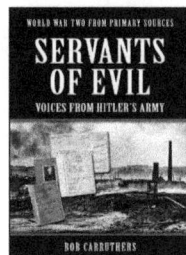